ISLAM IN TRANSITION

Young British Pakistanis live in a social world made up of many diverse elements. From their parents, they learn about Pakistan and about the way of life that is Islam. From Muslim and Pakistani friends, they learn much about their shared heritage. At the same time, they learn about the British culture of which they are a part and which is a part of them; but they discover too that, in the eyes of some, they can never be 'truly' British because of their dark skin and 'foreign' religion.

Islam in Transition explores the complex interrelationship between the ethnic, national and religious identities of young British Pakistanis. In particular, it focuses on the ways in which Islamic religion engenders powerful loyalties within a predominantly secular society and how, in their adherence to their religion, many young Muslims find a welcome sense of stability and permanence. The author presents material collected in a field-work study and quotes extensively from research interviews, in considering how it is that traditional sources of authority and allegiance survive in a world within which there seem to be abundant opportunities to challenge previously accepted concepts of identity.

Jessica Jacobson is currently working as a researcher for the Home Office.

ISLAM IN TRANSITION

Religion and identity among
British Pakistani youth

Jessica Jacobson

London and New York

First published 1998
by Routledge
11 New Fetter Lane, London EC4P 4EE

Simultaneously published in the USA and Canada
by Routledge
29 West 35th Street, New York, NY 10001

© 1998 Jessica Jacobson

Typeset in Baskerville by Routledge
Printed and bound in Great Britain by
TJ International, Padstow, Cornwall

British Library Cataloguing in Publication Data
A catalogue record for this book is available from the British Library

Library of Congress Cataloging in Publication Data
Jacobson, Jessica, 1966–
Islam in transition: religion and identity among British Pakistani youth /
Jessica Jacobson.
Includes bibliographical references and index.
1. Islam–Great Britain. 2. Youth, Muslim–Great Britain. 3. Pakistanis–Great Britain.
4. Islam–20th century. I. Title.
BP65.G7J33   1998   97–41696
305.235–dc21   CIP

ISBN 0–415–17085–0

For Kassim
with love and thanks

CONTENTS

ACKNOWLEDGEMENTS

This book presents the findings of field-work conducted in the London Borough of Waltham Forest. During the twelve months I spent as a field-researcher, I was entirely dependent on the kindness and good-will of the many people I met. Thus I owe a large debt of thanks to all who took the time to speak with me, provide me with information and introduce me to others. Above all, I must thank the young people who were the subjects of my lengthy research interviews; I hope that my account does some justice to their open, thoughtful and thought-provoking responses.

The research was originally conducted for a doctoral thesis, which I completed in the Sociology Department of the London School of Economics. Here I was privileged to study under the supervision of Professor Anthony Smith. I have benefited enormously from working with someone who offered not only outstanding scholarly insights, but also warm concern and ceaseless moral support.

I am grateful to the Economic and Social Research Council, which funded my doctoral studies.

For assisting with the transformation of the thesis into a book I wish to thank Anthony Smith (again); the examiners of my PhD thesis, Akbar S. Ahmed and George Schöpflin; the European Institute of the London School of Economics, which provided me with an academic home; Marie Gillespie, who offered encouragement and perceptive comments; and my editor, Mari Shullaw.

I must also say a word of thanks to my friends and colleagues in the Association for the Study of Ethnicity and Nationalism (ASEN) for all the distractions . . . which ultimately, I think, kept me sane. And a special thanks to a special friend: Atsuko Ichijo.

Finally, my family's patience and support made it all possible.

INTRODUCTION

The issues

The general problem addressed by this book is that of understanding the conditions of the survival and revival of tradition, especially religious tradition, in modern society. Social scientists have long been concerned with documenting the apparent fragmentation of traditional social ties and the decline of established sources of authority, both of which processes are assumed to be elements of the general 'modernisation' of societies. Today, many scholars reject earlier assumptions about the progress of societies towards a universal, modern form; they remain convinced, however, that traditional sources of allegiance and authority – such as the family, the nation, the ethnic group and religion – are playing ever diminishing roles in people's lives. Accordingly, in what is now a 'postmodern' world individuals have access to a multiplicity of identities; and new identities are constantly being created through the merging and intermingling of previously discrete social categories.

This study arose out of a concern with the questions of to what extent and why, notwithstanding the evidently widespread changes in patterns of identity that have occurred within Western nation-states, some traditional sources of social differentiation retain significance. My special interest has been in the ways in which, in particular, a minority religious tradition can act as a focus of allegiance in the face of what appear to be abundant opportunities to challenge the old bases of authority.

In contemporary Britain, Islam is a minority religion which is especially dynamic, and indeed seems in recent years to have been undergoing something of a revival. It was on these grounds that I decided to approach the question of the survival of religious tradition by conducting a study of attitudes among British Muslims. More specifically, I decided to focus on Pakistanis, who make up the largest sub-group within the heterogeneous British Muslim minority. This narrowing of the study would, I assumed, lend the project greater coherence, and would enable me to explore the interrelationship between commitment to a religion and attachment to a perceived place of origin as bases of identity. Furthermore, I decided to look specifically at the 'second generation' of British

1

Pakistanis – that is, young people whose parents emigrated to Britain from Pakistan – in order to investigate the ways in which the experience of growing up in Britain, with British nationality, influences attitudes to the minority religion and notions of ethnicity.

The research problem was therefore defined as follows:

> In what terms do second-generation British Pakistanis conceive of their own nationality, ethnicity and religion? Of these sources of social identity available to them, why does religion appear to have an especially strong appeal?

The aim of this study was to find some answers to these questions by conducting an empirical study of a qualitative nature, involving a series of interviews and discussions with young British Pakistanis. I decided to conduct the field-work within a single locality so that I could explore the social environment within which the respondents' identities have emerged, and compare the responses of the different individuals to what are broadly similar influences. The field-work was carried out in Waltham Forest, a London borough with a large Pakistani population.

It must be noted that the use of the term 'British Pakistanis' is somewhat contentious: I found that, for reasons that are discussed over the course of the book, a number of my respondents do not like to call themselves 'Pakistani' and/or 'British'. For the sake of clarity, however, it is necessary for me to use a specific and fixed term in referring to the subjects of the study, and it seems that the phrase 'British Pakistani' informs the reader – in a way that is concise, reasonably precise and as neutral as possible – that the respondents are of Pakistani background and have British nationality. The broader term 'Asian' is used throughout the book in the same way as it is used in popular discourse in Britain: that is, to refer to people from Pakistani, Bangladeshi and Indian backgrounds. The extent to which the respondents perceive themselves to be members of the 'Asian' minority in Britain is discussed in Chapter 5.

Another terminological note of caution that must be inserted here concerns the use of the phrase 'Pakistani community'. This phrase appears throughout this book because it is the shortest way of referring collectively to individuals of Pakistani descent living in Waltham Forest; however, it is a problematic term since those very individuals can at different times orient themselves towards different kinds of minority 'community': most notably the 'Muslim community' or the 'Asian community'. Indeed, the terms 'Pakistani', 'Asian' and 'Muslim' were frequently used interchangeably by my respondents in talk about the minority group, partly because the bulk of the population of both the Asian and the Muslim minority in Waltham Forest happens to be Pakistani. Baumann, in his study of 'discourses of identity' in Southall, writes at length about the degree to which Southallians 'regarded themselves as members of several *communities* at once, each with its own *culture*. Making one's life meant ranging across them' [original emphases] (1996: 5). Although, as Baumann writes, in most contexts the existence of five major 'communities' – Muslim, Hindu, Sikh, Afro-Caribbean and white – is taken for granted in Southall, a great many cross-cutting social cleavages have significance for the population of the area: including class, birth-place, own or parents' nationality, mother-tongue and preferred language.

Of course, my study is addressing the very question of how the respondents tend to describe and understand the social groups to which they belong; in particular, I have been interested in tracing the apparent differences between their own and their parents' definitions of the salient minority community. In writing of the local 'Pakistani community' I am thus referring to an entity whose parameters are shifting and evolving; and indeed my concern is primarily with the direction or directions of change. I have found it useful, when employing this problematic phrase, to keep in mind the comment made by one of my respondents in Waltham Forest in reply to a question about what it is like to live in a 'Pakistani community': he pointed out, 'No one got down and said – with pen and paper, books – oh we're gonna start a community up, who wants to join? It just happens.'

The framework

Social scientists have frequently sought to address questions relating to minority identity by referring to structural issues; in particular, gender, class and racism tend to be treated as explanatory factors. However, my intention in undertaking this study has from the outset been to develop an understanding of the issues which is based on an analysis of meanings imputed to their situation and articulated by the subjects themselves. The results of my research have persuaded me that while structural factors by definition shape any given social context within which identities are articulated, sociological understanding of issues of identity can be greatly advanced through a close examination of the ways in which actors, both collectively and as individuals, develop and manipulate the range of social concepts available to them.

My approach to the study of identity-formation among young British Pakistanis has produced many conclusions with regard to the respondents' conceptualisations of nationality, ethnicity and religion, and the reasons why religion remains a particularly significant source of identity for them. These conclusions have been ordered into an explanatory framework which comprises two closely interlinked lines of argument.

The first line of argument draws on the concept of 'social boundaries' as a tool for analysing the various ways in which young British Pakistanis differentiate themselves, or feel that they are differentiated, from non-members of the minority group. I have identified several boundary processes which help to shape the identities of young British Pakistanis. First, the young people position themselves in relation to 'boundaries of Britishness', which define what it is to be British and include, for example, ethnic definitions of the nation and definitions based on concepts of citizenship. Second, the older generation of British Pakistanis seek to

3

preserve what I term the 'parental boundaries', which encompass a relatively narrow definition of their minority community. This definition is predicated on the need for members of the community to maintain different standards of behaviour from the majority. Third, the young people are themselves in the process of reconstructing 'ethnic boundaries' through which they define themselves – in a manner different from and often looser than that of their parents – as Pakistani or, more broadly, as Asian in terms of cultural traditions and social patterns. Finally, young British Pakistanis, together with other British Muslims, are engaged in the process of constructing a set of 'religious boundaries' which enhance their own sense of identity as Muslims. It is in the nature of the teachings of Islam that these last-mentioned boundaries should be clear-cut and pervasive, which is in itself a source of their strength.

The second, closely related line of argument which I develop over the course of this book focuses on religion, and considers the role of Islam as a source of guidance in the lives of the young people. It is my contention that, as is evident from what has been said above, the social environment inevitably contains many contradictions for young people who have grown up in Britain as the children of immigrants from Pakistan. I would suggest these contradictions are a potential source of uncertainty; and that a large part of the appeal of religion to the young people lies in the fact that Islam provides a means of dealing with the ambiguities and dilemmas of their circumstances. For many of them, its teachings are a source of clear and coherent guidance on all aspects of day-to-day life.

As I have already suggested, structural factors relating to gender, class and racism are treated as background rather than foreground features of the analysis presented here. Gender is a theme that recurs in a variety of contexts in the pages that follow: it is made clear that to a large extent the men and the women of whom I write have different kinds of experiences, and make sense of them in different kinds of ways. However, there are also many commonalities in the experiences and attitudes of the men and the women, to which I draw attention. Gender is thus not treated as a key explanatory factor, but rather as an issue of special interest.

I deliberately chose not to look at the impact of class on expressions of identity; hence I decided to hold the variable of 'class background' constant by drawing my sample of respondents from what can be broadly described as a working-class population. It seems evident that an attempt to examine the relationship between class and identity would involve a much larger-scale empirical study than the one I have undertaken. Even within my relatively homogeneous sample there was a sufficient degree of diversity in terms of socio-economic factors to alert me to the fact that any analysis which seeks to incorporate a consideration of class must treat this as a complex and multidimensional phenomenon if it is to avoid crude reductionism. Such an analysis would have to take into account the levels of education and current occupations of the subjects as well as their family backgrounds.

Issues of 'race' and racism are, unlike class issues, of direct relevance to this study, given my general interest in the ways in which individuals define the social groups to which they belong. However, my analysis does not treat the power relations manifest in racism as key variables in themselves. It is clear to me that the study of structural issues on the one hand, and of individuals' definitions of their situations on the other hand, are alternative but equally valid levels of analysis. I hope that the arguments elaborated in this book – which are the outcome of determined efforts to let the subjects of the study speak for themselves and to develop an analysis closely grounded in and therefore relevant to their concerns – demonstrate the merits of this kind of project. Furthermore, it should be noted that my focus on the individual has not encouraged me to overlook the significance of issues of 'race'. Rather, it means that while I have not explored ideological structures of racism, I have paid attention to the impact of my respondents' *perceptions* of racism on their conceptualisations of 'Britishness' and, ultimately, on their ethnic and religious identities.

The structure of the book

The book has two main parts. The first sets the issues of primary concern in a broad theoretical and socio-historical context. The second part, which makes up the bulk of the book, is devoted to a detailed discussion of the findings of the empirical research and the general conclusions that I have drawn from them. In the presentation of the findings, I include many direct quotations from the research interviews, together with detailed overviews of what was said on each issue, in order to convey as accurately as possible the views of the subjects of the study, and demonstrate the grounding of my general conclusions in the empirical material.

It should be noted that the inclusion of direct quotations is useful not only because these convey interesting viewpoints, but also because in a great many cases the manner of expression is itself worthy of note. In much of what was said in the interviews, an interesting linguistic mix makes itself apparent, in the sense that colloquialisms common to all young people in London are tightly interwoven with the use of words and phrases that are specifically Muslim and/or South Asian in origin. While the instances of this linguistic mix are too common for me to draw attention to individual cases, the reader should look out for them as they are in themselves a vivid illustration of how different ways of communicating and thinking about the world can encounter one another and merge within individual lives.

The book as a whole is made up of seven chapters. Chapter 1 locates the research problem that this study addresses within theoretical debates on the subjects of identity, ethnicity and religion. Chapter 2 describes the background to the young British Pakistanis' expressions of social identity. It encompasses a brief account of the central tenets of the Islamic religion, and an overview of the circumstances of Muslims living in Britain. Chapter 3 describes the location in which I carried out the empirical study, the methodology adopted and the process of field-work.

Chapter 4 opens the discussion of the empirical findings with an analysis of two

boundary processes which give shape to the social circumstances of the respondents' lives: namely, the imposition of 'parental boundaries' by the older
generation of British Pakistanis, and the location of the young people in relation to
'boundaries of Britishness'. Chapter 5 is an account of the ways in which the
boundaries which frame the respondents' perceptions of their own ethnicity are
evolving. The final two chapters are specifically concerned with the subject of religious identity: Chapter 6 seeks to understand the significance of Islam in the lives
of the respondents by considering the ways in which it acts as a source of guidance;
and Chapter 7 presents an analysis of the 'religious boundaries' constructed and
maintained by the young people.

Part I

THEORY AND SOCIO-HISTORICAL CONTEXT

1

SOCIAL IDENTITIES

My aim in this chapter is to explore some of the theoretical issues which underlie the key research questions addressed by this study: that is, the questions of how young British Pakistanis perceive their religion, ethnicity and nationality, and why religion appears to have an especially strong appeal for them. It is not my intention to present here a fixed theoretical framework which can be said to have guided from the outset my field-work and my analysis of the empirical findings. Rather, there has been a two-way relationship between the empirical and the theoretical aspects of the study: that is, as the process of data collection and analysis progressed, I constantly reviewed the theoretical suppositions in the light of what was coming to the fore. Thus, the conclusions which I have reached on the basis of my field-work and which are presented in subsequent chapters both follow from and feed into the theoretical concerns which are considered here.

Identity

At the heart of this study is the notion of 'identity': a highly complex concept which has been considered from a wide variety of perspectives within the social sciences. Clearly it is impossible to provide an overview of these perspectives here; what I intend to do, rather, is to outline briefly the concept of 'social identity' developed by the social psychologist Tajfel (1978), which has clarified my own general usage of the term 'identity'. I shall then move on to consider some of the available and most useful means of conceptualising ethnicity and religion as sources of identity in the lives of the young people who are the subjects of the study.

According to Hutnik (1985: 298), most social scientific definitions of identity belong to one of two broad types. Personality theorists regard identity in terms of 'a sense of personal distinctiveness, personal continuity and personal autonomy . . . in other words, the totality of the individual's self-construal'. On the other hand, the conceptions which are more common in sociology and social psychology 'tend to stress the fact that a sense of identity is formed from the dialectic between the individual and society', and, more particularly, draw attention to the ways in which membership of *social groups* shapes or determines

9

individuals' perceptions of themselves. These are key themes in George Herbert Mead's work on the process by which the individual acquires a full sense of self: according to Mead, the self develops 'by organizing [the] individual attitudes of others into . . . organized social or group attitudes'. This means that the self becomes 'an individual reflection of the general systematic pattern of social or group behavior in which it and the others are all involved' (1964: 222).

Tajfel's theory of 'social identity' provides the basis for a systematic investigation of the relationship between individuals' self-definitions and their perceptions of the social categories to which they and others around them belong. Tajfel writes that there are three components to group membership: first, the cognitive (knowledge that one belongs to a group); second, the evaluative (assumptions about the positive or negative value connotations of group membership); and third, the emotional (emotions towards one's group and towards others who stand in particular relations to it). For Tajfel, social identity is, then, 'that *part* of an individual's self-concept which derives from his knowledge of his membership of a social group (or groups) together with the value and emotional significance attached to that membership' [original emphasis] (1978: 63).

According to this definition of social identity, the ethnic identity of any of my respondents is his or her knowledge, values and feelings in relation to membership of an ethnic minority that originates in Pakistan and/or the Indian subcontinent; the religious identity is, likewise, his or her knowledge, values and feelings relating to membership of the Muslim minority in Britain and also the global Muslim *umma* (community of believers); and the national identity is his or her knowledge, values and feelings relating to membership, as a British citizen, of the population of that country.

As the above definitions, and indeed my framing of the research problem, make clear, I am treating the young people's expressions of ethnic identity and religious identity as separate phenomena. In contrast, many scholars in the field of ethnicity tend to regard religion as a component of ethnic identity: for example, Nash (1989) lists religion along with nationality, shared history, language and 'body' – that is, assumptions about biological origins expressed in terms of genes, blood, flesh and so on – as the basic 'building blocks' of ethnicity. In the case of people of Pakistani descent, ethnicity as a source of identity is undoubtedly closely related to religion: the history of Pakistan – founded as a nation for India's Muslims – ensures that Pakistanis are likely to associate being Pakistani with being Muslim. In addition, given that Pakistanis make up the largest Muslim group in the area in which I conducted my field-work, there is little to distinguish the local 'Muslim' from the local 'Pakistani' community, and religious and 'ethnic' traditions are inevitably intertwined in day-to-day social practices.

That much said, my decision to treat religion and ethnicity as different bases of social identity, despite their being so closely intertwined, is partially based on the belief that there is a useful analytic distinction to be made between commitment to a universalistic religion with a global reach and membership of a social group defined with reference to a place of origin. Furthermore, as I shall demonstrate when I come to discuss my respondents' attitudes to their religion, this distinction accords with the views held by increasing numbers of young British Pakistanis and other British Muslims.

It should be evident from the definitions of the respondents' religious, ethnic and national identities outlined above that these social identities are necessarily multidimensional as well as interpenetrative: there are many aspects of the lives of all of the young people which can, potentially at least, both reflect and express their belonging to the given social groups. For example, regular religious practice, an adherence to Islamic values in day-to-day life, private study of Islam and feelings of solidarity towards fellow Muslims in Britain and overseas may together contribute to an individual's sense of religious identity. Ethnic identity, on the other hand, might be expressed through commitment to the norms governing South Asian family life, an interest in the culture and history of the Indian subcontinent and an attachment to Pakistan as a place that can, at least at times, be called 'home'. Where respondents perceive that they have a national identity as British, this might reflect assumptions about legal definitions of citizenship and the impact of a set of values associated with life in modern Britain; but, at the same time, an awareness of and resistance to racism on the part of many white Britons may provoke feelings of exclusion from certain definitions of 'Britishness'.

Tajfel's theory encourages a dynamic approach to identity on account of its emphasis upon 'the complex dialectical relationship between social identity and social settings' (Cairns 1982: 283). Tajfel does not treat the social identity of any individual as a fixed component of his or her life, or, for that matter, as necessarily the essential and defining aspect of the individual. Rather, according to social identity theory, an individual's self-concept is made up of varying self-images which 'can be construed as falling along a continuum, with individuating characteristics at the personal extreme, and social categorical characteristics at the social extreme' (Abrams and Hogg 1990: 4). The salience of an individual's social identity varies from situation to situation: in some cases, an individual's actions are primarily shaped by his or her membership of any one of the social groups to which he or she belongs; in other cases, behaviour is determined by personal characteristics.

The notion of social identity as dynamic is central to this study: both because, at a collective level, there appear to be significant intergenerational changes taking place in perceptions of nationality, ethnicity and religion within the Pakistani community of Waltham Forest; and also because, at the individual level, respondents have the opportunity to make certain choices between alternative sources of social identity and alternative expressions of any given social identity. The young subjects of this study can therefore be said to have 'identity options' – a term used by Rex and Josephides (1987) in referring to the situation of second-generation British Asians. Indeed, as will be evident from the continuing discussion of theoretical issues and from the presentation of my empirical findings which follows, one of the central concerns of this study has been to consider *to what extent* the respondents can be said to be exercising choices of this kind.

11

Social boundaries

Tajfel's conceptualisation of 'social identity' provides a useful starting-point for the analysis of my respondents' ethnic, religious and national identities; however, because of social identity theory's 'neglect of the specific meaning of social categories' (Billig 1995: 66), I have not chosen to employ this perspective in developing a broad framework within which to examine my empirical data.[1] The question therefore arises of how any attempt at an explanation of patterns of identity-formation among my respondents should proceed.

Some scholars who have sought to understand the persistence of ethnic ties in the modern world have developed what is often broadly referred to as a 'primordialist' approach to the study of ethnicity. These theorists stress that the apparent historical continuity of ethnic communities gives rise to intense emotional attachments to those communities. What Smith (1995) has called the 'extreme version' of primordialism is maintained by many nationalists, who assert that ethnic communities are 'natural' and fundamental units of human society. A more flexible primordialist position is maintained by scholars such as Geertz and Stack, who are less concerned with the 'facts' of ethnic group formation than they are with social actors' *perceptions* of their own ethnicity. Thus, Geertz argues that primordial attachments are those which stem from the *assumed* "givens" of social existence'; that is, 'congruities of blood, speech, custom, and so on [which] *are seen to have* an ineffable, and at times over-powering, coerciveness in and of themselves' [emphases added] (1993: 259). Stack finds that this perspective, in that it explores the notion of ethnicity as 'a powerful identity merging the individual with the group' (1986: 3), usefully highlights the extent to which ethnic ties can in themselves engender power and energy.

Even the more flexible primordialists have, however, been severely criticised for presenting an overly static view of ethnicity. Within any given ethnic community, perceptions of the origins, culture, significance and parameters of ethnicity are liable to change enormously over time; and all the more so, of course, when a group constitutes itself as a minority after a process of migration. The primordialist perspective thus appears to offer little to an investigation of second-generation British Pakistanis' understandings of their own ethnicity, although as shall be demonstrated below one aspect of their commitment to Islam seems to be their conviction that its teachings have a real historical continuity, and indeed a relevance for all eras.

The shortcomings of primordialist theories have been highlighted by scholars who maintain what is frequently termed the 'instrumentalist' perspective on ethnicity. They assert that in order to understand ever-changing patterns of ethnic group formation it is necessary to identify the underlying political and economic factors which shape the social environment. According to the instrumentalists, seemingly strong and sincere attachments to ethnic groups tend to arise out of their elites' and ordinary members' manipulation, for political or economic purposes, of pre-existing cultural traditions and institutions. This approach is commonly associated with the work of Abner Cohen (for example, 1974) and with Glazer and Moynihan; for instance, the latter argue in relation to ethnicity in New York that 'a man is connected to his group by ties of family and friendship. But he is also connected by ties of *interest*. The ethnic groups in New York are also *interest groups*' [original emphases] (1970: 17).

The basic instrumentalist approach, because of its emphasis upon political and economic factors, can do little to further my efforts to understand from the participants' perspectives the meanings that are seemingly inherent in ethnic and religious affiliations. More relevant to this study is the perspective on social identity known as the 'boundary' approach, which was pioneered by Barth (most famously in his 'Introduction' to the 1969 volume *Ethnic Groups and Boundaries*) and further developed and modified by many scholars working within social anthropology and the sociology of race and ethnicity.

This approach is sometimes subsumed under the general heading of 'instrumentalism' because, like the latter, it is a highly dynamic perspective, which asserts the malleability of ethnic identities. Also somewhat similarly to the instrumentalists, Barth argues that ethnic groups should not be regarded as isolated and distinct cultural units, but must be understood to have evolved within a wide context of social relations. It is quite wrong, Barth asserts, to analyse ethnicity in such a way as to suggest that there exists 'a world of separate peoples, each with their culture and each organized in a society which can legitimately be isolated for description as an island to itself' (1969: 11). Rather, the theorist should understand that

> categorical ethnic distinctions do not depend on an absence of mobility, contact and information, but do entail social processes of exclusion and incorporation whereby discrete categories are maintained *despite* changing participation and membership in the course of individual life histories.
>
> [original emphasis] (1969: 10)

Where Barth and others who follow his basic ideas differ from those theorists who regard ethnic groups as interest groups is in the primary focus of the analysis. For the latter, processes of ethnic categorisation depend on there being some political or economic gain to be had from affiliation with or mobilisation of the ethnic group, whereas Barth's focus is on the processes of ethnic categorisation *in themselves*, which he views as comprising the defining and ultimate bases of the existence of ethnic groups and relations. Thus, for Barth, it is vital that 'we give primary emphasis to the fact that ethnic groups are categories of ascription and identification by the actors themselves' (1969: 10). Where actors identify one another in terms of assumptions about general origins and background, these are ethnic ascriptions. Ethnic ascriptions therefore tend to focus on and highlight cultural differences; but this does not mean that ethnic groups can be defined with reference to any objective classification or set of cultural features. Rather, in any situation the actors themselves collectively determine which of many potentially significant cultural differences between groups are the grounds of ethnic distinctiveness.

It follows from Barth's perception of ethnic groups as 'categories of ascription and identification' and not as fixed and unique cultural entities that he argues that the focus of investigation should become the boundary between groups rather than their specific cultural contents: for the maintenance of a boundary is that on which the persistence of an ethnic category depends. Thus, he argues,

> The cultural features that signal the boundary may change, and the cultural characteristics of the members may likewise be transformed, indeed, even the organizational form of the group may change – yet the fact of continuing dichotomization between members and outsiders allows us to specify the nature of continuity, and investigate the changing cultural form and content.
>
> (1969: 14)

The process of dichotomisation depends upon a set of individuals making the assumption that they share particular 'criteria of evaluation and judgement', and that they therefore have 'a potential for diversification and expansion of their social relationship to cover eventually all different sectors and domains of activity'. In contrast, other individuals will be regarded as 'strangers' once there is 'a recognition of limitations on shared understandings, differences in criteria for judgement of value and performance, and a restriction of interaction to sectors of assumed common understanding and mutual interest' (1969: 15). Furthermore, that interaction which does take place between members of the different ethnic groups tends to be structured, such that the distinctiveness of the groups is enhanced. Barth writes that 'the organizational feature which . . . must be general for all interethnic relations is a systematic set of rules governing interethnic social encounters' (1969: 16).

Barth's concept of ethnic boundaries, and some of the many developments and critiques of his perspective, aid the analysis of my empirical data in a number of ways. Much debate in the field of race and ethnicity between the primordialists and instrumentalists has centred on the appropriateness of assuming that there is continuity in patterns of ethnic affiliations. It seems to me that the boundary approach allows one to advance from this debate, and from attempts to develop broad syntheses of the two approaches; for in advocating a focus upon actors' perceptions of identity and difference it encourages, as I hope to demonstrate, analysis of both continuity and change, while permitting consideration of the specificities of any given case under study. This focus on actors' definitions clearly ties in with my stated objectives of understanding young British Pakistanis' conceptions of their own ethnicity, nationality and religion, and the special appeal that religion holds for them.

Most importantly, the boundary approach is useful in the context of this study because it is clear that respondents' religious, ethnic and national identities emerge and take shape through the meeting, mixing and opposition of various cultures, values and lifestyles. Above all else, the study has focused upon the respondents' establishment of identities through various processes of learning, reinforcing and challenging several modes of differentiation between themselves and the people around them. Thus it is clear that an investigation of the boundaries which delineate the young people's social identities is vital to any understanding of the identities themselves.

The intention here is not to use Barth's concept of boundaries in an investigation of patterns of ethnic identity alone, but to consider the construction and maintenance of boundaries which delineate *several* sources of social identity. Thus I follow Hutnik's (1986) criticism of Barth's focus upon 'a system of dichotomization': she recognises, in the context of a study of British Asian identities, that patterns of identification are likely to be more complex than Barth appears to suggest, for most individuals position themselves in relation to more than just one social boundary (and the 'marginal individual' may perceive no clear boundaries at all). Wallman argues, similarly, that the multidimensional nature of boundary systems in modern industrial cities should be acknowledged; and that complexities are inevitable

> because a large city offers its residents a large number of reference groups to which they may belong, and from which they may be excluded; because . . . some proportion of urban dwellers will have brought 'other' symbolic structures and ties to their places of origin with them into the urban system; because the pace of change is characteristically faster in town than in the country; and because modern mass media of communication accelerate the spread of cultural and symbolic items with which people may identify, and by which they may differentiate themselves from others. In a complex urban setting . . . there are simply more boundary messages about.
>
> (1978: 214)

The markers of identity which comprise the various social boundaries under investigation here are drawn from the social environments and heritages of the respondents and those around them, and rest on a multitude of assumptions, beliefs and practices: presuppositions about 'race'; legal definitions; notions of group solidarity; a profound sense of 'right' and 'wrong'; emotional attachment to forefathers; language; customs relating to dress, music and food; collective memories; absolute religious truths; acts of worship, and so on. Some of these markers of identity are quite malleable and provide scope for diversity in their modes of articulation among individuals and groups. Others, on the other hand, reflect social structures and structures of meaning which have a real or perceived historical continuity and make up a broad and inevitably constraining context for individual expressions of identity.

This understanding of boundaries clearly presupposes that the social and cultural *contents* of the identities in question are manifest in the processes of boundary construction and maintenance. I hope that I have, by conceiving of boundaries in this way, overcome the important and common criticism of Barth that, since he focuses on 'the ethnic boundary that defines the group, not the cultural stuff it encloses' (1969: 15), he ignores the extent to which, as Eriksen points out, 'the cultural specificities or difference invoked in every justification of ethnic differentiation or dichotomization may (or may not) have a profound bearing on the experiential nature of ethnic relations themselves'. As far as Eriksen is concerned, it is important to remember 'that the medium is not necessarily the message, and that *the differences themselves* . . . should be investigated, and not only the form of their articulation' [original emphasis] (1991: 129). Talai argues along similar lines in complaining that Barth does not provide scope for understanding the meanings that membership of an ethnic community can have for its members: that is, the ways in which the members explain and justify to themselves the very existence of their community. The analyst, he argues, should recognise that

> [a] social boundary does not simply happen as a reaction of one system to another. It also reflects the traffic of symbolic meanings occurring within each of these systems or groups, in which the impact of external factors is refracted through the varied experiences of the members.
>
> (1989: 7)[2]

The empirical data produced by the present Waltham Forest study provide insight into the dynamics of four different boundary processes that play a part in the respondents' lives:

1   the construction and maintenance of inclusive and exclusive boundaries of Britishness within British society at large;
2   the construction and maintenance, by the older generation of the local Pakistani community, of boundaries which preserve a clear social distance between Pakistanis and white Britons;
3   the construction and maintenance, by my respondents and their 'Asian' peers, of boundaries which encompass a more loosely and broadly defined ethnic minority identity;
4   the construction and maintenance, by my respondents and their Muslim peers, of boundaries which delineate a religious identity.

This account of boundary processes rests on the assumption that not only are there different boundaries defining different forms of social identity, but also that any given form of social identity is shaped not by a single but by a *set* of boundaries. Each set of boundaries examined provides a range of definitions of the social identity in question; definitions which vary in their degrees of exclusivity, in the precise criteria upon which they are based, and in the groups or sub-groups that are primarily responsible for upholding the criteria. This view of boundaries

16

follows Ronald Cohen's argument that Barth's concept of ethnic boundaries is only useful if ethnicity (and, I would argue, other sources of social identity) is understood to arise through 'a *series* of nesting dichotomizations of inclusiveness and exclusiveness' [original emphasis] (1978: 387). Unless such a view is taken, Cohen suggests, there is a danger that Barth's approach reifies ethnicity: for although on the one hand Barth insists upon the need to recognise that ethnic groups change in form and content and arise through interaction rather than as isolated units, on the other hand his concern with ongoing boundary maintenance seems to imply that groups are fixed and almost concrete in nature.

Every one of the four boundary processes mentioned above involves more than a single boundary. Definitions of Britishness, for example, range from legal conceptions of citizenship which are inclusive of my respondents and other members of ethnic minorities, to definitions based on values and lifestyle which encompass those members of minorities who think and behave in certain ways, to assumptions that being British is a matter of ancestry and of being white. The boundaries maintained by the older generation are multifaceted: some of the older people are concerned with preserving the integrity of a narrowly defined social unit such as a caste or kin group rather than with the wider Pakistani community; some parents maintain stricter definitions than others of what is appropriate behaviour for members of the minority group; and many parents' perceptions of appropriate behaviour for Pakistanis vary according to whether they are thinking about their sons or their daughters. Similarly, members of the younger generation locate themselves within a range of ethnic boundaries: some prefer, for example, the self-definition of 'Asian' to 'Pakistani', and most tend to maintain different kinds of self-perceptions in different social contexts. Finally, the religious boundaries are, likewise, layered and shifting: sub-groups within the younger generation of Muslims exhibit differing degrees of religious commitment; furthermore, while some of the young people orient themselves towards a local Muslim community, others may feel strongly that they are a part of a national community, and still others may give primacy to the global Muslim *umma*.

There is much variation both within and between the four sets of boundaries in terms of where responsibility lies for boundary construction and maintenance. As some theorists have pointed out, a minority ethnic group can be defined in one way by its members, and in quite another way by outsiders. Jenkins, for instance, argues that a consideration of the ways in which minority groups are externally defined helps to counter-balance the tendency implicit in Barth's theory – arising from its concern with actors' definitions of their own ethnicity – to exaggerate consensus within ethnic groups and overlook the possible significance of unequal distributions of power between groups. Power relations may be manifest in a majority group's categorisation of a minority: that is, when the majority has the ability 'successfully to impose its categories of ascription upon another set of people' (1986: 176). This kind of situation arises, for example, in the extent to which British Pakistanis feel constrained by definitions of Muslims as an alien and threatening minority, or by definitions of the Asian population in Britain as a 'racially' distinct and inferior group. External and internal definitions of a minority group can of course reinforce each other: as is the case when majority categorisations of the British Muslim minority as threatening are countered by assertions of moral superiority from within the minority

It is important to recognise also that definitions of a given ethnic or other social group *within* that group can vary widely. Intra-group variations should be of special interest to researchers concerned with individual expressions of social identity rather than or as well as wider intergroup relations. All groups are likely to be internally differentiated to at least some degree, in the sense that individuals and sub-groups will probably vary in the strictness or specificity of expectations held of co-members. In the case of a group undergoing profound change, such as the Pakistani community in Britain, differences in the experiences of different generations are especially likely to be reflected in differences of opinion regarding the appropriateness of particular modes of identification with the group. Talai notes the extent of intra-group tension over identity within the Armenian community in London; a community which is, he argues,

> more than the aggregate of the choices of individual actors. Its orientation, cohesion, and structure is, at any one point in time, a reflection of a constant push and pull between the different views and stances of its members in the course of their manipulation of shared symbols.
>
> (1989: 5)

Religion and meaning

A primary objective of this study has been to provide a sociological understanding of the continuing appeal of religion as a source of identity to my respondents and their Muslim peers. The concept of religion is subject to various and contested definitions within social science; indeed, B.S. Turner suggests that 'the sociology of religion can be said to exist in order to define its subject-matter' (1991: 15). One of the most widely approved perspectives within this field, of which Durkheim has been the most influential advocate, focuses upon the function that religion performs for social order: that is, religions are defined as sets of beliefs and practices relating to the sacred realm which express and reinforce the social ties which bind individuals together into communities. Other sociologists of religion, whose studies have roots in the work of Weber, have paid closer attention to the ways in which individuals perceive and understand religion: these theorists regard religions as meaning-systems which provide people with answers to ultimate questions about existence and reality.[3] Some sociologists have favoured substantive over functionalist approaches to the problem of defining religion, and have sought to identify a set of characteristics that all religions share: such as a concern with the supernatural, a defined creed and set of practices, and some kind of institutional context within which the beliefs and practices are encouraged and made known.[4]

The broad question of how one should best define religion is not of direct relevance to this study, in the sense that the Islamic tradition to which my respondents adhere is self-evidently 'religious' according to all the major understandings of this term. Of the broad perspectives on religion that are most common in sociology, the one that has most directly informed my approach is that which treats religion as a meaning-system. The ways in which Islam provides meaning in the lives of my respondents will be discussed in subsequent chapters; however, in the context of this discussion of the theoretical issues underlying my empirical concerns, it is most useful to consider in general terms some of the insights provided by and potential problems associated with this particular approach to the study of religion.

The definition of religion as a meaning-system is, obviously, a very loose one; thus, within this perspective there is a wide variety of views on what kinds of social phenomena should and should not be termed 'religious'. Luckmann (1967) is responsible for taking this functionalist understanding of religion to what is perhaps its logical extreme, in that he develops an exceptionally inclusive notion of the religious sphere of life. Luckmann regards as necessarily 'religious' the universal process by which any individual, in conjunction with others around him or her, develops a sense of identity and a coherent biography which frame his or her identity. Specific, historical variants of religion have their roots in this process; and today, as the appeal and plausibility of traditional religions decline, individuals are developing for themselves personal systems of meaning referred to by Luckmann as forms of 'invisible religion'.

Luckmann is quite persuasive in arguing that an appreciation of the (broadly defined) role of religion in life is central to an understanding of the relationship between the individual and society, and thus to sociology as a whole. However, his conceptualisation of religion is problematic, largely because his understanding of what is 'religious' is so all-encompassing that it lacks explanatory value when applied to a study of a given religious tradition.

Some theorists have developed, similarly to Luckmann, inclusive notions of religion as a meaning-system, but are less inclined to regard as religious the entire process by which people become 'selves'. These theorists, instead, have a somewhat narrower interest in relatively coherent and integrated sets of concepts which deal with ultimate questions about reality and existence. Greeley, for example, who contends that 'the basic human religious needs and the basic religious functions have not changed very notably since the late Ice Age' believes that 'religion is an explanation of what the world is all about' (1973: 1, 55). For Bellah, religion is 'a set of symbolic forms and acts which relate man to the ultimate conditions of his existence' (1969: 263), although he notes that in the modern age these forms and acts are 'no longer the monopoly of any groups explicitly labelled religious' (1969: 287). Both Greeley and Bellah draw on the definition of religion outlined by Geertz, for whom

> [r]eligion is: (1) a system of symbols which acts to (2) establish powerful, pervasive, and long-lasting moods and motivations in men by (3) formulating conceptions of a general order of existence and (4) clothing these

conceptions with such an aura of factuality that (5) the moods and motivations seem uniquely realistic.

(1993: 90)

The rather more specific definitions of religion like that of Geertz are still inclusive enough to 'include as "religion" phenomena such as nationalism, Maoism, Marxism, psychologism, spiritualism, and even atheism' (McGuire 1992: 14). Such an approach to the study of religion therefore raises questions about the appropriateness of describing as 'religious' many social phenomena which according to common-sense understandings of the term are no such thing. This shortcoming of the 'meaning-system' approach might lead one to conclude that the sociology of religion is best served by a definition of its subject matter which has at least some substantive as well as a functionalist element. Such a definition might thus make some reference to the fact that the content of those belief-systems commonly deemed to be 'religious' are characterised by their positing of a relationship between the natural world and the supernatural. In the case of my respondents, for example, their concern with the 'supernatural' primarily focuses upon the concept of revelation, notions of judgement and the after-life, and the idea that it is possible to have a personal relationship with God.

Berger has developed an understanding of religion – which he himself describes as a substantive definition – which combines his concern with man's need for meaning with an acknowledgement of the supernatural character of specifically religious belief-systems. Like Luckmann, Berger is interested in the processes by which man, acting collectively, constructs a 'human world' through the production of culture, the purpose of which is 'to provide the firm structures for human life that are lacking biologically' (1969: 6). He differs from Luckmann, however, in asserting that not all processes of 'world-building' should be termed religious; rather, only those which occur 'in a sacred mode' and thus contribute to conceptions of 'the sacred cosmos'. In using the term 'sacred', Berger is referring to 'a quality of mysterious and awesome power, other than man and yet related to him, which is believed to reside in certain objects of experience'. Thus, 'the sacred cosmos is confronted by man as an immensely powerful reality other than himself. Yet this reality addresses itself to him and locates his life in an ultimately meaningful order' (1969: 26). Religion can, therefore, be described as that which 'implies that human order is projected into the totality of being'; or even, Berger suggests, as 'the audacious attempt to conceive of the entire universe as being humanly significant' (1969: 28).

The debate about which kinds of meaning-system can most usefully be described as 'religious' is one that cannot be resolved in any definitive fashion. The relevance to this study of the various discussions about religion and meaning lies mostly in the fact that my respondents seem to feel that Islam provides a framework within which they can make sense of their lives. More particularly, and as I elaborate in Chapter 6, I have found that the young people regard their religion as a source of meaning in that it provides clear and certain guidance on behaviour.

This conclusion rests partly on the assumption, articulated explicitly by some of the theorists cited above and implicit in all theories about religion's function as a source of meaning, that the need for order and fear of meaninglessness are near universal features of the human condition. Geertz, for example, writes that by presenting an image of order, religion supplies a means of dealing with problems of 'bafflement' and pressing questions of how one can make sense of suffering and evil. The effect of religion 'is not to deny the undeniable – that there are unexplained events, that life hurts, or that rain falls upon the just – but to deny that there are inexplicable events, that life is unendurable, and that justice is a mirage' (1993: 108). Berger argues that religion allows one to integrate into an overarching framework of meaning the kinds of marginal situations which are encountered in daily life and which have the potential of bringing into doubt the very reality of one's existence: for example, dreams, experiences of severe emotional trauma, and death. For Berger: 'The sacred cosmos, which transcends and includes man in its ordering of reality . . . provides man's ultimate shield against the terror of anomy' (1969: 27).

It is my contention that the particular circumstances in which my respondents live – as the children of immigrants, and members of a distinctive ethnic and religious minority which is generally accorded a low status within the wider society – are such that for some or many of them the meaning- and order-endowing potential of religion may have a special appeal. In other words, if all religions offer their adherents a way of explaining the world and their place within it, Islam performs this function particularly well for my respondents. This is not to suggest that they are inclined explicitly and self-consciously to ponder problems of 'meaninglessness' or the threat of 'anomy' and, consequently, to decide to take up the Islamic religion. Rather, my argument is that the likelihood of the respondents' wishing to be personally committed to Islam – the religion within which they were born and raised – is enhanced by the vital part it plays in their lives as a source of meaning. Or, to put it somewhat differently, this function of Islam diminishes the likelihood of the respondents' being persuaded by the apparently secular values of wider society that the religion of their parents and grandparents is irrelevant to their own existence.

My investigation of the empirical material relating to the respondents' religious identities must thus incorporate an examination of the ways in which the minority religious community provides a context for the development of individual expressions of religiosity. This consideration brings to the fore a theme that runs throughout the book: namely, respondents' understandings of the nature of the ties which bind them with the people around them. Furthermore, one aspect of my concern with the social context of the respondents' attitudes to Islam has been an interest in how the religious community operates, in accordance with the demands of the fundamental Islamic teachings, to preserve its integrity and internal coherence. In Berger's terms, this is the question of how the members of the community sustain the 'plausibility structure' of their religion: that is, the network of social relations within which the central religious beliefs and values are articulated and hence validated and reinforced.

'Postmodern' identities

Many social theorists argue today that global and, especially within Western nations, societal changes in the late twentieth century are producing radical transformations in modes of identity-construction among individuals. One of the transformations is said to be a growing and even widespread rejection of notions of fixed and unified identities.

The changes which are thought to have produced and to be manifest in the new, postmodern identities are many and interlinked. In particular, perceptions of unified national identities are, apparently, challenged by processes of 'globalisation' brought about by the huge expansion in activities of multinational corporations and by the technological revolution in the communications industry. Traditional sources of identity among dominant groups in Western societies are further challenged by internal processes of change, including the growing ethnic pluralism of urban centres and the fact that minorities are on the whole increasingly self-confident and assertive in comparison with immigrant communities, which are more inclined to tolerate low social status and a semi-segregated existence. At the same time, new social movements organised around issues such as gender inequality and the environment provide alternative foci of identification to those which have been taken for granted in previous eras.

Such processes as these have, in sum, produced 'a world of dissolving boundaries and disrupted continuities', writes Robins. In Britain new questions about identity are faced by all, for 'in a country that is now a container of African and Asian cultures, the sense of what it is to be British can never again have the old confidence and surety'. Indeed, to know what it is to be 'European' is difficult; for Europe is now 'a continent coloured not only by the cultures of its former colonies, but also by American and now Japanese cultures'. Ultimately, the question arises as to whether people are or will at all be able 'in global times' to preserve identities which are coherent and integrated; for 'continuity and historicity of identity are challenged by the immediacy and intensity of global cultural confrontations' (Robins 1991: 41). Back finds, among young people in the multiethnic environments of British cities, an 'embracing [of] diversity in seemingly inexhaustible combinations of form and content in ways that make Britishness or Englishness almost meaningless' (1996: 250).

Those theorists who detect the erosion of traditional sources of identity argue that new identities are emerging which are fluid and hybrid. S. Hall, for example, writes that the postmodern identity is 'a "moveable feast": formed and transformed continuously in relation to the ways we are represented or addressed in the cultural systems which surround us' (1992a: 277). Individuals now have access to 'a variety of possibilities and new positions of identification . . . making identities more positional, more political, more plural and diverse; less fixed, unified or trans-historical' (1992a: 309). The very nature of the historical background and current circumstances of the ethnic minority population in Britain would seem to suggest that the evolution of hybrid and fluid identities may be an especially evident process within minority communities. Gilroy writes of how Afro-Caribbean and Asian cultures in Britain 'have been created from diverse and contradictory elements apprehended through discontinuous histories. They have been formed in a field of force between the poles of under- and overdevelopment, periphery and centre' (1987: 218). But hybridity and fluidity are not characteristic of minority cultures alone: today all cultural forms are, it is argued, 'reflexively in doubt, unstable and lacking cognitive faith or conviction' (Werbner 1997: 2).

Some theorists assume that changing identities in the postmodern age reflect a profound shift that is occurring in the very notions of 'the self' around which individuals orient their entire lives. Today, it is said, people doubt themselves and their own world in a way that they never did before: there is a widespread recognition of the contingency of all aspects of life. The postmodern identity is one which, according to Connolly, 'treats as true the proposition that no identity is grounded in ontological truth . . . [It] assumes an ironic stance towards what it is even while affirming itself in its identity' (1989: 331). Theorists who plead for a 'cultural politics of differences' (for example, Rutherford 1990; West 1990) believe that this situation has a positive potential; but the new sense of self also has dangers associated with it. As Bauman notes: 'nerves of steel are the feature that a contingent being, conscious of its own contingency, needs most. Entertaining an unshared idea is an audacity that is flattering and exhilarating, but comes too close to madness for complete spiritual comfort' (1991: 245). Under such circumstances, Rutherford writes, '"Not belonging", a sense of unreality, isolation and being fundamentally "out of touch" with the world become endemic' (1990: 24).

The academic debate about 'postmodern identities' is by now extremely extensive and diffuse, and the language in which it is conducted is increasingly abstract and, arguably, often impenetrable. However, much of what has been written has a bearing on the findings of this study. Without doubt, the broad social environment in which the respondents are living is undergoing deep-seated social change: late twentieth-century British society is marked by a mixing and blending of cultures and traditions to a degree that in both quantitative and qualitative terms is peculiar to its time. Ethnic minority communities, like that to which my respondents belong, clearly contribute to this process; also, it is within these communities that the most obvious evolution of identities which challenge traditional allegiances and sources of authority is, perhaps, most likely to occur. I have in this chapter already discussed the fact that each of my respondents belongs to a range of social groups, and that each of these groups can, furthermore, be defined in different ways. It therefore seems self-evident that if one is to gain any understanding of the development of religious and ethnic affiliations among second-generation British Pakistanis, one must recognise that many parameters of identity are open to challenge.

Some of the arguments about postmodern identities are, nevertheless, problematic in that they overestimate the extent to which individuals, even in the latter part of the twentieth century, are able to pick and choose the various elements out of which they construct their identities. As I suggest above, individuals are likely to feel subject to certain definitions of identity which are (whether they are based on beliefs about race or descent, on cultural or religious expectations or on other factors) imposed upon them both by fellow-members of the groups to which they belong and by outsiders. Furthermore, many individuals may not feel inclined to challenge certain of the social definitions maintained by others. They may believe that it is highly important that they belong to a social collectivity, such as an ethnic group or a religious community, which they quite specifically perceive to be fixed and long-lasting, and of value precisely because they believe this is its defining characteristic; its very nature.

In fact, some of the writers who assert the significance of postmodern identities do recognise that not all individuals wish to make the most of the 'multiplicity of subject positions and potential identities' to which they have access in the 'post-modern, "wide-open" world': that many social actors, in the face of the uncertainties of this new world, display a tendency to retreat to the old securities of traditional allegiances (Rutherford 1990: 24). Robertson describes the 'almost globally institutionalised nostalgia' that is a product of contemporary processes of globalisation (1990: 55). Similarly, Parekh points to the fact that in the face of an advancing 'global culture' many societies 'display an understandable tendency to return to the security of the traditional way of life and to romanticise a past age' (1995: 147). Bauman writes of these matters with particular force: 'No wonder that postmodernity, the age of contingency *für sich*, of self-conscious contingency, is also the age of community: of the lust for community, search for community, invention of community, imagining community' (1991: 246). The postmodern age is thus an age, Bauman asserts, of 'neo-tribes'.

There is little to argue with in the suggestion that in the Western world today there is a widespread desire to belong that, paradoxically, accompanies the free-doms men and women are enjoying – perhaps for the first time – *not* to belong. But one can perhaps question the normative assumptions underlying the interpreta-tion of this desire to belong as nothing more than an empty and futile response to what are effectively overwhelming forces of fragmentation. For Bauman, neo-tribes 'inflame imagination the most and attract the most ardent loyalty when they still reside in the realm of hope' (1991: 249). What is more, 'the foremost paradox of the frantic search for communal grounds of consensus is that it results in more dissipation and fragmentation, more heterogeneity' (1991: 251). For Robins, the search for community is even potentially dangerous: it is no more than 'a mainte-nance of protective illusion'; a quest for 'purified identities' which can take 'the form of the resuscitated patriotism and jingoism that we are now seeing in a resur-gent Little Englandism' (1991: 41). Such normative goals, even as the notion of 'the norm' is denied, are no more evident than in West's call for us to 'trash the monolithic and homogeneous in the name of diversity, multiplicity and hetero-geneity' and to highlight 'the contingent, provisional, variable, tentative, shifting and changing' (1990: 19).

What dismissive or purely negative attitudes towards traditional notions of 'community' and 'belonging' tend to overlook is the fact that if individuals feel they are bound to certain grcups which are relatively fixed and have some historical continuity, and if they feel that the state of being bound is either inevitable or something to be sought after, then theoretical assertions about the non-essentialist nature of identity have little relevance to the day-to-day experiences of those individuals. As Friedman insists, the way in which life is experienced 'is neither true nor false; it simply *is*. The on-going history of the world cannot be interpreted as an intellectual conversation in which problems can be solved by convincing people that they have got it all wrong' [original emphasis] (1997: 88). Likewise, in a discussion focused on the specific case of British Asians, Modood points out that although social scientists are right to avoid 'ethnic absolutism', there are dangers of elitism and a consequent marginalisation of the majority of British Asians where the emphasis on 'new' forms of identity leads to an excessive concern with the *avant-garde*. He argues, further, that

[a] rejection of theories of primordial ethnic absolutism should not prevent us from accurately describing where most Asians are, regardless of whether it seems sufficiently 'new' or progressive. We must not pit 'new' and 'old' ethnicities against each other: we must avoid the elitism of cultural vanguardism that devalues and despises where the ordinary majority of any group or social formation is at – an elitism so thoughtlessly exemplified in Salman Rushdie's *The Satanic Verses*, to the loss of us all, new and old.

(1994: 873)

2

THE BACKGROUND

This chapter is concerned with certain aspects of the broad socio-historical context within which young British Pakistanis' expressions of religious identity are emerging. It is clearly far beyond the scope of this book to broach the vast subjects of the history and teachings of Islam, the evolution of Islam in South Asia, and the situation of ethnic and religious minorities in contemporary Western society. Therefore I have relatively modest aims here: namely, to highlight the teachings of Islam which appear to be at the core of my respondents' beliefs and to discuss the circumstances of Muslims in Britain.

Islam: the central tenets

As I shall demonstrate in the latter part of this book, my respondents' expressions of commitment to Islam are not, on the whole, idiosyncratic or highly personalised, but are rooted in an almost unquestioning acceptance of the key orthodoxies of Islamic thought. Hence, it is evident that any thorough understanding of the young people's views on Islam is dependent upon some background knowledge of the central tenets of the religion. This is not to suggest, however, that the respondents regard Islamic beliefs and practices as static and uniform: indeed, they made clear their awareness that there are different and often contradictory interpretations of the teachings of Islam, and that Muslims through the ages have tackled diverse problems in diverse ways.

The religion of Islam – today the religion of about one-fifth of the world's population – was established in seventh-century Arabia, on the basis of revelations received by Muhammad, the man deemed by Muslims to be the last or 'seal' of God's prophets. The teachings of Islam are derived first and foremost from the Qur'an, which is believed to comprise the direct words of God as they were perceived by Muhammad over the twenty-two years of his prophecy (the Arabic term *al-qur'an* translates literally as 'the reading' or 'the recitation'). During Muhammad's lifetime the revelations were preserved by oral tradition and as fragments of written text; the full text of the Qur'an was eventually put together after the Prophet's death. The Qur'an remains to this day the primary source of Islamic law and the focus of faith among Muslims. Its 114 *suras* (or chapters) combine spiritual and ethical teachings and guidelines for social and political legislation within the religious community.

The doctrines of Islam were further elaborated by means of reference to anecdotes about the words and deeds of Muhammad: he is deemed to have been a perfect man, who led a life which epitomised God's wishes for the whole of humanity. The *sunna* or 'example' provided by Muhammad is recorded in the form of *hadith*; that is, collections of reports on the life of Muhammad, including his sayings, which are believed to have been passed on from the members of the first Muslim community to subsequent generations.[1] Differences of opinion over interpretations of the Qur'an and *hadith* or over questions of how their teachings should be applied to particular situations led to the evolution of two further sources of Islamic law: namely, *ijma'* and *ijtihad*. *Ijma'* means 'consensus', and in practice is understood to refer to consensus of the *'ulama'* or religious scholars rather than all Muslims. The principle of *ijtihad*, or 'personal effort', allowed for the exercise of individual opinion in seeking solutions to religious problems; in time, emphasis was placed on the importance of *qiyas*, or reasoning by analogy, rather than on independent thought.

The teachings of Islam revolve around the notion of one transcendent, all-powerful and all-merciful God, Allah, who created the world and all that is in it with the command, 'Be'. The purpose of mankind is to worship God by following his universal law and submitting fully to him: the Arabic word *islam* means 'surrender' and *muslim* 'one who surrenders' (from the root *slm* which is 'peace'). Muslims are required to 'balance the world (*dunya*) with the principles of religion (*din*)'; they must, in other words, 'live in the real world but be guided by the principles of religion, by the idea of the afterworld' (A.S. Ahmed 1993: 29). All individuals are answerable for their deeds and beliefs at the Day of Judgement; those who have obeyed God's will are granted a place in Heaven, where they will enjoy pleasures of all kinds; the guilty are sent to Hell, a terrible, fiery place, where they will suffer eternal torment. God, throughout history, has sent prophets to his peoples to guide them, to show them 'the straight path'; but man, though he is dominant over all of nature, has many failings and often rejects God's messages.

Islam is commonly described as a legalistic religion for it is essentially through acceptance of the Divine Law, the *shari'a*, that one becomes a Muslim. Islamic law governs all forms of behaviour in which men and women engage: it covers matters relating to worship and ritual, family relationships and structures, economics, the nature and functions of the state, the minutiae of everyday life, the sanctions appropriate for those who contravene the rules, and much else. The *shari'a*, as it operates at the level of the collectivity, provides in its ideal form for rule in the name of God and in accordance with the wishes of God: rulers of an Islamic state have no secular basis for their power. The notion that Muslims should live as members of a community of believers – the *umma* – is thus crucial to Islamic teachings.

The all-encompassing nature of the *shari'a* ensures that, for the individual, all aspects of life are permeated with religious meanings. All actions carried out by individuals fall into one of five categories: namely, obligatory, recommended, neutral or permissible (this includes the vast majority of acts), disapproved, and forbidden. One therefore expresses devotion to God not only through religious ritual, but also through the general conduct of day-to-day life. Thus there are two basic categories of legal rights and duties: the first being duties to God, and the second duties to other people (Esposito 1991).

As regards the latter category, this means that Muslims in their daily lives should be guided by religiously-oriented moral concerns: they should, for example, give help to the poor and weak, live chaste lives (although celibacy is strongly discouraged), dress modestly (especially women who, according to most interpretations, are required to cover the whole of their bodies except their faces and hands), respect their parents, maintain loving marital relationships (men are permitted up to four wives, but only if they are able to act in an equally just manner towards each) and completely avoid alcohol and other intoxicants. Some religious prescriptions relating to day-to-day, general conduct are reinforced by harsh punishments for immorality, known as *hudud* punishments, which are defined in the Qur'an; other more general moral propositions are left as matters of conscience.

The key elements of ritual practice for Muslims are defined by what are known as the 'Five Pillars' of Islam. These Five Pillars are common to both Sunni and Shi'i Islam,[2] and adherence to the obligatory acts to which they refer is generally regarded as the defining element of an Islamic lifestyle. The Five Pillars are as follows:

Profession of faith (shahada)   This involves the utterance at least once in one's lifetime, in Arabic and with clear understanding and intention, of the statement 'There is no god but God and Muhammad is the messenger of God'.

Prayer (salat)   Five prayers are to be said in a day; ideally they should be said communally but can be offered individually. The times of prayers are defined as daybreak, noon, mid-afternoon, sunset and evening; and on Fridays a special noon prayer is held, at which a sermon is read. Before prayer, Muslims are required to wash their hands and forearms, face and feet. The prayers involve recitation of verses from the Qur'an, and are performed facing in the direction of Mecca. Each prayer entails a set series of movements between postures, including standing, bowing and prostration.

Alms tax (zakat)   Muslims are required to pay an annual tax which goes to help the poor. The details of the amounts which are owed and on what forms of wealth they should be paid vary according to the different schools of law. In some Islamic states *zakat* has been a tax that is collected by the government, and in others it has operated as a voluntary tax.

Fasting (sawm)   Muslims are required to fast throughout the ninth month of the Islamic calendar: the month of Ramadan. The fast entails abstinence from eating, drinking, smoking and sexual intercourse between daybreak and sunset. The celebration of *'id al-fitr* (the major festival of the year) is held at the end of the month.

Pilgrimage (hajj)   Every Muslim who can afford to do so is required to go on pilgrimage to Mecca once in a lifetime; this takes place in the last month of the Muslim calendar. The pilgrimage ends with the festival of *'id al-adha*, at which cows, sheep, goats and camels are sacrificed.

Ritual in Islam is more than just that entailed by the Five Pillars, and encompasses even the smallest mundane details of daily life; for example, Islamic scholars have been particularly concerned with outlining rules on personal hygiene. The attention to detail in part arises out of the special reverence that Muslims have for Muhammad, and the general wish to emulate all aspects of his life. Matters of ritual impinge upon diet: food that can be eaten is *halal*, and with regard to meat includes only animals that have been ritually slaughtered (that is, they must be killed with a single cut of the throat, and the kill should be consecrated with a blessing). There is, in addition, a complete ban on eating pork.

Notwithstanding the centrality of the tenets outlined above to Muslims in general, as I have already suggested it is important not to give a false impression of uniformity and consistency when writing of the teachings of Islam. There are today – as there have always been – many divisions of many kinds within the Islamic world. While the primary theological divide is between Sunni and Shi'i Islam, within Shi'ism itself there are many sects, of which the largest is Twelve Imam Shi'ism. Within Sunni Islam, various schools of law have offered differing interpretations of aspects of the *shari'a*; the four surviving Sunni schools of law are the Hanafi (which is followed in the Indian subcontinent and Central Asia), the Maliki, the Shafi'i and the Hanbali.

The rise of Sufism, which in the eighth and ninth centuries was a mystical movement among members of the Muslim elite but which in time developed mass appeal, brought about many expressions of belief which diverged from orthodox Sunnism. These expressions have tended to reflect indigenous forms of worship and cultural traditions in the societies within which Islam established itself. Diversity within the Islamic world arises also because the attempts of Muslim thinkers to respond to the dilemmas of modernity have produced a range of movements seeking, in various ways, to revive, reinterpret or return to whatever might be considered to be the essence of Islam.

The history of Islam in the Indian subcontinent provides many illustrations of the extent to which it has tended to diversify and to be infused with local traditions. Islam emerged as a religious force in South Asia through an ongoing struggle with Hinduism, and – even as Muslims were successfully establishing the powerful Mughal empire, which enjoyed its golden age under the reign of Akbar in the latter part of the sixteenth century – had to adapt to being a minority faith. By the time of the Partition of India in 1947 Muslims still numbered not more than about one-fifth of the total population of the subcontinent. What is more, in South Asia the Muslims were a minority in a population 'that was Hindu and polytheistic, *kafir* [infidel] by the strictest tenets of their faith' (F. Robinson 1979: 87). Within this broad context, a wide range of expressions of Islamic faith emerged: 'from the violent, pietist and assured to the pacific, introspective, and tentative', and within a wide range of settings: 'the individual conscience and conduct, the life of the sect, order or community, the courts of kings, the councils of legislators, [and] the conferences of politicians' (Hardy 1987: 390).

Various forms of Sufism, above all else, shaped the beliefs and practices of South Asian Muslims; Sufi orders in India proliferated, in particular during the time of the Delhi Sultanate (Lewis 1994). It seems that the gradual Islamicisation of non-Muslim tribes, which occurred predominantly in eastern Bengal, Western Punjab, the north-west Frontier and Baluchistan, was 'facilitated by the fact that the Sufis and their circles often established shrines on sites which had previously been venerated by Buddhists and Hindus'. Furthermore, the 'rich vernacular of the devotional hymns' developed by the Sufi brotherhoods had the capacity 'to root Islam in the hearts and minds of the majority, who were either unlettered or unacquainted with the languages of high Islamic culture – Arabic and Persian' (Lewis 1994: 33–4). Many Sufis were, nevertheless, unhappy with the persistence of practices among converts which they deemed unIslamic, particularly certain forms of worship at shrines involving, for example, animal sacrifice and intercessionary prayers to the deceased saints. Today, devotion to holy men and worship at shrines continue to be popular practices among the Muslims of South Asia and often provoke criticisms from religious leaders concerned about unorthodoxy.

The centuries of interaction between Islam and Hinduism in South Asia were followed by an extended period of close contact between the religions of India (which, since the sixteenth century, included Sikhism) and Western political and intellectual traditions. The thorough defeat of the Mughal empire by the British over the course of the nineteenth century was a shock which brought about among Muslim religious leaders 'a period of unusual creativity' as they pondered the question of what it meant to be Muslim in a society ruled by non-Muslims (F. Robinson 1988: 4). A number of religious reform movements came into being which provided a variety of answers to this question; among these movements, the Barelvi and, to a lesser extent, the Deobandi – both of which were established in the late nineteenth century – continue to enjoy extensive support today among British Muslims from South Asian backgrounds.[3]

Although I have warned that one must not simplistically regard Muslims as making up a homogeneous global community of believers, I nevertheless am content to conclude this discussion of the central tenets of Islam with the assertion that it is possible to conceive of Islam as, compared to other world religions, *relatively* monolithic. Certainly, most of the individuals who are the subjects of my own study spoke in such a way as to suggest that they believe the essence of their religion to be a unified and complete set of teachings. That these young people maintain such a view is due not to a misapprehension about their religion, but to the fact that Islam does encompass core elements which are consistent over time and place. In particular, this is manifest in the central and key assumption that the Qur'an comprises the direct words of God and that, therefore, its text can never be altered (even if interpretations of that text evidently vary widely). Furthermore, the 'Five Pillars' of Islam, although not set out fully in the Qur'an, were formulated within early Islamic thought and have remained throughout the Islamic world the basis of religious practice.

Thus it is that Roff, seeking to address the question of whether Islamic movements are 'one or many', argues that

> [a]ll social action by Muslims, *acting as Muslims* (acceptors of the *shari'a*), is constrained by the objectively invariant prescriptions of 'Islam', known to the believer first from the Qur'an and secondly (if more questionably invariant) the *sunna*. Though these prescriptions (and their elaboration by those learned in the *shari'a*) must be interpreted and applied by historically situated individuals (or collectivities), and hence do not exist outside of time or social context, it can be argued that they supply a major, sometimes determinative, part of the perceived objective conditions which direct or constrain action. Further, the common need to persuade, urge, teach, command or reason with one's fellows in pursuit of proper Muslim action ensures the frequent iteration of prescription and its embodiment in argument and discourse.
>
> [original emphasis] (1987: 31)

Muslims in Britain

Estimates based on census data suggest that in Britain there are probably between one and one and a half million Muslims, of whom nearly half are of Pakistani origin. There are also large numbers of Bangladeshi and Indian Muslims; the remaining Muslims are predominantly Turkish Cypriots, Arabs and Somalis (Peach and Glebe 1995). Some Muslim organisations have however argued that the British Muslim population is larger than is suggested by assessments based on census information, since the numbers of white and Afro-Caribbean converts to Islam are underestimated.[4] The large majority of South Asian Muslims in Britain are Sunni, and follow Barelvi or Deobandi traditions.[5]

Levels of interest in Islam

The starting-point of this study was an interest in the question as to why and how commitment to Islam persists in contemporary Britain. Clearly, then, a basic assumption that informed the formulation of my research questions was that Islam is a significant source of identity among British Muslims, and particularly among young British Pakistanis. The extent to which religion does indeed play an important role in the lives of my respondents, and the ways in which it does, are discussed in depth in the latter part of this book. It thus seems appropriate, prior to the analysis of my empirical findings, to consider whether the findings of related research support my claim that within the population of young British Muslims as a whole, Islam is a highly significant aspect of life.

Few attempts have been made to gather quantitative data on patterns of religious commitment and practice among British Muslims. However, *The Fourth National Survey of Ethnic Minorities* includes a valuable section on religion (see Modood 1997a): two-thirds of the survey's Pakistani respondents aged 16–34 stated that religion is 'very important' to the way they live their lives, compared to just over 80 per cent of those from older age groups; 65 per cent of Muslim male respondents (from Pakistani and other Asian backgrounds) aged 16–34 said they visit a mosque at least once a week, compared to approximately 80 per cent of older respondents.

Smaller-scale but more in-depth information is provided by a number of studies which, like this one, provide a view of the extent of interest in religion among certain members of given Muslim communities in Britain. While it is important to be cautious in generalising from these case-studies, I shall here give a brief summary of some of the ways in which, according to this literature, religion appears to be motivating young Pakistani and other Muslims in this country. I shall do so by highlighting four broad themes which are regularly discussed by other researchers and which, since they tally with the findings of my study, will be explored in detail in Chapters 6 and 7.

Learning to be Muslims

A number of researchers have found that a growing minority of young Muslims are developing an active interest in the study of their religion. While the Islamic education that is provided for children in mosques tends to be extremely traditional, with much emphasis for example on learning by rote, increasing numbers of young people appear to be committed to the notion that they should learn for themselves what it means to be a Muslim, rather than simply accept what they are told by their parents and the local *imams*. This attitude to Islam appears to go together with a willingness to question not the basic tenets of Islam, but aspects of traditional interpretations of the religion.[6]

Prioritising religious identities

Some studies have drawn special attention to what seems to be an increasingly common tendency for South Asian Muslims in Britain to emphasise the distinction between religion and ethnicity as sources of identity. These young Muslims argue that Islam is entirely relevant to their lives in Britain, whereas there is much less to be gained from attachment to, for example, Pakistan as a country of origin or 'Pakistani' traditions and customs which do not derive from the religion.[7] This approach to Islam is one which often goes hand-in-hand with a sense of the importance of religious study: many of the young people feel that it is only once they have learnt about their religion that they have the capacity to understand the differences between an identity that is based on religion and one that is based on ethnicity or 'culture'.

32

Protesting as Muslims

What appears from the literature to be a relatively recent phenomenon within British Islam is the articulation of a self-proclaimed Muslim identity by young men engaged in forms of political or social protest. This often vociferous assertion of the importance of Islam is not necessarily accompanied by a commitment to religious practice; and can, it seems to me, usefully be defined as the expression of an 'assertive Muslim identity'. It was in the context of the 'Rushdie Affair' that youth protests in religious terms first became noticeable, and they took many commentators by surprise; perhaps to a lesser degree this form of protest occurred also as an element of British Muslims' campaigns against the Gulf War.[8]

Radical Islam

In the literature on Muslims in Britain some attention has been paid to the development of radical or militant, or what are sometimes termed 'fundamentalist', approaches to Islam among a small minority of young British Muslims. These young (and also some older) men and women reject all aspects of Western life as morally corrupt and inherently worthless. They seek to promote single-minded and active devotion to Islam among their fellow-Muslims and also, quite commonly, to encourage conversion to Islam by non-Muslims.[9] The loudest voice of radical Islam in Britain at present is probably that of the organisation hizb-ut tahrir (discussed below).

The suggestion that religion is an important basis of social identity among young Muslims is certainly supported by the literature on Islam in Britain. As we have seen, data from the *Survey of Ethnic Minorities* indicate a slight intergenerational decline in levels of religiosity; nevertheless, it is clear that commitment to Islam remains relatively high among the younger generation. This is all the more apparent if one compares data on Muslims with data on other groups in Britain. For example, the survey cited above found that among the 16–34-year-old respondents, religion is 'very important' to only 5 per cent of the whites, 18 per cent of the Caribbeans and 35 per cent of Indians (of whom the large majority are Hindu or Sikh) (Modood 1997a). It can be noted also that, according to other survey data, no more than 16 per cent of the total British population attend religious services at least two or three times a month – although, perhaps surprisingly, 70 per cent claim to believe in God (Greeley 1992).

To the extent that generalisations can be made on the basis of the studies of particular Muslim communities, it seems that for significant numbers of young British Muslims religion is an increasingly important basis of social identity. It appears that there is a small but growing minority of young people who are especially devout – whether this devoutness is expressed in the form of Islamic activism and militancy, or in a commitment to a quest for knowledge about Islam, or simply in constant and thorough religious practice. There exist around this devout core many other young Muslims – probably the majority or even large majority of born-Muslims in Britain – who vary widely in their levels of belief and practice but maintain at least some degree of serious and self-conscious attachment to their religion both as the basis of a community to which they belong and as a source of teachings about their lives and their world. Again, the ways in which they express that attachment are many and varied: some do so through practice, some through protest, some through learning, some through the general manner in which they live their lives. It is clear also that while there are different ways of being a Muslim, there are no concrete categories which mark one kind of allegiance from another: young people change in how they think about and practise their religion as they grow older and their circumstances alter.

British Muslim organisations

One way of assessing the extent of interest in, and commitment to, religion among British Muslims of all generations is to consider the expansion of Islamic organisations in Britain. It is difficult to give an overview of institutional Islam, as there exists a complex and wide array of organisations, many of which are inter-related and have ties with bodies based outside the UK. Nevertheless, I will here present a sketch of three primary dimensions of organisational activity within British Islam: namely, activity relating to mosques, national organisations, and youth organisations.

Mosques

The mosque is the basic and essential religious institution within any Muslim community. For Muslims in Britain the mosque has thus become 'a symbolic representation of the land of Islam' (Joly 1995: 75). The mosque's primary function is to be the place where communal prayers are held, sermons are delivered and religious instruction is offered to children. The first mosque in Britain was probably the one founded in Woking in 1889; this became the early centre of Islamic activity in Britain (Lewis 1994). From the 1960s, as the Muslim population of Britain increased rapidly, so did the number of mosques which were registered with the Registrar General. By 1980 over 200 mosques were registered, and by the early 1990s the number had exceeded 500.[10] It should be noted however that there is no technical requirement for mosques to be registered, although it is generally beneficial for them to do so. Nielsen (1992) suggests that there are probably a few dozen more mosques functioning in the UK than have been officially registered.

National organisations

The majority of mosques in Britain were, according to Nielsen (1984), originally founded on a local basis (although most were linked within informal structures which made up Deobandi and Barelvi networks). But these were soon encompassed within various kinds of national organisations. Formal attempts to coordinate and promote Muslim activities at a national level have a long history; and there is now what Lewis refers to as 'a plethora of bodies presuming to speak for all British Muslims' (1994: 207). Many of these bodies have ties with institutions based outside Britain.

Among the most active national organisations in Britain is the Islamic Foundation, which is based in Leicester and was established by the Pakistani-based religious party Jama'at-i Islami. The Foundation is primarily responsible for conducting research and publishing books and leaflets on Islam including a lot of material for children; in particular, according to Andrews (1992), it seeks through its publications to promote and disseminate the views of Jama'at's founder, Mawdudi. Jama'at is also represented in Britain by the UK Islamic Mission, which has had as special goals 'the identification of young leadership, their education, and the provision of appropriate literature in English' (Lewis 1994: 102). It has also been active in liaising on behalf of British Muslims with local authority structures (Nielsen 1992). Both the Islamic Foundation and the UK Islamic Mission are also linked with some other bodies, of which the most influential is probably the youth organisation Young Muslims UK.

Three organisations which have all attempted in somewhat similar ways to act as federations of local mosques and religious groups are the Union of Muslim Organisations (UMO); the Imams and Mosques Council; and the Council of Mosques in the UK and Eire. The UMO was established in 1970 with the primary objective of furthering the political goals of British Muslims by lobbying the government and political parties. Both the Imams and Mosques Council and the Council of Mosques were set up as rival umbrella groups in 1984. The former has been sponsored by the Muslim World League in Mecca; the latter, which has links with the Libyan 'Call of Islam' Society and is under the chairmanship of Dr Zaki Badawi (who also set up the Muslim College in West London), has been successful in finding support among the Barelvi network of mosques (Lewis 1994; Nielsen 1992).

There are several other influential national organisations. These include the Islamic Cultural Centre which, largely on the initiative of the Saudi Arabian Ambassador, was opened by King George VI in 1944 in Regent's Park, London, and since 1977 has been housed within an expensive new complex which includes the well-known gold-domed mosque. Initially the Centre served Arab expatriates, although it has subsequently sought with limited success to represent the British Muslim population as a whole (Nielsen 1992). The South Asian reform movement Tabligh-i Jama'at is represented by a successful seminary established in 1982 in Dewsbury, West Yorkshire. The pro-Iranian Muslim Institute, formerly under the directorship of the late Kalim Siddiqui, has not had popular backing; but it has attracted a great deal of media interest, in particular as a consequence of Siddiqui's publicly-stated support for the Ayatollah Khomeini's *fatwa* against Salman Rushdie, and its role in setting up the so-called Muslim Parliament.

Youth organisations

Organisations which provide for Muslim youth seem to be growing in number and in scope. Activities for young Muslims are organised both at local and national levels; some projects are entirely local initiatives, but many are to varying degrees affiliated with or coordinated by national bodies. Projects run for and by young adults and children include Muslim youth groups which combine the provision of religious classes with the organisation of recreational activities such as sporting events, outings and summer camps; small study circles conducted in private homes; and series of talks and lectures held in mosques and local community centres.

A particularly active national youth organisation, which as mentioned above is related to the Islamic Foundation and UK Islamic Mission, is the Young Muslims UK (YM). It was founded in 1984 in Bradford after the demise of its forerunner, the Islamic Youth Movement which had been established (also in Bradford) in the early 1970s but had fared poorly. The YM, now a national organisation, runs a wide range of activities including religious talks and meetings, one-day and weekend conferences and summer camps; it also publishes a magazine, *Trends*. Andrews (1992) has argued that the YM draws its membership primarily from the Muslim student body, and has shown little interest in recruiting among working-class Muslim youth. More recently however, according to Lewis (in press: 10), Bradford members of YM have demonstrated a wish 'to shed something of their elitist image', and thus have, for example, been involved in providing leisure activities and extra tuition for (often under-achieving) Muslim children in schools. Furthermore, Lewis writes, YM has been committed to dealing with issues to which British Muslim youth can easily relate; with, for example, *Trends* addressing such subjects as the kind of information on Islam that is available on the Internet.[11]

Hizb-ut tahrir (literally 'party of liberation') appears to have been the most influential militant Islamic organisation in Britain over the past few years, and although it is not specifically or solely a youth movement it has directed its efforts primarily at young Muslims. This group was founded in the Middle East in the 1950s and has been banned in most Arab countries as a result of its subversive activities (Lewis, in press). In Britain, hizb-ut tahrir operates mostly from East London, and has been especially active in distributing literature, tapes and videos and organising meetings and lectures; it also publishes a magazine. Its activities are devoted to the self-proclaimed goal of establishing – apparently as soon as and wherever possible – *khilafah* (the title of its magazine), or Islamic rule. Hizb-ut tahrir has apparently enjoyed its greatest success in taking control of a large number of Islamic Societies in universities and colleges, including further education colleges, across the country. This has led, in some cases, to these societies or the group itself being banned on account of its distribution of literature, which has been deemed anti-Semitic, racist and homophobic. As Lewis (in press) points out, the danger posed by such an organisation is twofold: first, the inflammatory nature of its literature serves to reinforce negative stereotypes of Muslims among the non-Muslim population of Britain;[12] second, it undermines support for groups such as YM which, rather than setting themselves up in opposition with all things 'Western', are interested in engaging with wider society.

Another youth initiative which has enjoyed some success in recent years is the newspaper *Q News*. This is an English-language weekly paper which began publishing in London in March 1992, having earlier existed in the form of the magazine *Muslimwise*. The goals of *Q News* have more in common with those of YM than those of groups like hizb-ut tahrir, to the extent that while it is certainly dedicated to promoting sincere and determined adherence to Islam, it also encourages young people to think about ways of being British *and* Muslim, and does not demand outright confrontation with 'the West'. According to Lewis, *Q News* 'appeals to young, educated Muslims, impatient of sectarianism, and is able through an international language, English, to access innovative and relevant Islamic scholarship' (1994: 207). The newspaper includes a bi-weekly advice column by Sheikh Syed Darsh offering answers to a diverse range of readers' questions: issues broached in this column have included homosexuality and Islam, prostitution, and questions as to whether it is appropriate for Muslims to be involved in British party politics and to undertake jury service in a non-Islamic judicial system (Lewis, in press). *Q News* is also associated with other projects such as An-Nisa, a women's group which has been involved in various activities including the organisation of Islamic classes and cultural exhibitions. The 'Mind, Body and Soul' project grew out of An-Nisa; this is a loose network of young Muslims, and was set up to discuss and examine aspects of British Muslim identity.

Political activities and issues

It is also possible to gain some insight into the levels of interest in Islam in Britain by looking at the extent of political mobilisation of British Muslims around issues relating to their religion. From the mid-1980s, religiously-oriented political action has been increasingly evident, the most important focus of which has been the opposition to Salman Rushdie's novel *The Satanic Verses*. By its very nature, political activity is carried out by the Muslim leadership rather than the bulk of the British Muslim population (although some popular protests against *The Satanic Verses* did take place). However, the growing political participation of the leadership can be said to reflect some quite generalised concerns, and at the same time to promote religious awareness at the grass roots level. Given the indivisibility of the religious and the political sphere in Islamic thinking, it is to be expected that British Muslims should make some efforts to exert an influence on public policy – notwithstanding the ambiguities (in terms of Islam) of their position as members of a very predominantly non-Muslim society,[13] and the fact that because Islam does not have formal recognition in the UK, Muslim rights have tended to be recognised only on a piecemeal basis within particular areas (Dwyer and Meyer 1996: 220).

The Rushdie Affair

Of all the issues affecting race relations and Muslims that have come to the fore in Britain over the past decade, what is generally known as the 'Rushdie Affair' has aroused the most interest and concern among both Muslims and non-Muslims; among academics, journalists, religious leaders, policy-makers and ordinary people.[14] Salman Rushdie's novel, according to its author,

> celebrates hybridity, impurity, intermingling, the transformation that comes of new and unexpected combinations of human beings, cultures, ideas, politics, movies, songs. It rejoices in mongrelization and fears the absolutism of the Pure . . . *The Satanic Verses* is for change-by-fusion, change-by-conjoining. It is a love-song to our mongrel selves.
>
> (1991: 394)

But it is also a book that has brought to the surface the conflicts and the turmoil in 'our mongrel selves'; and the tensions and antagonisms within our hybrid societies.

In Britain, initial objections to Rushdie's novel, published by Viking/Penguin in the UK in September 1988, were quietly voiced by middle-class Asian and Arab Muslims in London, who made representations to the publisher and the government (Modood 1990). An apparent indifference to the issue on the part of the media was ended when, in January 1989, street demonstrations were held, at one of which (in Bradford) the book was publicly burnt. British Muslim anger over the book remained high, and was given greater energy and produced among many non-Muslims intense alarm when on 14 February 1989 the Ayatollah Khomeini of Iran issued an Islamic ruling, or *fatwa*, sentencing Rushdie to death for apostasy. This was welcomed by many Asian Muslims in Britain; not because, Modood claims, the majority wanted Rushdie killed, but because the Ayatollah 'was considered to have stood up for Islamic dignity and sensibilities against the West and in contrast to Arab silence' (1990: 155).[15]

Campaigns in Britain against *The Satanic Verses* continued and took various forms including demonstrations, the circulation of petitions and extensive lobbying of MPs and the government. A wide range of organisations was involved in the protests; almost all were 'united in their demand that the book should be withdrawn from circulation, destroyed, and not be re-published in any form' (Joly 1995: 19). They campaigned also for the extension of the blasphemy law to cover Islam. The UK Action Committee on Islamic Affairs (UKACIA) was established in October 1989 specifically for the purpose of protesting against the book, and has proved to be quite effective at putting pressure on the government through its lobbying of the OIC (Organisation of the Islamic Conference) and the involvement in it of Muslim ambassadors in Britain (Lewis 1994).

The scale of the offence caused by Rushdie's book is extremely difficult, if not impossible, for non-Muslims to comprehend. Modood discounts Rushdie's argument that the *mullahs* had stirred up Muslim anger for their own political ends: 'The truth is that all the religious zealots had to do was simply quote from *SV* for anger, shame and hurt to be felt' (1990: 54). Ruthven has tried to understand, from the perspective of a non-Muslim, the basis of this anger, shame and hurt. He points out that the book both challenged the authority of the Qur'an (its title, it should be noted, refers to some verses of the Qur'an that, according to certain accounts, were inspired by the Devil and subsequently removed) and appeared to question the Prophet's moral integrity. He suggests that it was this latter insult which was the most dangerous, for in hitting out at the Prophet – and, what is more, in language deemed in itself to be highly offensive – Rushdie attacked what, for Muslims, 'has become an integral part of their identity' (1990: 162). The fact that Rushdie gave the name Mahound, which means false prophet, to the character in the book who is identified with the Prophet further inflamed Muslim anger; as did Rushdie's description of a brothel in which the prostitutes had the names of Muhammad's wives (Lee 1990).

One of the most striking aspects of the Rushdie Affair in Britain was the depth of the anger expressed by Muslim youth (especially young men), who were well-represented in demonstrations against the novel. Many of these young people appeared to be articulating a self-conscious identity as 'Muslim' for the first time (even if in most cases this was not accompanied by increasing levels of religious practice), and seemed to feel as acutely as their parents that Rushdie's book was an intolerable affront. For the young people in particular, the sense of insult was without doubt greatly fuelled by an awareness of racism and experiences of exclusion.[16]

The failure of the government to respond to the concerns of the Muslims further exacerbated their feelings of marginalisation and alienation, as did the fact that the large majority of non-Muslims appeared not to recognise that the Muslims might have grounds for anger. Indeed, the protests of the Muslims seem to have greatly increased hostility towards Islam among non-Muslim Britons; they also, as Lee (1990) points out, confirmed what appeared to be one of the basic premises of the book: that is, that Islam is intolerant. Since the Rushdie Affair, anti-Muslim feeling in its crudest form has been expressed in an increased number of physical attacks on Muslims in several parts of Britain (Anwar 1991). In the media, criticisms of Islam – especially from members of Rushdie's own literary world in the 'serious' press and broadcast media – have had a particular intensity. In much of what was publicly said and written about the Rushdie Affair, it was clear that many liberals found that they did not know how to respond to this situation where a minority group was appealing against oppression, but, in doing so, was expressing *religious* anger and questioning the principle of free speech and, what is more, showing some support for a death threat to a British citizen issued by the leader of Iran.

Education

No political issue has aroused such widespread concern within the British Muslim population as the Rushdie Affair, but several others have provoked ongoing debates and campaigns. The educational needs and rights of their children is a topic which, in particular, has aroused much concern among the older generation of Muslims. As immigrants, many of whom risked a great deal in the pursuit of economic advancement, Muslim parents are often greatly ambitious for their children (especially their sons), and view education as one of the keys to future success. However, as Nielsen (1984) points out, British schooling is seen also as a threat: it is in school, parents feel, that children are most likely to learn values which subvert those of the home.

Nevertheless, a number of Muslim demands for special provisions in schools can be, and often have been, quite easily met. Some schools have, for example, adapted uniform rules to allow girls to wear *shalwar kameez* (loose trousers with a long shirt) in school colours, or trousers with school skirts. Although the wearing of head-scarves by girls has at times been opposed by school authorities (Anwar 1991), there has been in Britain less controversy over school uniform issues than in Belgium and France where, in particular, the matter of head-scarves provoked much anger among the general public (Rath *et al.* 1991). Other relatively straightforward issues which schools and local education authorities have dealt with to varying degrees include demands for the provision of prayer facilities and *halal* meat in schools, time off for Muslim pupils to attend Friday prayers at the local mosque and Eid celebrations, single-sex PE lessons (where the preferred option of a single-sex school is not available) and the withdrawal of Muslim children from sex education lessons.[17]

Religious leaders' concerns about the general orientation of courses taught in schools raise issues which are far more complex than those discussed above. Although many provisions for Muslim pupils, such as those just mentioned, can be granted in accordance with the stipulations of 'multicultural' education, some of the basic tenets of multiculturalism are themselves problematic for Muslims. Parker-Jenkins (1991) asserts that many Muslims feel their own identity is challenged and undermined by a school curriculum which reflects cultural diversity. Ruthven also discusses this problem, which is clearly of particular relevance to religious education: he argues that a perspective of cultural relativism, when applied to the teaching of religions, 'runs directly counter to the widely held Muslim belief in the superiority of Islam over all other faiths' (1990: 80).

The anxiety of many Muslims about various aspects of the British educational system has led to an increasing number of demands for the establishment of voluntary-aided Muslim schools, of a similar kind to the Church of England, Roman Catholic and Jewish schools that are already in existence. The campaigns for separate schools have been long-running but thus far have had little success; however, at the time of writing Muslim campaigners are hopeful that the Islamia Primary School in Brent, north London, and the Al-Furqan School in

Birmingham will shortly become Britain's first state-funded Muslim schools.[18] Opposition to the campaigns for separate schooling has operated at two levels, as Nielsen (1992) reports: it is argued, first, that Muslim schools promote social segregation and, second, that the quality of education in Muslim schools is likely to be poor. Dwyer (1993) points out that the debate over separate schooling brings into sharp focus the contradictions between different conceptions of multiculturalism. Thus, for example, Muslim campaigners have argued that multiculturalism in education has not gone far enough to meet their needs, and have had support from conservative groups which are intensely opposed to the very concept of multicultural education on the grounds that it is secular and liberal. At the same time, the Muslim campaigners have met opposition from anti-racists who see little relevance in religion and insist that racism should be tackled on the basis of a shared 'black' identity.

Other political issues

British Muslims' concerns in relation to family law and the ritual slaughter of animals have produced two further significant instances of Muslim involvement in public policy debate. The UMO, with some support from other organisations, has since 1975 consistently campaigned for the introduction of a separate system of family law for British Muslims, which would cover such matters as marriage, inheritance and custody of children. According to Nielsen (1992), the UMO's campaign has not attracted widespread interest within the British Muslim population, and nor has it been favoured by the British legal authorities; however, some experts have suggested that it could be possible for the legal system to become more flexible with regard to minority cultural traditions. On the matter of ritual slaughter of animals, both Muslims and Jews have successfully campaigned (and engaged in some limited cooperation in doing so) for the continuation of the exemption of *halal* and kosher butchers from the statutory requirement for the stunning of animals prior to slaughter (Kaye 1993). Various other issues on which Muslims have campaigned, at national or local levels, include the matters of provisions for Muslim burials, planning permission for mosques, and the availability of *halal* food in institutions such as prisons and hospitals.

In January 1992, Kalim Siddiqui gave the inaugural address to the so-called 'Muslim Parliament', the establishment of which appeared to be an attempt by British Muslims to enter the political arena by means of setting up an alternative political structure. The Parliament, which comprised 155 'MMPs' ('Muslim MPs'), provoked a great deal of press interest and hostility, particularly in the wake of Siddiqui's statement that 'Muslims will oppose and if necessary defy any public policy or legislation that we regard as inimical to our interests' (Kaye 1993). However, despite its being called – undoubtedly for the specific purpose of attracting attention and controversy – a 'parliament', the new institution appears to have been set up as, essentially, an umbrella body that could represent and lobby on behalf of British Muslims. The Muslim Parliament has not attracted popular

41

support from the Muslim population of Britain, and indeed has been criticised by Muslim leaders, especially on the grounds that its members are unelected. Since the death of Kalim Siddiqui in April 1996, doubts have been expressed by a number of Muslim leaders over whether the Muslim Parliament can indeed survive.

Of concern to some Muslim campaigners has been the fact that anti-discrimination measures in Britain have tended to prioritise 'ethnic' or 'racial' over religious groups (Modood 1990). This is an issue frequently raised by the newspaper *Q News*: the editorial of 25 March 1994, for example, insisted that 'the anti-racist movement in Britain . . . must stretch out its arms and be prepared to embrace Muslims as Muslims: not as "Asians" or any other false categorisation'. The *Q News* 'A to Z of British Muslims' (24 December 1993) included 'A is for . . . "Asian" – the CRE [Commission for Racial Equality] catch-all mutant label that judges you by curry and colour not beliefs'. That there are anomalies in anti-discrimination legislation is clear: the Race Relations Act outlaws discrimination against Jews and Sikhs – but not against Muslims *qua* Muslims – on the grounds that Judaism and Sikhism are the religions of particular ethnic groups; and religious discrimination over employment matters is unlawful in Northern Ireland but not elsewhere in the UK (Runnymede Trust 1997: 20).

This discussion of political issues can perhaps best be concluded with the suggestion that although many of the efforts at political mobilisation may not have gained the support of the majority of the Muslim population, and most Muslim initiatives may not have achieved the desired results, the scope of political activity within British Islam demonstrates that Muslims make up an increasingly self-confident and articulate religious minority. Furthermore, with regard to the anti-Rushdie protests in particular, this minority has presented itself as much more united than it had ever done in the past.

It is against this background of political ambition and debate that my respondents' expressions of religious commitment are emerging, although most of the young people did not on the whole indicate a deep concern with those political issues that have a bearing on their religion. The general lack of attention to Muslim politics may partially be a function of the age of the respondents: interest in educational matters, in particular, will presumably increase once they have children of school age. A subject which did frequently provoke lengthy responses of one kind or another was the Rushdie Affair: comments on this will be reported upon in the chapters that follow.

3

THE FIELD AND FIELD-WORK

I have by now set out the major issues that were addressed by the field-work I conducted in the London Borough of Waltham Forest. The subject of this chapter is the process of field-work itself: where and how it was conducted, the backgrounds of my respondents and the difficulties I faced in carrying out the research.

The field[1]

The London Borough of Waltham Forest

The London Borough of Waltham Forest was chosen as the field for my research partially because it has a large Pakistani population and I was interested in exploring aspects of life within a sizeable minority community. It seemed appropriate to work in this area also because I had the opportunity of moving there: I lived in Waltham Forest for the year I spent as a field-worker; that is, from summer 1992 to summer 1993.

Waltham Forest took its name from the earlier name of Epping Forest. It is situated to the north of the East End; it is bordered by the boroughs of Enfield and Haringey to the west, Hackney and Newham to the south and Redbridge to the east; Essex is to its north. The River Lea runs through the western side of the borough, and Epping Forest encompasses its northern and eastern boundaries. The borough was created in 1965 out of the former municipal boroughs (now its three parliamentary constituencies) of Leyton in the south, Walthamstow in the middle and Chingford in the north. The southern part of Waltham Forest derives much of its present form from the latter part of the nineteenth century, when row upon row of terraced houses were built; since then this area has seen some limited redevelopment, which included the building of a few high-rise blocks of flats in the 1960s and 1970s. Chingford and north Walthamstow (which make up the northern part of the borough) were largely developed as residential areas in the 1930s and 1940s, and contain more spacious housing and greater extents of greenery than the areas to the south. Most of many fine eighteenth- and nineteenth-century buildings which once graced what is now Waltham Forest have gone; but since the 1960s attempts have been made to preserve what is left of them, and the old village of Walthamstow has been designated a conservation area.

From the time when the Waltham Forest area was first heavily built up, it has been a place within which immigrants to Britain have made their homes. In the late nineteenth and first part of the twentieth centuries, many of the 'outsiders' who settled there were Jews who had come to Britain to escape persecution in Central and Eastern Europe and, after initially having lived in the East End of London, were making their way to the more affluent northern outskirts of the city. The largest influx into the area from overseas took place, as elsewhere in Britain, in the postwar years, with the arrival of immigrants first from the Caribbean and then South Asia, particularly Pakistan. Other immigrants who, mostly since the Second World War, have settled in the borough include Africans, Mauritians, Chinese, Greeks, Turks and Irish; the most recent newcomers from abroad have been refugees from Somalia and the former Yugoslavia. Today, the non-white ethnic minority population of the borough makes up one-quarter of the total.

Any visitor to Waltham Forest can immediately see that Chingford, with its larger houses and gardens and wider roads, is the wealthiest part of the borough. Chingford extends into Essex, and was once the constituency of the Conservative MP Norman Tebbit (famous, among much else, for his complaint that many British Asians fail the 'cricket test' – see Chapter Four). The population of Chingford is predominantly (92 per cent) white, although increasing numbers of ethnic minority, especially Asian, families are making the northwards move there from Walthamstow and Leyton. The narrower, terraced streets of these two southern parts of the borough house a more ethnically mixed population than the streets of Chingford: approximately 70 per cent and 60 per cent of Walthamstow and Leyton, respectively, are white.

There is little, either in the relatively prosperous suburbia of Chingford, or in the terraces and ethnic mix of most of Walthamstow and Leyton, to make Waltham Forest stand out from many of the other London boroughs, although it does have more open spaces than most on account of the preserved areas of forest land and the reservoirs of the Lea Valley. Walthamstow as a place-name is perhaps associated in the minds of most Londoners with, above all else, its Greyhound Stadium. The borough also boasts what is often claimed to be the longest street market in Europe: this is situated in the High Street in Walthamstow Central, and at weekends is crowded and noisy and a place within which the great diversity of Waltham Forest's population – that is, not just the diverse ethnicities but also the mix in terms of age, class, styles of dress, ways of talking, and general demeanour – is clearly visible.

The Pakistani population of Waltham Forest[2]

Waltham Forest has the largest Pakistani population of all London boroughs: 13,000, or just over 6 per cent, of the borough's residents are Pakistani. This is a tiny fraction of Britain's total Pakistani population, which numbers just under half a million, of which 50 per cent is British-born, and is on the whole oriented towards the north of England and the Midlands. The Pakistani population of Waltham Forest is most concentrated in Walthamstow, where it comprises almost 10 per cent of the population. The South Asian population of the borough includes, in addition to the 13,000 Pakistanis, some 7,000 Indians and under 2,000 Bangladeshis. The Muslim population of the borough encompasses the vast majority of the local Pakistanis (who are very predominantly Sunni Muslim; there are also small numbers of Shi'ites, Ahmadis and Christians among the Pakistanis) and Bangladeshis, a significant proportion of the Indian population, and smaller numbers of Mauritians, Turks and African Muslims.

The Pakistanis who settled in Waltham Forest, like those who made their homes in other parts of Britain, came predominantly from rural parts of northern Pakistan: more precisely, from Mirpur in 'Azad' ('free'; that is, Pakistani) Kashmir and from nearby Jhellum in Punjab. The first Pakistanis to settle in Waltham Forest in significant numbers – again as was the case elsewhere – were, for the most part, men who were taking advantage of the job opportunities provided by Britain's booming postwar economy. The majority took up manual work; in particular, jobs in local factories and with London Transport were common. Although most had initially planned to stay in Britain only for as long as it took to accumulate sufficient savings, they became increasingly enveloped in locally based social and economic networks, and were eventually joined by their wives and children who started to come to London from Pakistan in large numbers in the late 1960s.

The general socio-economic and demographic profile of today's Pakistani population of Waltham Forest is broadly similar to that of the Pakistani population in Britain as a whole. Among the characteristics of the Pakistani population of the borough which differentiate it from the white majority are the considerably younger age structure of the Pakistani population; the larger average size of Pakistani families; the fact that Pakistanis tend to live in more overcrowded housing; and the higher rate of owner-occupation among the Pakistani population. With respect to their position within the local economy, Pakistanis in Waltham Forest are not concentrated in any particular sector of employment, which in part reflects the fact that the borough does not have any dominant industries. Just under half of all the men who are working are engaged in manual work; and, as is true for the British Pakistani population as a whole, the economic activity rate among Pakistani women in Waltham Forest is low, with just over one-quarter of Pakistani women of working age economically active, compared to just over three-quarters of white British women.[3]

Unemployment is a problem for the general population of Waltham Forest, and is a particularly acute one for the Pakistanis and members of other ethnic minorities. The unemployment rate (that is, the proportion of the economically active population that is unemployed) among white men in the borough is 12 per cent and among Pakistani men is just under 30 per cent. That the economic characteristics of the Pakistani population of Waltham Forest may be undergoing some significant change is suggested by the fact that while a relatively low proportion of this ethnic minority has educational qualifications, there is a high rate of participation in further and higher education among young Pakistanis: 40 per cent of Pakistanis aged 16–24 describe themselves as students, compared to only 16 per cent of white young people. However, it is difficult to estimate to what extent educational qualifications will translate into improved employment opportunities for the young Pakistanis living locally.

Processes of chain migration – whereby the first immigrants encouraged and sponsored others from their families and villages to join them, who in turn brought over more people from home – have ensured that tight-knit social networks between kin and (former) fellow-villagers have been maintained within the borough. The general visibility of the Pakistani minority in Waltham Forest, especially in Walthamstow, is heightened in certain small parts which have dense concentrations of evidently Pakistani (or, more generally, Muslim and/or South Asian) businesses: in these streets, solicitors' offices and doctors' surgeries have Muslim names on their doors; small butchers' shops advertise their *halal* meat; clothes shops display *shalwar kameez* and saris; the occasional branch of a Pakistani bank can be spotted; and travel agents' windows proclaim special deals on flights to Karachi.

The Pakistani community of Waltham Forest encompasses, in addition to the kinds of businesses and services just mentioned, an elaborate and extensive structure of formal and informal organisations which provide social support of all kinds, opportunities for socialising and arenas within which internal political conflicts can be played out. These organisations, some of which receive funding from the local council, have been established by and are under the control of a network of community leaders. Some groups are defined as specifically 'Pakistani', while others are described as 'Muslim' or 'Asian' and thus cater – officially at least – for a wider segment of the population. The organisations range from the highly active to the more-or-less defunct, and perform a wide variety of functions: they include groups which provide welfare and legal advice, local branches of Pakistani-based political parties, women's groups, youth groups, musical and literary societies, sporting societies, religious associations, organisations for the elderly, for the disabled, for the mentally ill, and at least one Muslim funeral society. The *Directory of Ethnic Minority Organisations* compiled by the Waltham Forest Race Relations Unit lists forty-nine groups in its 'Pakistani' section, which are supplemented by groups listed under the headings of 'Indian' and 'Asian Umbrella' organisations.

The community leaders who head the local organisations are middle-aged and elderly individuals who are relatively well educated and command some degree of respect within the community as a whole. Some of these individuals – among whom there is a significant minority of women – hold or aspire to formal positions in the community such as that of local councillor or officer in some department of the local authority. A large majority of the community leaders appear to be engaged in ongoing struggles with one another in their attempts to extend their influence over the community and to acquire funding from the Council or other sources for their various projects. These internal political conflicts are generally conducted between shifting alliances of individual leaders, who are quick to assert quite publicly the lack of competence and corrupt methods of their rivals. In recent years one particular site of conflict within the Waltham Forest Pakistani (and wider Asian) community has been the 'Asian Centre', which was originally founded in 1984 as a general resource for all Asians in the borough.[4]

For the Pakistani and the general Muslim population of Waltham Forest the local mosques, as would be expected, are significant institutions. At the time I conducted my field-work, there were five functioning mosques in the borough (all Sunni) and two in the process of being established. None of the local mosques is purpose-built; the largest is a converted factory on the Lea Bridge Road which regularly holds well over a thousand people for Friday prayers. Each mosque has one or two *imams* and is managed by a committee made up of local community leaders. The mosques have limited facilities for the attendance of women at Friday prayers and prayers on special occasions; in general, mosque attendance is male only. In addition to acting as places of communal worship, the mosques provide religious and mother-tongue classes for children; some also provide space for religious talks and lectures and for study and discussion groups run by and for young men. The *imams* who lead the prayers in the mosques in Waltham Forest include some younger men who may have been educated in Britain, but the majority, as in most mosques in the UK, are elderly and from the Indian subcontinent. The fact that there are at least some younger, British-based *imams* has encouraged a tendency for the sermon that accompanies Friday prayers to be given in English as well as Urdu or, as is the case in a mosque in Leyton, Bengali.

The field-work

The process

My aim of exploring the ethnic, national and particularly the religious identities of young British Pakistanis necessitated, I believed, the use of qualitative methods. These methods are most appropriate where a researcher intends to acquire insight into the subtle and complex meanings held by social actors. Qualitative methods also tend to be associated with the kind of open-ended or 'theory-building' approach to data collection that I wished to undertake: that is, I planned to develop analytic categories on the basis of whatever empirical material was collected, rather than impose preformulated concepts on that material.

More specifically, at the outset of my field-work I decided to make in-depth interviewing the central element, because 'identity', the primary concept under investigation, exists as an *abstract concept* not only to the social scientist but also to the social actor. Thus it seemed necessary to ask the subjects explicitly about how they define the groups to which they belong and their position within those groups. Furthermore, as it is through social action that an identity takes shape and is manifest – for example, a 'religious identity' may manifest itself, in large part, in

47

religious practice – it was vital that as well as inquiring about attitudes and values in the research interviews, I should ask about patterns of behaviour and past experiences.

The major part of the field-work in Waltham Forest was, hence, a series of in-depth, semi-structured interviews with young British Pakistanis living locally. These young people were the 'core respondents' of the field-work process; and it is their responses to the interview questions that make up the largest part of the empirical material discussed over the course of this book. By inquiring about a great many aspects of the respondents' day-to-day lives, I aimed to address the following key themes and questions in the interviews:

Religion
- What is the significance of religion in the lives of the respondents?
- How do they express their commitment to religion?
- What do they feel that they gain from the religion?
- What does it mean to be a Muslim in a non-Muslim society?

Identity
- How do the respondents define their own identities?
- What does being British mean to them?
- What does being Asian or Pakistani mean to them?
- In what ways does Islam act as a source of identity?

Family and community
- How do the respondents' definitions of what it is to be British, Pakistani and Asian differ from those of the older generation of the minority community?
- To what extent do the respondents feel that there are contradictions between the expectations of family and community and the demands of wider, British society?
- What are their responses to such contradictions?

In addition to the interviews with the core respondents, I decided to carry out three supplementary field-work activities. First, I held informal interviews and discussions with other young local people from the Pakistani and wider Asian or Muslim population; these were to deal with some or most of the issues raised in the formal interviews or, more generally, with questions about the local Pakistani/Muslim/Asian 'community'. Second, I observed social activities and patterns of interaction in the locality: a process which was part of my day-to-day life since I was living in Waltham Forest throughout the field-work period. Finally, I spoke with local 'community leaders' from the Pakistani or wider minority population about their concerns and, in particular, about their views on developments within the younger generation. My decision not to use the interviews with the core respondents as a method in isolation, but to engage also in supplementary field-work, was made on the grounds that this would allow me to gain a better insight into the extent to which what I heard about 'identity' in the formal interviews was related to concrete patterns of social life in the local community.

The various elements of the field-work involved my building up an extended network of contacts in Waltham Forest – a process which by definition was haphazard, and involved various strands of activity. I made many approaches to formal institutions or services within the Waltham Forest local authority: these included the borough's Race Relations Unit (my first point of contact), social services, the youth service and the three further and higher education colleges in the borough. I visited a large number of Pakistani, Muslim and Asian community organisations. I attended a number of local social events and activities, where I was able to meet people informally: these events included four *melas* (Asian fairs) held in the local showground, an Asian fashion show, an 'Asian Sports Day', the celebration of the Prophet's birthday held at a local mosque and the wedding party of one of my respondents. I also arranged, with another researcher working in the area, a two-day 'Asian youth workshop' at the Town Hall to which young Asians were invited to engage in discussion about questions of identity; unfortunately the attendance at this event was low, but nevertheless some interesting issues were raised and explored over the course of the two days.

I left 'the field' at the point when I felt that I had gathered sufficient material to provide some answers to the research questions I had set myself. By this time I had held lengthy formal interviews, all of which were taped and transcribed, with thirty-three 'core respondents' (details of whom are provided below). In addition, I had spoken informally with approximately thirty other young respondents – all of whom were Asian, and most of whom were Pakistani. These young people I met in various contexts; some I spoke to quite briefly and others at length; some singly and some in small groups; in two cases the discussions were taped, but in all other cases I simply took hand-written notes. This latter group of respondents included five young men whom I met when they were selling Islamic literature at several local events; another three men with whom I spoke at a mosque during a celebration of the Prophet's birthday; a number of both male and female students who attended the 'Asian youth workshop' mentioned above; and four young men and four young women who can be described as youth workers, who were working with local young Asians in various capacities.

As is stated above, one of my goals as a field researcher was to interview a number of 'community leaders' as well as young people. I was able to speak with a total of eighteen community leaders: twelve men and six women, several of whom were employed in various capacities by the local authority (for example, as officers in the borough's Race Relations Unit and Race Equality Council and an officer in the Education Department with special responsibility for race issues). Two of the other individuals were, at the time I talked with them, local councillors with the Labour Party. All the community leaders were or had been involved in more than one (and often several) voluntary organisations, including the Waltham Forest Islamic Association, the Muslim Funeral Society, the Asian Family Resource Centre, the Muslim Women's Welfare Association and the Muslim Ladies' Circle.

49

From my conversations with community leaders I acquired a certain amount of useful background knowledge about local politics, the nature of intergenerational tensions and the history of the Waltham Forest Pakistani community; however, the specifics of these conversations will not be reported upon in this volume since my major concern here is with the attitudes and values held by young people.

The core respondents

Since the bulk of the empirical material discussed in this book derives from the formal interviews held with the thirty-three core respondents, it is vital that I provide some information here about the backgrounds of these individuals together with an account of the interview process. It should be noted that the respondents were assured, prior to their interviews, that there would be no breach of confidentiality; hence, all the names used here are pseudonyms, and no information is given about the individuals that would allow them to be identified.

The sample of core respondents comprised eighteen women and fifteen men, twelve of whom I met through community organisations or community leaders, seven through the colleges they were attending, and fourteen through personal introductions by fellow-respondents. At the time of the interviews, all were aged between 17 and 27, and over half of them under 20. Only three of the male (Hanif, Majid and Yusuf) and three of the female (Masooma, Sara and Zubaida) were married; of the married respondents Yusuf and Zubaida had children. Hanif, Yusuf and Zubaida were living with their spouses away from their parents' homes; all the other respondents were living in the parental home, with the exception of Khalida who, at the time of the interview, was staying in a refuge for Asian women after having run away from home.

Among the core respondents there were four pairs of siblings; thus a total of twenty-nine families were represented by the thirty-three young people. The majority of these twenty-nine families were large by British standards: twenty contained four or more children, and five contained at least eight children. It is interesting to note also, in relation to family patterns, that only two of the respondents – Abida and Mariam – had parents who were divorced.

As would be expected given the general patterns of Pakistani emigration to Britain, most of the respondents' families came originally from the rural north of Pakistan: more precisely, from the districts of Jhellum, Mirpur, Sialkot and Gujrat, which are on the border between Punjab and Kashmir (Mirpur is inside the Kashmiri border). A few of the families originated in or near the city of Lahore, and there was one family from each of the cities of Karachi, Islamabad and Multan. All the respondents' parents came to Britain as adults with the exceptions of Mustafa's and Tahir's fathers, both of whom emigrated at the age of thirteen, and Abida's mother who made the journey at the age of ten. In most cases, the respondents' fathers came to Britain alone in the 1960s, and were subsequently joined by their wives. Five of the respondents were themselves born in Pakistan and came to Britain at very young ages; and two (Hanif and Masooma) were born in Britain but spent extended periods of their childhoods in Pakistan.

Eight of the respondents had one or two parents with professional occupations: these included two accountants, two social workers, an engineer, a civil servant and a local authority education officer. The remaining respondents could be said to come from broadly working-class backgrounds. Nine of the respondents' fathers were at the time of interview unemployed or out of work for health reasons; twelve were currently or had been in the past factory workers; seven owned or had owned small businesses (in two cases, a dry-cleaning business and, in three cases, a grocery); six were working or had at one time worked for London Transport or British Rail. The majority of the respondents' mothers were not working outside the household, but at least six of them were doing sewing work at home.

Among the respondents themselves, nineteen were at the time of the interview in full-time further or higher education. Many of both the men and the women indicated that they were quite ambitious with regard to career plans, and believed that they were in a position to enjoy a great many educational and job opportunities that their parents had never had. Six of the respondents (Hanif, Rafiq, Shahid, Khalida, Masooma and Zareena) already had or were studying for university degrees, and thirteen had plans to undertake studies at university; the subjects in which there was the greatest interest were law, business studies and medicine. Among the respondents who were most evidently 'upwardly mobile' was Sara, whose father had been a factory worker and was currently on invalidity benefit; she was working as an administrative officer in the Treasury and was shortly to undertake a part-time law degree. Hanif, whose father owned a small greengrocer's, had recently acquired an MSc in computing and was working in the personnel department of a large company; he hoped eventually to run a business engaged in the transfer of information technology to Third World countries. The respondents included also a trader in Walthamstow Market (Majid), a telesales assistant (Mustafa), a trainee hairdresser (Amina), a printer (Ilyas), a young woman running a jewellery-making business (Jamila) and four unemployed young people (Yusuf, Zaheer, Abida and Rasheeda).

All the interviews with the core respondents lasted between sixty minutes and two and a half hours. The questioning was guided by an interview schedule which was constructed after initial pilot research had been carried out in the form of unstructured interviews with a number of British Pakistani students at the London School of Economics. These pilot interviews enabled me to identify both the empirical issues that had to be raised in order that I could acquire information relevant to my research problem and the most appropriate ways of asking the necessary questions. The schedule was used in a flexible manner: many of the questions did not have fixed wording, and the order of questions was changed where this allowed the discussion to proceed more fluently. Both general questions and more specific prompts were included; naturally, where respondents were particularly talkative there was no need to raise many of the more detailed points as these tended to be covered spontaneously.

The interview schedule opened with a number of questions about the respondent's background, concerning for example educational history, current and previous occupations, and interests. The next section of the interview dealt with the respondent's family and family relations: the questions here also covered attitudes to authority, gender relations, marriage and the status of women. The next set of questions explicitly addressed the subject of ethnicity and identity: here, as well as asking very open questions such as 'How would you describe your identity?', I asked more specifically about what it means to be Pakistani, Asian and British, about experiences of racism, and about aspects of life within a fairly tight-knit minority community. The final section of the interview covered religion: questions were asked about levels of religious practice, religion and morality, and the respondent's views on particular issues (such as the Rushdie Affair).

The respondents were given the opportunity both before and after the interviews to question me about my study; some were keen to ask why I was looking at questions of British Pakistani identity and what I had found out to date, but a majority did not show great curiosity about my research. On the whole the respondents appeared to enjoy the interviews, as most spoke with great alacrity about the topics raised and took time to ponder some of the more abstract questions. Several told me after the interviews that they had enjoyed being compelled to think about questions of identity which under normal circumstances they had little or no cause to reflect upon. In two cases only – the interviews with Yusuf and Nazia – the respondents clearly found it difficult to think of much or anything to say in answer to many of the questions, and seemed to find the stated purpose of the research puzzling. ('They're hard questions. Hard questions. Really I don't know what to answer that question. I had a long night last night – I'm tired now!' Yusuf told me, laughing, at one point; and Nazia greeted the end of the interview with an unrestrained 'Yippee!') Nevertheless, along with all the others Nazia and Yusuf responded with warmth and good humour as well as patience to my long list of questions.

Field-work problems

The field-work process was lengthy and often stressful, since it demanded that I constantly introduce myself to people I had never had contact with before and, further, request favours from them. That the research was productive was thanks to the fact that those requests were almost invariably met with remarkable generosity. All the same, the field-work inevitably had its shortcomings associated on the one hand with the general methodology adopted and, on the other hand, with the specifics of the situation in which I found myself. These shortcomings by no means invalidate the findings of the research, but must be taken into account in any consideration of the general conclusions drawn. The reader may wish to bear in mind, in particular, two sets of problems: first, problems of representativeness and, second, the implications of my 'outsider status' as a researcher.

Representativeness

Many researchers who gather qualitative data by means of small-scale field-work face the charge that their findings are not generalisable to the full researched population. In the case of this study, such a criticism has some validity: I held interviews and discussions with a relatively small number of individuals, and I did not follow a systematic sampling procedure. Indeed, my sample of respondents was biased in several ways because of the manner in which I contacted the young people.

The most significant problem with the sample was that it was weighted in favour of young people who were inclined to identify with the Pakistani community in one way or another. This bias was unavoidable: it simply was not possible for me to come into contact with individuals who had completely cut themselves off from the minority, given my 'snowballing' approach to building up a network of respondents and the fact that many of my initial points of contact were community groups. (One of the female core respondents had, in fact, run away from home, but even she was staying in a hostel for young Asian women; the interview with her was arranged for me by the voluntary organisation that ran the hostel.)

However, from what was said to me by a great many of my respondents and other contacts in Waltham Forest, I gained the strong impression that cases of young people who break all ties with the community are rare; furthermore, the findings of related studies (which are referred to throughout the book) suggest that in terms of their general attitudes towards family and community my core respondents were not, on the whole, atypical. It should be noted that several of the young men with whom I spoke informally – such as those I met when they were selling Islamic literature at local events – came into contact with me directly as a result of their involvement in religious activities; indeed I was interested in talking to them precisely on the grounds that I wished to learn something about attitudes held by the small minority of 'radical' British Muslims.

Just as I was not able to speak to young people who had nothing to do with the minority community, it was also on the whole not possible for me to talk to those who were, in a sense, the most embedded within it: I was not able to gain access to young women from the most conservative backgrounds, as they were unlikely to be in college or much involved in community organisations, and their parents would not have permitted me to approach them directly. It is difficult to assess the ways in which the attitudes of young women from highly conservative families would vary from the attitudes of those who have had comparatively liberal upbringings. On the one hand, many of the former might be less inclined to reflect upon and question certain aspects of life within the minority community as they experience it; on the other hand, some of those who are most restricted in their lifestyle might be particularly drawn to the idea (if not the reality) of rebellion against parental norms and values.

A disproportionately large number of my respondents were or had been students in further and higher education, partly by virtue of the fact that I made contact with some of them through the local colleges. Again it is difficult to gauge the impact upon my findings of the fact that the sample was skewed in this manner, since the size of the sample was too small, and the average age of the men and women too young, to permit any systematic examination of the relationship between attitudes and level of education. It was in any case apparent from what I heard from my respondents that this relationship is unlikely to be straightforward. To a certain extent participation in further and higher education might be expected to lead to a weakening of allegiance to the minority community, as students are subject to a wide range of influences. At the same time, because Islamic societies are highly active in many colleges and universities (and certainly several of my respondents mentioned being involved in college or university Islamic societies, or attending their meetings), Muslim students may find that they have a great deal of opportunity, and are strongly encouraged by their peers, to learn about their religion.

In carrying out the field-work in Waltham Forest it was never my aim to gather information that would enable me to estimate the numbers of British Pakistanis who hold particular views. Rather, my objective was to identify some broad patterns or trends in my respondents' articulations of religious and ethnic identity: patterns or trends which one might expect to be reflected within the wider population. I am happy to acknowledge that the explanatory framework I have developed on the basis of the empirical findings – elaborated over the course of the following chapters – is preliminary and speculative. It is my hope that this framework can act as the basis of further and more broadly based empirical work.

Outsider status

A problem to which I have already alluded is that of parental suspicion: my access to young people who could act as respondents was partially hindered by the fact that many parents were likely to worry that I might in some way stir up trouble if I was allowed to interview their sons or daughters. As an 'outsider' to the Pakistani community of Waltham Forest – that is, as a member of the white British majority – it was always possible (understandably enough) that I would arouse particularly acute suspicion among some parents. This problem was aggravated by the fact that I often could not explain my position to parents because of the language barrier: many of them did not or were reluctant to speak English, and I had no knowledge of Punjabi or Urdu.[5]

The fact of parental suspicion not only prevented me from speaking at all with young women from highly conservative backgrounds, but also was the cause of some difficulty on several of the occasions that I did manage to arrange interviews. On the whole I preferred to hold the interviews with the core respondents in their family homes, both because this was usually convenient and because it enabled me to catch a glimpse of family life; but in some cases this simply was not possible because of likely parental disapproval. Sometimes when I did visit a family home for an interview the atmosphere was noticeably strained: a mother or father would look at me anxiously as the son or daughter welcomed me in the front door, and I would find myself able to offer little by way of reassurance. From this kind of experience I learnt something about the wide social gulf that exists between the less confident members of the older generation of British Pakistanis and their white British neighbours and work-mates. As I found myself on one side of this gulf, my intended respondent would struggle to bridge it, by simultaneously placating a parent in Punjabi and offering me a cup of tea or coffee with an embarrassed or apologetic smile.

'My Mum kept going – "Who is she? Is she after you, is she after you?"' Faruq, my first male respondent, said of his mother's response to my telephone call to his house to arrange the interview with him. He laughed as he spoke of it, but added the serious suggestion that I should avoid ringing up potential respondents unless I knew in advance that their parents would not react badly to a call from an unknown, white female (advice that I subsequently followed). A two-hour interview with another male respondent, Zaheer, was conducted in the front room of his parents' terraced house while his father determinedly swept and swept again the small front yard: in order, or so I assumed, to keep an eye on the proceedings.

My outsider status inevitably also had an impact upon my interactions with the respondents themselves. In the interviews with the core respondents, it was during the discussions about racism that I felt my ethnicity probably had the greatest significance. I noted for example that Sara, while in the middle of speaking of the racism of her colleagues, inserted the phrase, 'you know, no offence at all'; this made me wonder how many others among the respondents were holding back from making certain comments about the racism of white Britons out of fear of offending me. Nevertheless, the majority of the young people did speak at some length about racism among whites in response to my explicit questioning on the subject.

On a more positive note, I gained the impression that many of the young people were at ease talking to me about personal matters precisely because I was an outsider: they were able to speak in an open and free manner, without worrying that what was said would somehow get back to their parents or other members of the community. Several of the female respondents in particular seemed to like having the opportunity to talk about family problems to someone from whom they were socially distant. In addition, I felt that a number of the young people found it an interesting and enjoyable experience to explain to an outsider aspects of the minority culture and religion. Perhaps, from their point of view, my very ignorance meant that I was likely to have more sympathy for their own views and perceptions than would somebody who was personally associated with the minority community.

Among some of the most devout young people with whom I spoke (mostly informally) during the field-work process, there seemed to be some suspicion or guardedness in relation to the fact that I was a non-Muslim apparently interested in Islam. My most direct experience of this (which is recounted in Chapter 7) was when I was told by one of my contacts that some young men of his acquaintance did not wish to be interviewed by me because, in the wake of events in Bosnia, they felt that Muslims in Britain should be wary of researchers gathering information about them.

A different kind of hesitancy was in evidence on the occasion when a young man selling Islamic literature told me quite explicitly that he would speak to me only if I wished to learn about the religion for its own sake and not merely in order to 'get good grades at college'. Another young man who had initially agreed to a formal interview with me subsequently refused to answer any of my questions until I answered *his* questions about why I would not accept that the existence of God was a logical necessity. (I never did reply to his questions in a manner that satisfied him.) In such circumstances as these I found it difficult to steer a middle path between, on the one hand, displaying a genuine interest in Islam and, on the other hand, avoiding the pretence that I was contemplating conversion.

But certainly not all of those who displayed a proselytising zeal did so in such a way as to make me feel uncomfortable. Majid, a core respondent, told me several times over the course of the interview that if I wanted to take up Islam he would help me 'one hundred per cent'. He was insistent that I should meet his brother-in-law who, he explained, was especially knowledgeable about Islam and could tell me anything I might want to know. For his part Amir, the brother-in-law, spoke to me at length about his beliefs with an air of quiet conviction and kindly concern, as his two small daughters played around us.

That a researcher investigating topics as complex as religious and ethnic identity will misunderstand, overlook and fail to appreciate much of what she sees and hears is inevitable. No doubt the risks are all the greater for a researcher who is situated very much outside the community with which she is concerned. 'Who am I to be pondering these problems, asking these questions?' was a constant refrain in my head as I arranged meetings, held interviews, visited people, nagged my contacts. But I persisted with my task, in the belief that it is little short of senseless to expect social scientists to investigate only those social groups of which they are a part, and that the best way of starting to understand patterns of identity-formation and social interaction in contemporary Britain is to take the time to listen to the people in whom one is interested. That this particular endeavour was worthwhile, notwithstanding difficulties encountered along the way, will I hope be demonstrated to the reader over the chapters that follow.

Part II

EMPIRICAL FINDINGS

4

THE CIRCUMSTANCES

This chapter examines certain key aspects of the social environment within which the respondents' ethnic and religious identities have evolved. My focus is on two boundary processes which, to a large extent, shape that social environment. First, I consider the 'parental boundaries' as these are perceived by the respondents: that is, the efforts made by the older generation of the Waltham Forest Pakistani community to define and preserve the distinctiveness of the minority group. Second, I am concerned with the positioning of the respondents in relation to 'boundaries of Britishness': boundaries which reflect various definitions of the British 'nation' and nation-state. This chapter can be described as an account of how the respondents orient themselves in relation to two poles of identity which are rooted in, respectively, the place of departure and place of destination of the immigrant journey undertaken by their parents. In the final part of the chapter, I consider the implications of these boundary processes for the respondents' self-perceptions.

Parental boundaries

Restrictions

The respondents and their peers are sharply aware of their parents' wishes to maintain and even enhance the distinctiveness of the minority community, although the very definition of that community can vary between families and between contexts. For example, while the primary concern may be with the 'Pakistani community' as a whole – a community which may itself be defined as, alternatively, local or national – the focus may at times be, more narrowly, on the need to preserve the integrity of the kin or caste group.

For the members of the older generation, commitment to the minority appears to be a commitment to the traditional lifestyle and values of its members, the preservation of which in part depends on there being limited social interaction with outsiders. Thus the older generation can be said to be engaged in the process of constructing and maintaining relatively impermeable and fixed social boundaries.[1] For the young people, these boundaries are most clearly manifest in 'restrictions' arising from parental views of the special standards of behaviour that are appropriate for members of the minority community.

The respondents – especially the young women – quite frequently complained of the extent to which their parents impose restrictions upon their behaviour. In total, about half of the female core respondents spoke in strong tones about problems that they have had in dealing with the demands of their parents in relation to general behaviour. In contrast, none of the men spoke with the same degree of exasperation about parental expectations, but most did indicate that they have or have had in the past some disagreements with parents about what is and is not acceptable behaviour. From all that was said, it would seem that conflict with parents arises most commonly in relation to the subjects of marriage (more specifically, over the appropriate criteria for marriage partners and the right of parents to choose their children's partners), dating, going out at night and – among women – dress.

Some of the respondents indicated that they simultaneously resent and respect the restrictions imposed by their parents: none more so than Naveed, who told me,

> My mother wouldn't like us to mix with the British society because of various influences and social ideals which people have here which she doesn't agree with – as in going out a lot, or raving, or drinking.

When it comes to thinking about how he would treat his own children Naveed clearly has mixed feelings:

> Supposing they grow up here in Britain – er – I suppose they would have a lot more interaction with other kids [than I had]. No, *less* interaction with other kids, because external influences should be as small as possible. But then that would be like imprisoning them in my own house – that would be wrong.

Three of the female respondents – Jamila, who is now in her mid-20s and running her own small business, and Ghazala and Khalida, both of whom are aged 20 and are students – spoke at length of having faced particularly stringent parental demands. Jamila described not being allowed to cut her hair when she was a girl, and being made to wear Asian clothes which she found difficult because there were few other Asian girls in her class: 'I felt really left out'. After she left school there was a period of several months when she was not allowed to go out of the house on her own: 'I wasn't even allowed to go to the sweet shop without having a brother taking me – that's how bad things were'.[2] Indeed, Jamila talked of having felt that the very fact of her being Asian meant, above all else, that she was severely restricted in what she could do. When she was small she was constantly told: 'You're Asian, you're not white: you can't do anything that they do.'

Ghazala appeared to be quite nervous about my interviewing her, and was insistent that I should not meet her at her home (even though I had previously interviewed her brother in the family's front room); she also did not want to come for interview to my own flat as she said it was too near to where she lived and someone might see her going there. She complained that her mother does not allow her to go out to socialise, but does always ask her to do the shopping: 'If she needs me to go out to do shopping and things like that, she never thinks – oh somebody's going to hurt you then.' Khalida was living in an Asian women's refuge when I interviewed her; she had run away from home after her father was violent towards her. She talked of what her parents wanted of her: 'To be obedient, to never ask questions about why I can't do that, can't do this, to stay quiet and just do the housework, do the cleaning, ask no questions, never ask to be allowed out.'

That the kinds of experiences described by Jamila, Ghazala and Khalida are not too rare was made clear by what was said by several other respondents who, while commenting that their own parents are not excessively strict, made the point that many young people in the local community are subject to extremely severe restrictions. This illustrates clearly the complexity of parental boundaries: the older generation of Pakistanis in Waltham Forest quite evidently do not maintain a single definition of the 'right' values, lifestyle and behaviour. Rather, different parents seek to impose different levels of control over their children's behaviour – even if the basic values they maintain are broadly similar – and thereby participate in the construction and maintenance of a series of boundaries which are of varying degrees of exclusivity.

Male–female differences

It was clear from much that was said by the respondents that transgression of the minority community's boundaries by females is perceived by the older generation as a much greater threat to the survival of the group and its values, or of the individual family within the group, than is male transgression. A family's *izzat*, or 'respect' (a concept to which I shall return shortly), is seen as highly important within Pakistani and other South Asian communities and is to a large extent dependent on the perceived chastity of the females in the family. Many of my respondents, including some of the young men, spoke explicitly about the fact that their parents are a great deal stricter with their daughters than they are with their sons. Yasmin, for example, complained,

> It's fine for my brother to go out [on dates] but then when it comes to me, I'm a girl and that's completely different. Like my brothers, they've got girlfriends, and one's a Sikh, and these Muslims can't go out with – specially Sikhs, cause they're a different culture, completely. And my mum – she don't say nothing. But if she found out I was going out with a Pakistani guy she'd go mad.

The special concern of members of the older generation of the Pakistani community with the behaviour of young women was discussed at some length by several of the respondents who are involved in youth work. They talked about the fact that when they have sought to organise groups and activities specifically for Asian girls and young women, they have tended to meet suspicion and general opposition from parents and community leaders. Shazia, for example, told me that once some community leaders had written to the parents of girls she was working with to tell them that she was involved in teaching the girls how to make love. Mumtaz spoke about complaints received by the Asian women's refuge in which she works from community elders who accuse the project of encouraging young people to leave home. Jamila, a core respondent, told me about her own intentions to set up a group for young Asian women: a plan that is in part motivated by her experience of being involved in a women's organisation which has excluded younger people from certain activities – such as a seminar on AIDS – because of worries about gossip in the community. Her own youth group, Jamila said, would try to exclude the 'fuddy-duddy' older women who are prone to being 'scandalised' by anything and everything.

It was quite frequently pointed out in interviews that young men tend to support their parents in insisting that the women in their families should adhere to a particularly strict code of behaviour. A few of the male respondents admitted, in one or two cases with some ambivalence, that they themselves are guilty of having double standards:

> I don't see anything wrong with dating. I mean, I've been brought up really strict, and like if I see my sister going out with her geezer, I wouldn't really like it. I dunno, like in English society, is that what they do?
> *Yeah* —
> They don't mind really, do they? Like with me, I wouldn't like it. But then again, that's being a hypocrite, because if I was to go out with a girl, I wouldn't see nothing of it, and still that girl's somebody's sister, so – in that way it's a lot confusing.

> (Zaheer)

> If the boys don't come up Muslim-wise, the girls should be. Like if the boys run off with the next girl, it doesn't really bother you. If the girl went off with the next man, then that bothers you – then it's a shame on the whole family.

> (Yusuf)

Among the female respondents who spoke of the double standards of their male peers was Bushra, who told me that Asian boys at college criticise Asian girls who are friendly with men for being 'a bit too modern'. Amina talked at some length about the intolerance of Asian boys at her college. She commented,

> I haven't actually worn a skirt . . . it wouldn't feel right. 'Cause being an Asian, if I wore one, the Asian guys would never let me hear the last of it.

My friend wears them, and I've always thought, why don't you wear it at college, and she goes she can't, because if she goes into college, the guys there they just go on and on and on and on – Asian guys – *they're not your brothers*, nothing, but they just go on . . . . If I wear something like a dress, even if there's a cardigan, they're always saying – you shouldn't be wearing that, why don't you wear your own *shalwar kameez*.

(The highlighted phrase draws attention to Amina's apparent assumption that one's brothers have a certain right to comment on one's dress.)

That young men can be even more stringent than parents in imposing restrictions upon their sisters was stressed particularly strongly by Khalida, who told me that her brothers take the same view as her parents of her running away from home, and 'are just wanting to kill me'. She complained of Asian young men generally who 'have just got one big chip on their shoulder, one big attitude problem when it comes to girls. They believe girls should be at home. . . . They believe girls are inferior, that's the way God intended it to be.' Mumtaz, a worker in the refuge at which Khalida was staying, said that as far as young Pakistani men are concerned, 'the culture works to their advantage'. They are able to have girlfriends and generally do whatever they like, and yet are still regarded as good Muslims: all the guilt is passed on to their sisters. Mumtaz commented that she knows young women who have been abducted from Asian women's refuges and brought home by their brothers.

The 'community'

Parents' efforts to maintain relatively fixed and stable boundaries around the minority group appear to be reinforced by the facts of life in what is an apparently close-knit community, in the sense that many respondents feel that even when they are beyond their parents' gaze, their parents' friends, relations and neighbours scrutinise their behaviour. A majority of the female respondents spoke about being subject to this kind of social control; among them, some spoke fervently about the claustrophobia of community life:

> To be a Pakistani means – I think . . . like being expected – not to do certain things. Like if I was to go out with a few boys and girls, just a mixed group, even a woman who doesn't know me will stare and just stare – thinking what's she doing? Like if a black girl, a white girl, someone else done that – a Western girl – the Asian woman would not stare.
>
> (Amina)

> It's disgusting the rate the gossip gets around! Like – one of my friends was walking up towards the market with a guy from college. They were just friends – there was nothing wrong with it. But somebody saw them, who knew her, and he told his uncle, and his uncle told his brother, his brother told his wife, his wife told her Mum! And they were just friends –

it was fine. It's just that everybody puts two and two together and comes up with two thousand!

(Mariam)

A few of the male respondents also spoke of the sense of being under scrutiny that comes with life in a community; most notably, Zaheer complained: ' 'Cause I've rebelled against everything, other people have seen me and they just write you off. If they see you on the road, they just wouldn't want their kids to go about with you.'

But the close-knit nature of the community can in fact, as Mariam explained to me, work to the advantage of young people, for it enables them to give each other a special kind of support. She explained,

> We [young people] don't know each other the same way our parents know each other. We all have – it's like a silence. It's like, some people aren't allowed to go out to the cinema – something like that. And say we have an afternoon off, we might decide to go to the cinema. And these people's parents think that they're still at college. And they all get home on time; their parents are happy. And we don't tell our parents about it, so it doesn't get to the older generation at all. It's like a silence. ... It's like an unsaid rule, an understanding. Everyone's really tight on that.

Gener gap.

In a number of interviews, it emerged that some respondents believe their parents to be less concerned with the actual behaviour of their sons or daughters than with the need for their children to be *seen* by others to behaving well. This suggests that boundaries are transgressed only where evidence of the breach becomes visible. The overriding importance of appearance was stressed, for example, by Yasmin, who told me that her father had once seen her talking to a male friend in his car and subsequently said to her, 'I know he was just your friend, but if someone else had seen you it would have looked really stupid.' Mustafa, similarly, told me that when he is at a wedding and acts in a friendly way with girls his mother 'just says – don't do it in front of other relatives: they'll get the wrong idea'.

Between two cultures?

In the 1970s and early 1980s a number of empirical studies, mainly of an ethnographic nature, were conducted on Pakistani and other South Asian communities in Britain. Discussions about second-generation Asians in these studies tend to focus on the young people's responses to the many contradictions between the expectations of the minority community and the demands of wider, Western society: hence it is often said that this literature presents a 'between two cultures' model of British Asian identity.[3] This model generally focuses on the various ways in which the structure of traditional Asian families brings into sharp focus the differences between 'Asian' and 'British' cultures. Two features of British Asian family life which are frequently examined in the literature are, first, the continuing importance of the extended family and wider networks of kin (or *biraderi*); and, second, the emphasis in Asian families upon 'respect', or *izzat*, a concept which conveys both the sense that children (and particularly daughters) must behave in a decent manner and thereby avoid bringing shame on their families, and also the importance of young people behaving with respect towards their elders.

The empirical material discussed above would seem to support the idea that intergenerational conflict is quite frequently a result of the contradictions between the 'two cultures' within which my respondents are living. But it is important to consider also recent critiques of the 'between two cultures' model, which suggest that this perspective encourages a view of the young people as passive victims of their circumstances. Drury, in an article about young British Sikh women, argues that the 'between two cultures' approach 'implies that young people are simply caught up in a vacuum, in some sort of no-man's cultural desert' (1991: 388). Bhachu also complains about the portrayal of second-generation British Asians, in the media as well as academic literature, as young people who lead 'between and betwixt' lifestyles, and can do little but suffer their parents' imposition upon them of alien cultural values (1985: 172).

Bhachu is one of a number of scholars (including some of the earlier researchers) who have stressed that family ties within South Asian communities in Britain tend to be close, notwithstanding the very apparent and sometimes realised potential for conflict between generations.[4] There is much literature that suggests that a majority of young people in Britain from South Asian backgrounds display intense loyalty and attachment to their families, despite frequently being ambivalent about certain demands made of them by their parents. Hence, within many communities, modified patterns of traditional family behaviour are emerging: for example, many young people are insisting upon greater freedom of choice over marriage partners but do not fully reject the arranged marriage system; and respect for parents is maintained alongside a willingness to challenge the authority of the older generation on certain issues.

The evidence of my own field-work indeed indicates that it would be quite wrong to assume that the young people necessarily resist all or most of their parents' efforts to preserve the distinctiveness of the minority. Rather, as I shall be demonstrating in subsequent chapters, they are modifying and reshaping but not abandoning traditional modes of differentiation between the minority and the majority. Furthermore, even though some of the more stringent demands made by parents do provoke varying degrees of resistance among the young people, it would appear from what was said by most of the respondents and by my other local contacts that while there is often considerable tension in family relationships within the Pakistani community of Waltham Forest, there is little outright family breakdown.

The 'between two cultures' model can be criticised not only for exaggerating the tendencies for intergenerational conflict within British Asian families. Its 'implicit notion of "culture" as a bounded, impermeable, monolithic entity' and presentation of reality 'in terms of binary oppositions' is also a gross oversimplification, as Gillespie points out (1995: 206). There is in Britain no single culture that

is 'Asian' or 'Pakistani'. As has already been noted, even within the older generation of Pakistanis in Waltham Forest different conceptions of the minority
community co-exist. This applies all the more strongly to the younger people, who
are aware of many different ways of defining the minority group *vis-à-vis* the white
British majority. And when it comes to the 'British' side of the equation, as we shall
now see, there also exists a wide range of cultural formations.

Boundaries of Britishness

In the interviews with the core respondents, explicit questions were asked about
what it means to be British. These questions provoked a great variety of responses:
a full spectrum of views were expressed by the individuals on the matter of
whether they themselves are British, with some completely rejecting the notion,
others expressing ambivalence and uncertainty, and others affirming their own
Britishness. The following different replies were offered to the question, 'Do you
consider yourself British?'

> No, not at all. . . . No! I hope not, anyway. . . . 'Cause I'm not, am I?'
>
> (Rafiq)

> I think I'd have to describe myself first and foremost as a Muslim. I
> couldn't say I'm British at all.
>
> (Shazia)

> Umm – yeah and no. 'Cause I consider myself British, but then I can't
> consider myself British because I like the way things are done in my
> community.
>
> (Zaheer)

> Er [pause] yeah, sometimes. Depends on the situation.
>
> (Salim)

> I'm British, I'm obviously born and bred here. But I do consider myself
> Pakistani – so I'd say I'm a British Asian.
>
> (Sara)

> Predominantly I'm British; I was born here and I've lived here – this is my
> country.
>
> (Hanif)

> Yeah. . . . Just like, I was born here, I'm from here. That's it.
>
> (Amina)

Because of the diversity in the respondents' comments about Britishness, one might be tempted to argue that the only conclusion to be drawn from the data is that, for young British Pakistanis at least, 'Britishness' is a complex, multidimensional phenomenon which means something different to each individual. If one looks more closely at the views of the respondents, however, it becomes evident that within their social world Britishness is not a concept that is subject to limitless reinterpretation. Rather, even if for them there is no single set of criteria of Britishness, there are *various sets* of criteria; or, to return to the theme of boundaries, the respondents locate themselves in relation to several different 'boundaries of Britishness'. These boundaries, or modes of distinguishing the British from the non-British, are constructed and maintained by members of the white British majority and, to a lesser extent, by members of ethnic minorities. Some of the boundaries encompass individuals such as my respondents and members of other minority groups, while others are exclusive.

Citizenship

The concept of British citizenship acts as a formal boundary (perhaps the only one of those discussed in this book that can be described as a formal and thus distinct boundary) which is inclusive: all my respondents are British citizens. In about a third of the interviews the respondents, in answering questions about their own Britishness, referred to the fact that they have British citizenship or 'nationality'. In most of these cases, however, the young people spoke in such a way as to suggest that they believe citizenship to entail a kind of belonging to British society that is official but not truly meaningful.

Some, for example, seemed to reduce the advantages or the meaning of being British to a matter of travelling on a British passport: Faruq remarked, when considering what it means to be British, that it 'is an advantage at airports, stuff like that'. The most explicit expressions of reluctance to associate any inner feelings of allegiance with the fact of British nationality were voiced by Ruksana and Ilyas who are quoted, respectively, below.

> It just – doesn't ring true, when, you know, nationality – I am British because I'm born here, but it just doesn't mean anything, to say I'm British – it doesn't conjure up an image, it doesn't hit me *here* [*she puts her hand to her heart*] or anywhere.

> I'm a British citizen, so I have to consider myself as British. You know, like in school, you have to be labelled as 1M, is your class. But really you're just mucking about and you're always jumping about from this class and that – it's like, yeah, I'm there as a British citizen, but inside I'm Asian. . . . Pakistani.

If many of the respondents have doubts about the significance, as a source of identity, of British citizenship, one subject which allows for a ready expression of these doubts is sport. A few respondents described their support for Pakistani sportsmen, or lack of support for British teams, as indicative of their feelings that they are Pakistani rather than British. Two commented, in somewhat disapproving tones, on the enthusiasm with which many of their peers support the Pakistani team, and suggested that, for these youngsters, knowledge of Pakistan comprises knowledge of Pakistani sportsmen: 'When Pakistan win the cricket they're proud of it, and they'll walk around with the flag', said Faruq, 'and as far as they're concerned, that's what their roots are.'

The question of sporting loyalties is in itself a fraught one: what has become known as the Norman Tebbit 'cricket test' (arising from remarks made by the Conservative MP in April 1990 about the lack of loyalty towards England displayed by British Asians during test matches) has ensured that a heightened sense of significance is often attached to assertions of support for Pakistan in cricket.[5] This support can signify a self-conscious rejection of demands, by those who share Tebbit's views, for allegiance to the British State; and hence is also recognised as an act which may provoke hostility in others. The dilemmas involved in this were apparent in most of the comments that were made about sport, including the following (consciously self-contradictory) remark from Yusuf:

> When it comes to cricket, people say – you're from England, you should support your English team, no one should support Pakistan, but end of the day you've got to support your own home country! This [England] *is* our home country . . . this is where I was born, but I still end up supporting Pakistan.

Only one respondent, Shahid, explicitly mentioned the Tebbit 'cricket test', telling me that his father 'semi-passes the Norman Tebbit test' in that he will support England as long as they are not playing Pakistan. Shahid later commented, in response to questions about his own identity, that thinking about whether or not one is British is not important; but one can perhaps detect some over-anxiety in his desire *not* to be anxious:

> It's like, when Norman Tebbit makes a speech and he says something like how many of them would pass the cricket test, I didn't give that a second thought. But if I sat there and started brooding about it, and started thinking about whom I'm supporting – should I really be this, should I really be that, would I be more accepted if I had this attitude – then I'd just get myself down.

While the respondents quite frequently indicated that for them citizenship does not automatically bring about a sense of real belonging to British society, they do on the whole seem to be satisfied that their citizenship is secure: they did not speak in such a way as to suggest that they feel in danger of losing their rights as British citizens. However, some of them did say that their parents are not confident of their legal status in this country; for example, Faruq commented, 'Some Asian parents still think, oh we're going to get kicked out of the country – we shouldn't be too visible because we're going to get kicked out.' And Adnan said of his mother,

> She's just waiting for the day when the British kick us out of England – she's been saying that for many many years. She's going, get your education before – you don't know, any time the British can throw us out; this is their country.

Values and lifestyle

A number of the respondents seem to feel that they live within an inclusive boundary of Britishness not simply because of their status as British citizens but also insofar as they have adopted, as a result of having grown up in Britain, a way of life and set of values which they characterise as typically 'British' or 'Western' rather than Pakistani. Here they can be said to be engaged in the process of upholding an inclusive cultural boundary of Britishness. However, although many of the young people spoke about having a different view of life to that of their parents on account of their British backgrounds, little was explicitly said about the extent to which they feel themselves to be British in terms of some of the values or the lifestyle they have adopted.

Nevertheless, some degree of self-categorisation as British in these terms was evident in a number of replies given to questions about visits to and life in Pakistan. About half of the respondents, when asked if they would like to live in Pakistan, said that they would miss the way of life and general social environment which they know in Britain, and/or that they would feel somewhat alien among Pakistanis in Pakistan. Thus, in much of what was said there was an implicit or fairly explicit association of Britain with a real sense of home, as in the following two examples:

> Once you've settled in this country, it's hard to forget it. I mean, I've been back to Pakistan twice now, and you say oh, I'm gonna go to Pakistan and I'm gonna settle down there – but how long are you gonna be over there for, because when you're born and bred in a country, you're used to it, you can't go to another country and live for the rest of your life there, especially a country where it's so behind and so poor.
>
> (Zaheer)

> When I go to Pakistan – I'm lost. I don't fit in. I can enjoy it for a while, but I am different from them at the end of the day. I'm a lot different from them.
>
> (Jamila)

A sense of inclusion within those boundaries of Britishness which define a way of life was apparent also in some replies to questions about the nature of British society and the advantages of living in Britain. Notwithstanding the evident and sometimes very marked ambivalence of most respondents towards aspects of British culture and society – expressed in comments about exclusion and racism, the perceived low standards of morality among many white Britons and the various benefits of membership of the ethnic and religious minority community – almost all of them raised at least some positive points about life in Britain, and in so doing seemed to express a degree of personal commitment to this kind of life. Only one of the core respondents – Rafiq, who was the most 'radical' in terms of his religious views – voiced nothing but disdain for all things British. ('When you speak about England . . . then I'm saying yeah, it's a vile country', Rafiq said to me.)

In what was said about the positive aspects of British society, two basic themes frequently emerged. The first, mentioned by many of the women and a few of the men, was that people in Britain, and particularly women, are able to enjoy a great deal of freedom and independence with respect to the way they lead their day-to-day lives. Many of the female respondents stressed that were they to live in Pakistan, they would be denied whatever freedom they enjoy (or strive to enjoy in the face of parental resistance) in Britain. 'Being British means having a bit more independence, being able to voice your opinions . . . like I'm doing now', I was told by Bushra, who evidently felt that she was acting as a British person even in the very way in which she was responding to the interview question. Ghazala said that a female cousin of hers in Pakistan almost never leaves the family home, 'so I think that's one advantage to staying [in Britain]. Even going to Sainsbury's is enough for me, 'cause at least I get out the house.' In Britain, Zubaida commented, 'a woman can have so much rights'. British people have problems like everybody else, she went on to say, but at least in Britain – unlike in Pakistan – problems are discussed openly and are not hidden away. The openness in Britain means, she said, that a person's 'inside soul and outside soul is the same thing. Not that on top you're one thing and inside you're something else.'

The second theme that was frequently raised in discussions about the benefits of the British way of life was that of the advantages associated with life in a society that is, relative to Pakistan, well ordered and prosperous; in relation to this, reference was sometimes made also to the fact that Britain is politically stable and democratic. The following were among the comments made:

> *What do your parents like about living in Britain?*
> The laws, the way of treating the human being as a human being. Like the British manner of living – like to respect this person, to respect the house, to respect the Queen – like the way it's – just it's organised.
>
> (Ilyas)

> In this country you get pension, income support. People get help. Back home, if you was unemployed, you had no money, no one would help you. . . . But here no one starves. No matter what your circumstances are, at least you get money for food.
>
> (Zubaida)

[In Britain] people care about people – they treat them as humans. . . . Like the way people care about children – you get things like Save the Children – and the hospitals. People really care. Like hospitals, you can just get up and go to them.

(Amina)

Exclusive boundaries

As I turn now to the subject of exclusive boundaries, my aim is to look at the respondents' reactions to social boundaries which define them and the minority to which they belong as 'other' or 'alien'. In discussing Britishness here I do not have a particular concern with theoretical debate about the highly contested concepts of race and racism, nor indeed with the question of what my respondents' experiences can tell us about contemporary British race relations. Rather, my interest is in the respondents' perceptions of racism and, most importantly, in the impact upon their own sense of Britishness of what they regard as common-place assumptions made by white Britons about the interconnections between 'race', 'heritage' and 'nation'.

Exclusive boundaries of Britishness, in the eyes of my respondents, reflect the seemingly popular view among white Britons that being British is a matter of 'race' and 'culture'. According to racial definitions, Pakistanis, like members of other non-white minorities, cannot be 'properly' British because, in the first place, the colour of their skin is evidence that their ancestry is not British; indeed, for some, it is evidence that there are intrinsic and immutable differences – in terms of their biological and psychological make-up – between the minority Pakistani and the majority white population of Britain.[6] The exclusive cultural definitions of Britishness are rooted in the assumption that Pakistanis lack British credentials because their 'culture' is not indigenous to Britain. The term 'culture', it should be noted, is used in this context to encompass such diverse phenomena as religion, language, family patterns, styles of dress, food preferences, and so on.

Writers on ethnicity and race relations in Britain have drawn attention to the tendency within the mass media and right-wing political circles towards conceptions of Britishness which leave little room for a recognition of the rights and contributions of ethnic minorities. Gilroy, for example, writes of the assumptions that are made about the 'most profound difficulties [that] are uncovered by trying to dilute our nationhood and national culture so that they can accommodate alien interlopers and their formally but not substantively British children' (1987: 60). Parekh asserts that the politician Enoch Powell's famous warning, in 1968, of the dangers of mass immigration, had the effect of promoting widespread notions of Britain as 'a cohesive and unified society, a "nation", held together not only by allegiance to a common authority, but also by common commitment to a shared body of values and a shared way of life'. This is a nation within which ethnic communities are 'alien islands', insisting as they do upon following lifestyles incompatible with the norms of mainstream British society, and threatening the very survival of Britain as a nation (1990: 62).[7]

71

Just under half of the respondents made explicit comments about their feelings that they, or non-white people generally, are not accepted as fully 'British' by white Britons. For example, Hanif remarked that

> there are times when I've felt regardless of how much I've done in my life to integrate I've still been left out. And that does hurt. . . . And I think, down to the bottom of my heart, if I ever think that it's ever going to go away, I'd be foolish.

Shahid said that one advantage of living in Pakistan would be that 'There, nobody will look at me, and say – he doesn't belong here, we don't want him'. Being Asian means, according to Bushra, being 'someone who'll never be considered a British person'. And Zubaida commented, 'Just because of our skin colour we're different, and we're looked upon as if we're – God knows what – aliens or something.'

Several of the young people raised the issue of colour in terms of a question that has no easy answers: must one be white to be British? Ruksana, when asked if in some ways she does not feel British, answered, 'Yeah – when I look in a mirror. Then I can say maybe I'm not British.' Bushra responded to the same question by saying, 'It's an interesting question, but what does being British mean? What does it mean – being white? I'm not white, you know. As I've said, it's a label, 'cause I was born here.'

A few respondents explicitly discussed the ways in which cultural difference can be the basis of the exclusion of Pakistanis or Asians in Britain from popular concepts of Britishness. Khalida, who herself had rejected almost all aspects of the religion and culture of her parents, made reference to how 'English people' find Asian culture 'very strange . . . very alienating. . . . They think it's really weird.' Shahid spoke of how Asians are expected to lead a certain lifestyle, if they are to be considered British. He said that he himself would never give up his culture, but that there are Britons who say Asians should speak English and should eat fish and chips instead of curry, if they are living in this country. Shahid went on to argue that in America, a country of immigrants, the situation is different: 'When you're American, you're American. There's no – you're this kind of American, that kind of American.' This is because, he said, Americans 'don't own that country anyway. They took it off the Indians.'

Perhaps the most heartfelt complaint about cultural expectations was voiced by Kabir, who argued,

> [b]ecause of the colour of the skin, and the cultural backgrounds of people, 'cause you don't go to the pub or eat hamburgers or hot dogs, you are not one of them. You cannot be one of them. And they don't like – some people don't like that. If you live in this country, you've got to do what we do. You have to live how we live. Dress how we dress. You've got to talk the way we talk. You've got to write the way we write. And things like that. Silly little things. And that breaks – that pulls you down a lot. So

you have to fight them. You have to say, no, I want to be myself. You can't tell me what to do. That way, they're ruling your lives, instead of you ruling your own life.

Like Kabir, Ilyas spoke in such a way as to suggest that he has thought a great deal about questions of exclusion. He recounted at some length the story of an encounter he and an Asian friend once had with a drunk man on a train:

It was about 6 o'clock in the daytime, and we were coming back from work. . . . He [the drunk] starts pointing out the window and he said, I'm going past my heritage here, East End of London, and we said, yeah. And he said, and I see you two people, and it really makes me angry. And I said, why is that? He said, I get angry 'cause I think you're gonna talk in your own language . . . and then, he goes, why don't you build up your own country? And he kept saying oh I'm sorry, I'm sorry.

The impact this encounter had had on Ilyas is indicated by his response, at a much earlier point in the interview, to a question about his parents' sense of identity. He said that although they do not forget they are Pakistani, they also feel they are British: 'British is the way we wouldn't go outside, singing our own songs or anything, *not speaking our own language on the train and that, 'cause it's not nice*' [emphasis added]. Ilyas also spoke (similarly to Shahid, quoted above) of there being different attitudes to ethnic minorities in America: 'If you say I'm an American, it's different, you won't relate to them as being white. . . . He can be black, Asian. Here if you say you're English, you're British, they look to you to be white.'[8]

Racism

The interviews revealed that experiences and awareness of racism – tangible manifestations of exclusive boundaries of Britishness – have impinged on the lives of almost all the respondents, including those who did not speak directly about exclusion. As has already been mentioned, the term 'racism' is a contested one within the social sciences, but none of my respondents requested clarification when asked in the interviews about the subject: they appeared to maintain a common-sense understanding of the term, and used it to refer to all forms of hostility and discrimination experienced by members of the Asian minority in Britain which evidently arise from the fact of their being visibly different from the majority population.

The general comments made about racism indicated that most of the young people perceive it to be a serious problem for Asians in Britain today. The respondents' accounts of how racism has impinged on their own lives revealed a wide variety of experiences. Among the women, two mentioned what might be termed violent incidents. Yasmin described having been 'beaten up' by two white girls and a black girl at the age of eleven. Jamila, although she commented that she did not see racism as a big problem, told me that the previous year 'I had a glass bottle thrown at me. And to see that bottle hit the floor, on the pavement, and smash, really was a shock to my system.' The experiences of racism mentioned by other female respondents included that of being called a 'Paki' when younger ('But I thought, you know, it's just a word, and I'm quite proud of it anyway', Abida added); having 'skinhead boys take the mickey out of you or the way that you dress' when walking down the street (Rasheeda); having suffered with the rest of the family racist comments from neighbours 'when we would have our clothes hanging up on the line' (Zareena); and seeing stall-holders in Walthamstow street market 'taking the mick out of [blacks and Asians] behind their backs' or 'snapping at you because you're an Asian' (Ghazala and Bushra, respectively).

As might be expected, more of the male than the female respondents talked of having faced racist violence. Zaheer said that he has had 'a helluva lot of fights off racists', and that when he used to work as a cab driver he had been at the receiving end of much racist abuse. He was the only respondent to mention having come across racist police officers. Kabir told me that he had encountered quite a lot of racism at school, and that his family had had problems with neighbours when they were living on a local council estate. They had, he added, managed to move out of their flat 'just in time': just before two particular families moved into the estate who would have given them even greater trouble. Shahid said that among other experiences, one he remembers clearly was an incident which occurred when he was aged about 15. He was walking down the street with his parents, when some boys started throwing eggs at them from a bus that had stopped in the traffic. 'And I've never been able to forget that, you know.'

One aspect of racism which was discussed in some depth by several respondents was the tendency, maybe becoming increasingly prevalent, for prejudice and discrimination to be expressed in a covert manner. 'Hidden racism' is clearly felt by some to be especially troubling precisely because it can rarely be detected. For example, Faruq complained that in an area containing a large Pakistani community 'the racism gets driven deeper – it's harder to pick out'. He argued that this makes the prejudice all the more difficult to combat, because there is little that can be done 'to let people know that the ideas are dodgy'. He said that there are many individuals who would not be openly racist, but when they go to the pub at night they sit around saying things like, 'I was talking to them, bloody Pakis, eating curry again . . . the place stinks . . . '. Later in the interview Faruq commented, 'The worst form of racism is when no one says anything, but you know what it is. The other kind of racism I can handle: if someone calls me Paki, picks a fight with me, I can handle that.' Echoing Faruq, Shahid told me,

> I see racism as really deep. You see, the worst kind of racism is the one that doesn't show itself on the surface. I mean, I don't mind a skinhead standing before me, right, because I know he's a racist. But it's people who go around with, like, a mask, and deep down they're racist. And they're the ones I feel I've got to be careful of. And they're the ones I really hate.

74

Among the women, Sara spoke with the most bitterness about 'hidden racism'. She said that when she is at work (in the civil service): 'I never feel that I'm totally fitting in . . . with the white people there.' She told me that her colleagues 'wouldn't blatantly be horrible', but that

> it goes deeper than that. . . . They do it in other ways, which – I don't know if it's better for them to do it openly. I mean, maybe it is, 'cause at least you know where you stand with them. But if they're doing it very quietly, I'd rather not know them, 'cause they tend to be stabbing you in the back.

And if she was ever to complain, she pointed out, she would be accused of being hyper-sensitive. Bushra spoke of the 'undercover, indirect racism' that is sometimes manifest in discrimination against Asian people seeking employment; but none of the respondents, it is interesting to note, spoke at any length about this kind of institutional racism.

Another theme to emerge in a number of interviews is the idea that one can be protected from serious racism by living in an area (such as Walthamstow or Leyton) in which there is a large Asian population. The protection that is offered by a large Pakistani population can be of a physical kind, as is suggested by Faruq's comment that there is 'strength in numbers', and Adnan's remark that 'You feel a bit safer when you walk down the street – like if there's a lot of Asians, you know if you get in trouble they'll help you'. A large Asian community, some respondents indicated, also provides support in the sense that this allows them to feel inconspicuous within the locality. 'When you get out of this place', said Tahmeena, 'there are some areas where there's no Asians at all, and when you go in it, people stare at you.' Faruq described his experience of going into a pub in Chingford to get help when his friend's car broke down:

> It was the longest I ever spent in a pub – 15 minutes. . . . Some little girl, she said, 'There's an Asian!' – and I'm like – where am I?! It's like something out of [the film] *Mississippi Burning*, you know! I thought in a minute there'd be someone – 'Excuse me Mr Asian, can you leave our white women alone. . . .'

A majority of the core respondents said they feel that in Britain as a whole racism, or at least overt racism, is becoming less of a problem. Of these, a total of eight made reference to the fact that some years ago 'skinheads' or 'the National Front' were more evident in the local area. Ghazala, for example, commented, 'I remember the National Front – I can remember them, and I was just a kid, and it happened in T-Street where we live'. Yusuf spoke of the early 1980s, 'which was the riots time, and there used to be skinheads down there, and life used to be hell when we used to be children. . . . I know the times we went through were very hard'.[9]

Racism and cultural difference

In writing about exclusive boundaries of Britishness above, I demonstrated that the respondents feel culture as well as colour can act as a basis of exclusion. Likewise, discrimination and prejudice on the part of white Britons can stem from preconceptions about the minority culture as well as or together with assumptions about biological or genetic differences between races. Some social theorists have argued that 'racism' predicated on cultural difference has become increasingly common in modern Britain; for example, S. Hall suggests that 'a culturally constructed sense of Englishness . . . [is] one of the core characteristics of British racism today' (1992b: 256). Gilroy writes, also in the context of a discussion of race relations in contemporary Britain, about 'new, cultural definitions of "race" which are just as intractable [as older biological definitions]' and lead to a 'new racism': that is, a 'cultural racism' which is sometimes not recognised as racism precisely because of its emphasis on culture (1987: 60).

It may, however, be problematic to conflate within the concept of 'racism' biological assumptions about race with cultural prejudices. It is useful to bear in mind in this context the definition of race provided by van den Berghe (cited in note 6): for him, a 'race' is necessarily a group that is defined in terms of physical criteria. He thus asserts the importance of distinguishing 'race' from 'ethnicity': ethnic groups, for van den Berghe, are 'socially defined . . . on the basis of *cultural* criteria' [original emphasis] (1967: 9). According to such a perspective, to write of cultural racism is to run the risk of confusing 'racial' with 'ethnic' elements of prejudice; and the fact that racist individuals (and probably most of their victims) generally fail to make any distinction between these elements does not justify a lack of clarity on the part of the analyst.

Modood, more sensitively than those theorists who write without qualification of 'cultural racism', suggests that it is appropriate to speak of 'cultural racism' only where this is understood to *presuppose* 'biological racism': his argument is that

> cultural racism builds on biological racism a further discourse which evokes cultural differences from an alleged British or 'civilised' norm to vilify or marginalise or demand cultural assimilation from groups who also suffer from biological racism. Post-war racism in Britain has been simultaneously culturalist and biological and while the latter is essential to the racism in question it is, in fact, the less explanatory aspect of a complex phenomenon.
>
> (1997b: 155–6)

Modood proceeds to argue that non-white minorities which, like British Asians, are seen to have distinct and 'alien' cultural characteristics are likely to 'suffer an additional dimension of discrimination and prejudice', particularly where they wish to assert the importance of certain aspects of the minority culture (1997b: 164).

Of forms of cultural prejudice in Britain today, arguably the most pervasive is anti-Islamic prejudice, or 'Islamophobia', which, according to the Runnymede Trust, 'has become more explicit, more extreme and more dangerous' over the past twenty years in the Western world in general (1997: 7).[10] For Modood, there is little doubt that 'Muslimphobia is at the heart of contemporary British and European cultural racism' (1997b: 163). And certainly, most of the comments made by my respondents about cultural prejudice focused on white Britons' attitudes towards the minority religion. Among various remarks made about general anti-Islamic prejudice were those of Faruq, who talked about media representations of Islam which encourage people to think that Muslims are all 'fanatics, terrorists, Palestinians, bombers'. Likewise, Rubina complained that the impression most people have of Muslims is gained from television pictures of Iranians who 'have all got black on, and they're all waving their hands. You know, when you get the Shi'ahs.' Sara spoke of the attitudes of her work colleagues to Islam and its teachings: she talked about how 'people tend to mock you. . . . I mean I've had it said to me at work – "Oh, don't be stupid, that can't make sense!"'

As was discussed in Chapter 2 above, the publication of Salman Rushdie's *The Satanic Verses* precipitated a series of events which can be said to have brought into sharp focus the extent to which unease about cultural difference on the part of the majority population can be tightly interwoven with racism. It is interesting to note that in a number of interviews, answers to questions about Rushdie's book indicated a particular concern with the issue in terms of what it revealed about, or its impact on, relations between the Muslim minority and the majority population. The publication of the novel, and the fact that it was not banned when the extent of Muslim anger became apparent, were interpreted by some respondents as constituting an attack on, or at the very least revealing a lack of tolerance for, the Muslim population of Britain. This kind of perspective on the Rushdie Affair is evident in the following answers that were given to the question, 'Why did Rushdie's book cause such a great deal of anger among Muslims?'

Mainly because Asians are an ethnic minority, and someone has attacked their main beliefs and values . . .

(Salim)

Because it again highlighted the fact that we're not wanted – that we're different . . . that we were looked down upon. Our religion wasn't valid. . . . I think it's more anger at the government for not banning it.

(Faruq)

Because it's so blatant really. . . . And this is someone comparing him [the Prophet] to a dog, literally, and comparing like his wives and that to whores – and saying these things blatantly. *And nothing was being done about it – it was just perfectly legal, and everyone thought it was fine.*

(Mariam [emphasis added])

Some of the respondents who spoke of the negative repercussions that the Rushdie Affair has had for community relations complained that non-Muslims had not even tried to understand the intense anger that Muslims felt. Shahid told me that people now think Muslims are closed-minded and cannot take criticism; in fact, he said, Muslims are perfectly able to tolerate challenges to their religion, but not 'abuse' of the kind Rushdie's novel amounts to. Mariam commented, 'At school, everyone thought there was nothing wrong with [the book] at all – it was a whole load of mad fundamentalists running around. . . . They didn't understand what was actually in the book.' Jamila talked in a similar fashion about class-mates who failed to recognise what the true concerns of the Muslims were:

> When the Salman Rushdie book came out I was in college at that time, and it was a major issue, because they had a Muslim girl in the class, so everyone was firing questions at me, and they couldn't understand why I hated it. And it was really bad – because when they said that they wanted to kill him, and put a reward out or whatever, I remember turning round and saying, well he's gonna get what he's asked for – and one of the girls saying, 'I can't believe you're saying that . . . '

Several of the young people said that they feel the demonstrations against Rushdie's book have made people in Britain think more badly of Muslims than they did before, and it was sometimes suggested that Muslims themselves are primarily responsible for creating a bad impression of their own community. Naveed, for example, spoke of the Muslim demonstrators having done nothing but lose 'a whole chunk of what little bit of good will they had from the Western community'. Abida was quite impassioned as she said to me:

> OK, he swore at our Prophet – but he is gonna get punished. Burning the book – I mean it's stupid, really. I mean he wrote it, OK. Let him write it if he wants to – he's a writer. . . . I mean, they went as low as him, really. . . . I think it's stupid. You can't exactly kill him, can you? You can't do this in London! They think it's Pakistan! You know, the laws here are different, you have to abide by the laws. I mean – it's embarrassing!

Ambivalence over identity

In the chapters which follow this one, I shall be looking at the ethnic and religious identities of my respondents, and shall seek to understand the ways in which these identities appear to have been shaped by their experiences of being raised by generally traditional parents within a tight-knit Pakistani community, and of living, at the same time, in a modern Western society which seems both to embrace them as part of itself and to exclude them on account of their 'otherness'.

First, however, I wish to consider in more general terms some of the implications of the boundary processes described above for the respondents' sense of who they are. My contention is that these boundary processes promote a certain ambivalence over identity: that is, as a result of the social circumstances in which they are living, the individuals have a tendency to view themselves as subject to various and, to some extent, opposing definitions of self. A certain degree of ambivalence over identity is quite possibly an inevitable and significant part of life for members of all low-status minority groups, but for the children of immigrants the ambivalence may be heightened because the minority to which they belong is, by definition, in a state of transition or even crisis. Therefore, the process by which a member of the second generation negotiates or determines his or her position within the minority and within the wider society is likely to feel like a peculiarly open-ended and uncertain project.

We see this ambivalence in many of the comments analysed above. It is evident in the expressions of frustration over parental demands and expectations; in the doubts about the meaning of Britishness; in the perceptions of racism and prejudice. Almost all respondents articulated at least some degree of self-doubt or uncertainty with regard to questions of identity, and some spoke quite self-consciously about the fact that such questions do not have clear-cut answers.

In the more explicit reflections on ambivalence, three themes emerged: the first of which was the notion that a single individual can contain at least two different selves. As such, one might appear, on the surface, to be a particular kind of person and yet be someone else on the inside; or one might find oneself switching between roles from situation to situation. For example, Ghazala said, 'When I walk outside the front door, I sometimes think of myself as British, because I'm fighting for things I want to do, like studying. And once I step inside the front door again, I've turned Asian again.' Asya told me, 'It might sound weird and that, but deep down I'm just a normal Pakistani, you know. Even though I've been born here, I've been brought up here, still deep down I'm Pakistani.' Asif commented, 'There's part of me says I'm Pakistani and then there's part of me says I'm British because I'm born here, and basically everything I know is from England.' And Faruq joked, while talking about how difficult it would be for him to live in Pakistan, 'Maybe I'm a coconut: brown on the outside, white on the inside. There's a white man dying to get out here – take me to the pub, *please!!*'

The second theme was one of uncertainty: several of the respondents raised rhetorical questions about the general concept of identity as such, and some made it clear that they could give no definitive answers when asked whether or not they are British and/or Pakistani. As Adnan said, 'I dunno what is British and what is Pakistani. I can't understand it. It's not like an object, it's not like clothing, is it?' And Naveed commented,

> What is British? I don't know. I suppose I would probably be more British than the average British person sometimes. But then at other times I would be not at all British, at all. I can't class myself as British. But then I can't class myself as being Pakistani. important

79

Zubaida commented, in response to the question 'Do you feel British?':

> I don't know how to answer this question. I mean, it's a bit hard. I know
> I'm Pakistani. But out of all my sisters I think. . . . I'm a bit more broad-
> minded than them. They see me as different, but I'm not, and at the end
> of the day I am a Pakistani, and I wouldn't count myself as a British
> Pakistani.

The third theme concerned the difficulties of being forced, by family and
community pressures, to live one kind of life, when another seems more appealing.
This view was voiced most strongly by Jamila and Rasheeda, who are quoted,
respectively, below:

> I get confused. Because I would like to be a lot more Westernised. I'd like
> to dress up a lot more Westernised. I can't do that, so I end up getting
> confused sometimes, and I've got myself into a right rut sometimes. I've
> had tantrums over it, I've cried over it.

> Sometimes I'm mixing both [a British and a Pakistani way of life]. And
> sometimes I don't really like it. I prefer one, I do. And sometimes I don't
> prefer none of them at all – always mixing. . . . And sometimes when
> I'm by myself, I think what am I doing down here in this world.
> Sometimes I think – what do I really want in life – should I be born in an
> Asian family? That's what I really think. Should I be born in an Asian
> family, or shouldn't I?

In arguing that the respondents' social circumstances produce a tendency
towards ambivalence over identity, and that in some cases this state of mind is associated with a degree of tension or anxiety in the individual, it has never been my
intention to suggest that these young people are taking up a passive or helpless
stance in the face of the perceived 'culture clash' they are experiencing. If this had
indeed been the implication of my remarks, I would in effect have been endorsing
the 'between two cultures' model of British Asian identity; whereas in fact I have
concurred with those who have criticised the model for overemphasising the
passivity of young British Asians and exaggerating the extent of intergenerational
conflict. Some of the critiques have stressed that, far from feeling that they are torn
between alternative ways of life, young British Asians demonstrate a striking
capacity to mix and blend elements of the various cultural forms within which
they participate or with which they come into contact. This allows them to move
with reasonable ease between alternative social settings while presenting what is
deemed an appropriate image or appropriate behaviour within each.

R. Ballard, for example, refers to the 'code-switching' of young British Asians
who act 'as skilled cultural navigators, with a sophisticated capacity to manoeuvre
their way to their own advantage both inside and outside the ethnic colony' (1994:

31). Another, related kind of 'code-switching' is evident in the articulation by many of the young people of hybrid expressions of cultural identity: with regard to fashion or styles of music, for example, different strands of different traditions are brought together in new combinations. Somewhat similarly to Ballard, Bhachu writes of British Asian women as 'cultural entrepreneurs' who have taken up 'roles as innovators and originators of newer cultural forms' which combine reformulated elements of 'ethnic' traditions with aspects of class and local cultures (1991: 402). Gillespie describes the skills of 'cultural translation' acquired by young Asians in Southall, West London, who often find themselves 'negotiating from context to context between various cultures and various positions within each' (1995: 207).[11]

Indeed, some of my respondents spoke in a positive manner about dual or mixed identities which serve them as a kind of social resource. Apparently they feel that in their daily lives they have recourse to alternative courses of action or modes of understanding, between which they are able to choose in accordance with the needs of a given social context. Among those who spoke in this manner was Ruksana, who said that to be a British Asian means: 'You mix the two cultures together, you can have your own culture, and have a Western culture – a choice – do what you want.'

When I come to the subject of the respondents' ethnic identities, more will be said about this kind of positive response to dual identities: for it is clear that the young people's conceptions of the 'ethnic' culture are wider than those of their parents, and that there is within the minority community a growing openness to cultural and social influences that emanate from outside it. New forms of identity are thus being created, and the more traditionalist conceptions of ethnic identity held by parents and also long-standing notions of 'Britishness' are being challenged and reshaped. Furthermore, with regard to religion there is evidence of a willingness among the respondents to question some aspects of what they learn from their parents, in the light of their experiences of growing up in Britain, and to reformulate (albeit to a limited extent) certain religious ideals in ways which ensure that they have greater relevance to lives spent in a modern Western environment.

What we see, then, is that while their exposure to a wide variety of styles of life and ways of thinking can cause stress or uncertainty for the respondents, it also offers them the opportunity to be independent-minded and self-assertive with respect to their ethnicity and religion. There is much scope for creativity and self-expression, even idiosyncrasy, in the processes of ethnic and religious 'translation'. But I would stop short of claiming, as those of a postmodernist frame of mind might be inclined to, that the desire to be creative, inventive, spontaneous is bound to be the overriding or primary response to the tensions and contradictions of life in a multicultural setting. Along with invention and self-assertiveness, I shall argue below, there is also a readiness and sometimes an eagerness to retain certain traditional modes of communal belonging and structures of meaning. After all, the constraints imposed on individuals by parents, by community, by the social and cultural structures of modern Britain – for all the resentment and mixed feelings they often arouse – cannot be easily overridden or ignored. Moreover, is it not highly conceivable that perceived continuities should be all the more valued when so much in life appears to be fluid and discontinuous?

I shall close this chapter with a brief quotation that gives one cause to think about many of the issues that have been raised. Shahid's response to a question about his socialising habits was the following:

> When I'm with my English friends, I don't feel out of place. Maybe in a pub I would, *but when I'm talking to them and stuff I don't let them see that I feel out of place, or they're talking to somebody who's not like them.* . . . And then again I can switch back to my Asian friends. And I think that's a good balance – I like to keep a good balance.
>
> [emphasis added]

Here Shahid talks in a positive way about his ability to move between different kinds of social circles, but at the same time points to the tensions implicit in such a habit. That he feels – even though he can hide it – 'out of place' in a pub with his English friends, that he is 'not like them', is no doubt partially due to the influence of parental words of warning about the perils of alcohol and of mixing too freely with white people. It may be due also to a sense that no matter how welcoming his friends appear to be towards him, they will never fully accept him as one of them in the same way that they accept each other. The question of how, in response to these manifold external pressures, Shahid and his peers have started working out for themselves what it means to be Pakistani, Asian and Muslim in London today, is what I turn to next.

5

ETHNIC BOUNDARIES

The previous chapter was concerned with two sets of boundaries which, to a large extent, frame the social environment within which the respondents live. Here the focus is on boundary processes, which are continuous with those dealt with in the previous chapter, yet separable from them for purposes of analysis. I am now concerned not so much with external definitions of ethnicity, community and nationality as with the respondents' own definitions of the minority ethnic group of which they are a part.

In constructing and maintaining ethnic boundaries, the respondents are not of course creating a new social collectivity, but are drawing upon the pre-existing understandings of what it means to be Pakistani and Asian. In particular, they are reshaping the definitions of the minority group upheld by their parents. The empirical material to be presented in this chapter will demonstrate that the ethnic boundaries drawn by the respondents contrast with those maintained by the older generation in two vital respects. First, the younger generation boundaries are *wider*, in the sense that the young people tend to feel loyal to, and to orient aspects of their behaviour towards, the Pakistani or the even larger Asian community of Britain, rather than to smaller sub-ethnic or caste groups which have significance for many of their parents. Second, the boundaries have become *semi-permeable*, in that they are increasingly easy to cross in certain situations, and generally do not insulate the minority from other cultural influences. This latter process can also be described in terms of a burgeoning of dual identities.

Ethnic boundaries can be described as comprising those aspects of the respondents' and their peers' lives which mark them out – to themselves, to other members of the community and to outsiders – as members of a minority which has its origins in the country of Pakistan and/or the Indian subcontinent. The findings of my field-work indicate that there are three important dimensions to these boundaries. First, there is the conceptual dimension, which refers to the respondents' tendency to categorise or perceive themselves as members of the Pakistani or Asian minority in Britain. Second, the social dimension encompasses the pattern of interpersonal relations which reinforces their belonging to the minority. And third, the cultural dimension reflects their behaviour and activities which relate to various aspects of the culture, traditions and languages of their families' place of origin.

As pointed out in Chapter 1, it is common for scholars of ethnicity to subsume religion as one aspect of ethnicity; however, in this study I am distinguishing between religion and ethnicity as sources of identity – both for the sake of analytic clarity and, more importantly, on the grounds that many of the young people with whom I spoke (and, according to other studies in the field, many young Muslims throughout Britain) are today emphasising that being a 'Muslim' and being a 'Pakistani' or 'Asian' are different, if related, matters. The nature of the distinction between religion and ethnicity is discussed in some depth in Chapter 7.

The conceptual dimension

It should be clear from the findings presented in Chapter 4 that most of my respondents feel there are few fixed parameters to their ethnic and national identities. As Hutnik writes in her social psychological study of ethnic identities among young British Asians,

> The issue of ethnic identification is not a simple either/or matter. In most cases, it is not a simple preference for one group to the exclusion of the other; it is a delicately graded balance of identification with both the ethnic minority group and the majority group.
>
> (1991: 156)

Indeed, respondents' replies to questions such as 'Do you consider yourself to be Pakistani?' and 'Are there any ways in which you feel you are not Pakistani?' were quite diverse, and produced a certain amount of equivocation. Nevertheless, the respondents' statements make it clear that ethnic boundaries survive in the sense that the vast majority of the young people are willing to describe themselves as ethnically distinct from the majority population of Britain. Of the thirty-three core respondents, half told me that they definitely call themselves Pakistani; compared to twelve who accepted the term with strong qualifications only; and five who said they do not consider themselves Pakistani. Ten respondents indicated that they favour the term 'Asian' over 'Pakistani' in describing themselves; ten favoured 'Muslim'; and only four 'British'. (These latter three categories of response, it should be noted, are not mutually exclusive.)

Whatever the extent to which the young people within the Pakistani community of Waltham Forest continue to refer to themselves as Pakistani, it might be expected that they have a different perspective on this term from that of their parents. I have stated above that ethnic boundaries among the younger generation appear to be wider and more permeable than those maintained by their parents. And certainly, the boundaries manifest in respondents' self-definitions can be regarded as semi-permeable to the extent that, as we have already seen, many of the young people describe themselves as British as well as Asian or Pakistani, and are willing to accept that British values have influenced their lives.

84

The question of whether there is among the younger generation a widening of ethnic self-definitions is not easy to address. Even among the older generation it might be expected that the immigration process would have led to a broadening of definitions of the salient community. The experience of settling on foreign soil as members of a minority group was bound to lead to perceptions of commonalities across groups which previously would have defined themselves as discrete entities. Nevertheless, there is evidence that with respect to South Asian emigration to Britain in general, processes of chain migration did ensure that to some extent old loyalties to kinship, caste and regional groupings persisted within the first generation.[1] The question here is, then, to what extent are these old loyalties breaking down among the children of the immigrants?

From what was said by my respondents, it would seem that most certainly regard kinship ties as important: many had members of the extended family living locally or in other parts of Britain, and spoke of frequently attending family gatherings and spending a great deal of time with cousins. As will be discussed below in relation to the social dimension of ethnic boundaries, there appears to be, however, a growing reluctance to acquiesce with parental wishes for intra-family marriage. With regard to caste, it appears that this is something to which the respondents generally do not accord particular importance: most of those who mentioned the caste system at all spoke of it as something which older but not younger people tend to worry about in relation to marriage.

Only six of the core respondents discussed caste in any detail, and all of them implied that it is something of diminishing relevance to life in Britain, as the quotations below illustrate.

> You might see us, Asians, as all the same, or they're all Pakistanis, but a lot of people wouldn't get married outside their caste. There's farmers, there's shoe-makers, there's people who wash clothes. . . . They don't have to necessarily *be* tool-makers or farmers, but it's the caste which has been brought back from ages and ages, and they've been brought up into that caste. . . . I don't see anything wrong in me getting married to a different caste.
>
> (Zaheer)

> You know like tribes? That's how it's split in Pakistan. . . . But nowadays – my background up there [in Pakistan] is a big person, is top – but now like here, I'm just doing a little job, I ain't on top of no one, and my dad just says to me so often – a human being is a human being.
>
> (Ilyas)

As was the case with caste identities, regional affiliations were not discussed by the vast majority of the respondents when they were faced with questions about identity issues. However, it would be misleading to suggest that they necessarily perceive Pakistanis in Britain to be a homogeneous group, since some evidence did emerge of rivalries among the younger generation based on sub-ethnic groupings. Adnan, whose family are from the area of Mirpur (like a great many of the Pakistanis in Waltham Forest and elsewhere in Britain), spoke quite bitterly about attitudes among his peers towards Mirpuris:

> When I was at school, all the other Pakistani kids weren't Mirpuris, or the ones that were, they'd deny it, and they'd make a joke about MPs being backward – they used to just take the mick out of us, saying how we save all our money, and we send it back home and that.

From a different perspective to that of Adnan, Shahid also spoke of, or at least hinted at, the existence of this kind of tension. He remarked, 'My parents know every single Pakistani family on this street. Even though they're mostly from Mirpur – they don't really like us. No! That was only a joke!!'

A further few respondents indicated that the precise region of origin of one's family is considered less important than the question of whether the family originates from a rural or urban area. Tahmeena, for example, made it clear that she considers herself to be quite different from people who have rural backgrounds:

> You have two types of Pakistanis. There's one which are from the town area, and there's one from the villages. . . . And I'm from the town area, and I try to mix in with the town people. Because when it comes to mixing with the villagers – I suppose I don't mind, but I try not to.

And Yusuf, discussing the question of modest dress, said that according to 'the proper Islamic way', a woman should allow only her husband to see her face; but

> we don't follow [the religion] *that* much – that's putting too much, man – we've still got freedom. If you're from a village, man, then you're in trouble. We're from – it's like the same thing we're from London – it's a big town we're from.

(It is interesting to note that in the above two quotations, both young people – who were born and brought up in London – use the present tense and first person in describing their Pakistani backgrounds.)

Notwithstanding the evidence of some sub-ethnic rivalries, it is fair to conclude from the ways in which most respondents spoke of their ethnicity that they are generally more inclined than their parents to be oriented to the broadly defined 'Pakistani' ethnic community. A further widening of boundaries at the conceptual level is apparent when one notes that on the whole the young people approved the self-designation 'Asian', and quite frequently used this more general term interchangeably with 'Pakistani'. Again, of course, it must be borne in mind that many of their parents are also likely to define themselves, at least from time to time, as members of the 'Asian community' in Britain; but it can be argued that this is a more meaningful term for the younger people, given the emergence of a generalised 'Asian' or 'British Asian' youth culture (to be discussed below). Baumann points out that while one should not assume that 'the forging of an *Asian* post-immigration *culture* [is] the preserve of youngsters alone', among Southall Asians from Hindu, Sikh and Muslim backgrounds there is 'an articulate awareness . . . that being "young and born here" involves them in, and qualifies them for, the conscious creation of a comprehensively *Asian culture*' [original emphases] (1996: 154).[2]

crucial.

For my respondents, to be 'young and born here' entails, also, a very different relationship with Pakistan from that of their parents. As has been observed by a number of researchers looking at South Asian communities in Britain (for example, V. Robinson 1986; Murphy 1987), for the older generation of Pakistanis in Britain, Pakistan remains a 'home' to which many of them dearly wish to return. Most of my core respondents told me that their parents plan or would like to go back to live in Pakistan for good; several of them added, however, that their parents are discouraged from doing so because of financial problems and the fact that they have children settled in Britain.

As far as their own views on Pakistan are concerned, a number of the core respondents told me, as noted in Chapter 4, that they would find it difficult to adapt to life in Pakistan; however, most spoke about their experiences of Pakistan , or about what they know of it from their parents, in such a way as to suggest that it still holds considerable appeal for them. (All except one had visited Pakistan at least once; three had been there only as young children.) Memories of visits to Pakistan, and the stories of parents, grandparents and others about the lives they spent there, seem to provoke in the minds of the young people potent combinations of diverse opinions and feelings about the place: this is a country which is, to them, both exotic and very close; which both attracts and alarms them; and which is home but is at the same time quite obviously not home.

That there are elements of fantasy and nostalgia in so many of the young people's visions of Pakistan was expressed by Zareena, who told me: 'I used to always think that Pakistan was above the clouds'. Perhaps what Salman Rushdie writes of Indian expatriate writers can apply generally and with even more force to the children of immigrants from India and elsewhere:

> If we do look back, we must also do so in the knowledge – which gives rise to profound uncertainties – that our physical alienation from India almost inevitably means that we will not be capable of reclaiming precisely the thing that was lost; that we will, in short, create fictions, not actual cities or villages, but invisible ones, imaginary homelands, Indias of the mind.
>
> (1991: 10)[3]

Over two-thirds of the core respondents spoke of some of the intense pleasures of living in Pakistan. They told me, variously, that on visits to the country they have enjoyed its healthy environment, spacious homes, easy-going way of life and friendly people. For example:

> It is so natural. You work and you eat it yourself. . . . Everything there's fresh. And everything is good for you. Even the air's good for you, the water, it's spring water – a proper spring – I've seen it. I mean, I saw this bit of water, and there's a spring, and I was thinking how does that happen? It's just there, natural – innit.
>
> (Ilyas)

> Basically what it is up there – hardly anyone works there, and there's very cheap things – they don't have to pay no electricity, no rent or nothing – they just do farming and make their money out of that . . .
>
> (Hanif)

> The men go out to work and the women sit in their gardens and they cup the peas and they socialise. Over there, it's like near the beach, you're always out, it's always sunny. . . . You wake up at the crack of dawn, and you hear the *azan* [call to prayer]. . . . And you can hear chickens and cows and lambs and everything, and kids playing . . .
>
> (Shaheena)

Nevertheless, many of the respondents – including a number of those who also had much that was good to say about Pakistan – spoke of aspects of the country which they find disturbing and alienating. Over half of them discussed various drawbacks to life in Pakistan. The men tended to talk of the poverty and squalor, poor welfare provisions and corruption that are, they said, a part of life in Pakistan. Zaheer's memories of the poverty he encountered were especially vivid:

> like there's lepers, and beggars on the road with no arms, no legs. . . . And like for people up there, it's just a normal everyday thing seeing them, but when you come from here, you don't wanna look at them and look away, you wanna have a good look, cause you're never gonna see something like that again. . . . There's a lot of flies over there, sitting on food, which – in this country, if you see that you throw it away or something, but in that country there's flies just sitting on fruit as if it's a normal thing. . . . And, it's like you've got buffaloes walking about and donkeys walking about. And in this country it's like a big thing innit – you see a buffalo walking past you!

While several of the female respondents also spoke of poverty and corruption, their most common complaint was that women in Pakistan have little or no freedom. For example, Jamila, commenting on her six-month stay in Pakistan at the age of 17, said,

I couldn't go anywhere. You can't walk around there on your own. And I was just like sitting indoors all day killing time. And the heat and everything. I remember I was crying – literally crying, like begging them to let me come back.

Several female respondents also asserted that women in Pakistan suffer endless sexual harassment: in Ghazala's words, 'You wouldn't just get young boys after a girl in Pakistan – you'd get old men, you'd get people in their eighties up there, after a girl.'

Despite the various reservations expressed about life in Pakistan, as many as sixteen of the core respondents said that they might settle in the country and four that they definitely plan to do so. Nearly all of the young people expressed a keen interest in continuing to visit Pakistan: suggesting that a significant aspect of their ethnic self-definitions is a sense of attachment to their country of origin. In contrast, only one of the core respondents – Khalida – asserted that she would 'never again' visit Pakistan; because of, she said, 'the way the men are – they're so disgusting and dirty'.

The social dimension

Friendships

It has quite commonly been assumed by scholars in the field of ethnic relations that such processes as 'assimilation' and 'integration' can in part be understood in terms of the extent to which members of minority groups socialise within their own communities, or develop personal networks that extend beyond the group.[4]

My respondents' accounts of their friendship groups indicate, quite clearly, that ethnic boundaries are manifest in their socialising patterns. Over three-quarters of the core respondents told me that most of their friends or closest friends are Pakistani or Asian. It is from both sides of the ethnic cleavage, several of the young people seemed to suggest, that a certain social distance is maintained between themselves and their non-Asian peers. Several of them implied that, for their own part, they have some difficulty in communicating with or developing any profound sense of fellow-feeling towards non-Asians. From the other angle, a few of the respondents said explicitly – and others implicitly, in talking about racism – that white people show little interest in making friends with members of ethnic minorities; and several commented that white people are, in fact, generally disinclined to form close relationships with anyone. ('They're very formal – they never get too personal with someone, even if they're a relative', Naveed said of white Britons.)

Of those respondents who spoke about their own hesitation regarding interethnic friendships, many – particularly the women – explained this with reference to the fact that only other Asians can truly understand when they talk about family problems and related matters. As Khalida put it: 'With the English people, when you tell them about arranged marriages, they're really interested, but they could never understand, because they've never lived in that culture.' Several respondents also talked about the limits placed on friendship with non-Asians arising from differences in socialising habits: Bushra, for example, commented, 'If you were to want to go out with English people, there would be a major clash in the hours you're allowed out. So I don't bother in a manner of speaking. Save yourself from the embarrassment!' And Shahid complained, 'With my English friends, the primary conversation used to always revolve around how drunk they were the night before! And you just sat there – oh right, OK.' Another point often raised was that with other Asians it is possible to talk and laugh about various aspects of the minority culture. Asya said, 'Mostly with us lot we talk about everything and anything. Even about our culture – we talk about it, piss-taking. But with whites you couldn't, you know.'

Respondents' general comments about their friends seem to support my claim that ethnic boundaries among the younger generation are widening, for most of them talked in terms of having 'Asian' rather than 'Pakistani' friends. However, only a minority specified that they have friends who are non-Pakistani Asians; as far as the others are concerned, it is difficult to judge the extent to which the use of the term 'Asian' actually reflects the existence of Asian-wide social networks.

The talk of predominantly Asian or Pakistani friendship groups notwith-standing, the majority of the core respondents told me that they have or have had in the past many non-Asian friends. Two said that all their friends are Muslims, from a range of ethnic backgrounds. In many cases, respondents emphasised that interethnic friendship has a special value; for example, Ilyas told me,

> In my school there was me, an English boy, and a black boy. Best friends – for so long. They made me learn a lot – about how to respect this person, how not to say the wrong thing at the wrong time, and this and that.

That so many respondents stressed that they maintain interethnic social contact points again to what I have termed the increasing permeability of ethnic bound-aries. This also alerts us to the arguments of Hewitt (1990), who complains that theorists of race and ethnicity have tended to overlook the 'extremely common' phenomenon of mixed-race friendship among working-class youth in Britain. According to Hewitt, this friendship emerges out of the young people's common experiences of a shared social environment and the appeal of certain 'black' (that is, Afro-Caribbean and Asian) cultural practices to white youth.

Marriage

Endogamy is a vital element of boundary-maintenance for most ethnic groups. For the first generation of Pakistanis in Britain, the tradition of marrying within the caste group and, more narrowly, within the kinship group or *biraderi* has acted to preserve the integrity of smaller social units as well as the Pakistani community as a whole. Marriage between first cousins has, in fact, been very common in

Pakistan, and is a tradition that to a large extent has until now survived in Britain.[5] The findings of my research interviews suggest that marriage within caste and family group is indeed still favoured by the older generation of the Pakistani community of Waltham Forest. Of the eleven of the core respondents already married or engaged, six have partners who are family members; and a further twelve of the young people explicitly mentioned their parents' preference for marriage within the caste or family.

There is, however, evidence that among these young people and their peers there is an increasing willingness to challenge their parents' narrow criteria for marriage partners.[6] As has been mentioned above, several respondents said that they believe the concept of caste in general to be somewhat outdated. Furthermore, a few also indicated that they are not keen to marry within the family. For example, Kabir commented,

> I've told my parents that I will not marry none of my cousins! It's just that you're mixing up the family – you don't know who's who then. . . . I want to expand the family, not just stay in one little corner of the room.

And Abida, who told me of the immense pressure she had been put under by her grandparents to marry a first cousin, asserted,

> I don't believe that you should marry cousins. . . . My cousins, they're like brothers, and then one day, I grew up and the other boy grew up, my cousin, and they said – you have to marry him. And I'm thinking – *excuse me!*

A few respondents stressed the problems for young British Pakistanis associated with one particular aspect of family marriages: namely, that they tend to be arranged with cousins living in Pakistan.[7] Adnan was one of the respondents to voice his disapproval of this kind of arrangement, saying: 'My dad wants me to marry his brother's daughters, who are Pakistani. It will be too much of a culture clash, and I don't want to do that. I'll be ruining some girl's life forever. I can't do that.' Khalida talked of the difficulties that arise when someone 'really educated from here' marries someone 'really sort of backward' from Pakistan, as has happened to cousins of hers who were raised in Britain and 'have had to marry some dickheads from Pakistan'.

Perhaps somewhat surprisingly only one respondent mentioned the possible implications of the tradition of family marriage for physical health.[8] Amir raised this issue when asserting to me in general terms that members of the older generation tend to be ignorant about their religion and, consequently, about how they should bring up their children. He commented,

> [The parents] think they know how it's supposed to be done, but like Asian families, you find that they marry very close in families. I mean, there's even a saying of the Prophet Muhammad, right – peace be upon

91

him – that if you're to be married, don't marry very close into families.
Reason why, because . . . then you can have handicapped children.

Amir's wife elaborated this point, explaining to me that her sister, herself the product of a marriage between double first cousins, married her own double first cousin, and has had two children who are both handicapped.

Many of the young people indicated their openness to the possibility of marrying not only outside the family and caste, but outside the Pakistani community itself. Almost half of the core respondents, in total, said that they feel it is important to marry a Muslim, but not necessarily a Pakistani. This compares with a third who favour a Pakistani partner, and a few others who implied that marriage within the wider 'Asian' (Muslim and non-Muslim) community is acceptable. However, in contrast, not one declared that colour, culture and religion are all unimportant when it comes to choosing a partner for life. Most, or even all, respondents, then, seem to feel that 'mixed marriages' are inherently problematic; though their definitions of 'mixed marriage' vary. Some spoke explicitly about the difficulties faced by people who marry outside their own religion or 'community'. For example, Amina commented,

> The only reason I don't like couples marrying from a different religion is because when they have children, they don't know which religion are they. . . . And when [the parents] are praying, they're praying differently, and some would even have an argument over it.

And Yasmin told me, 'If I got married to a Muslim Gujerati – the way they talk, the way they eat, the way they sit – it's completely different. I won't be able to adapt to that.'

In general, my findings relating to the subject of marriage indicate that, although reservations about 'mixed marriages' remain among the younger generation, intergenerational change in attitudes is occurring at quite a rapid rate. But it is clear that however much the respondents assert that they maintain wider criteria for marriage partners than do their parents, the extent to which their claims translate into action is limited (as would be expected, given the fact that the arranged marriage system survives, if in a modified form). Even parental insistence upon marriage within the family or caste appears to be extremely difficult to oppose in practice, as the following two examples illustrate.

Hanif said that his older brother had argued with their mother, who wanted him to marry her own brother's daughter.

> He [my brother] said no, because he treated her as a sister really, and he goes, I can't think about it like that. So he got married to my dad's – er – [niece] . . .
> *So he married another cousin?*
> Yeah, you have to get married in the family – you can't do it out.

A young woman told me that she knows it is wrong, according to Islam, to worry about caste, and that her parents know it is wrong; but even so she herself would not go against the tradition of marrying within the caste. This is just how things are done, she said, and how they always have been done. 'Specially in our caste', she added. 'We're very strict about it.'

If many of the young people ultimately acquiesce with parental wishes regarding marriage within family and caste, few are likely to withstand pressures to marry within the Pakistani community in favour of creating wider units of endogamy based, for example, on religion or a general 'Asian' ethnicity. A small number of respondents did, however, mention that they know people who have married non-Pakistani Muslims or non-Pakistani (Muslim or non-Muslim) Asians.

Two of the respondents were themselves hoping, at the time I spoke to them, to marry outside the Pakistani community. The difficulties they were facing reflect the barriers to wide-scale change in marriage patterns that still exist. Bushra was engaged to her Bengali Muslim boyfriend, and complained that she would be given a 'hard time' by the older women in the Pakistani community when they found out that she was to marry a Bengali, and that although her own parents had come to accept the marriage, her fiancé's parents had not. Zaheer told me about his girlfriend, a young woman from a Sikh background who had recently converted to Islam. He said he would like to marry her, but his parents disapprove.

> I keep telling them, she's turned Muslim – what's wrong with her? . . . It's hard to find – you have to go out and find a girl who's from the same caste, the same colour, the same religion – you can't do it, because you can't feel for somebody who you're looking out for, what they are on top. It could be an ugly person, but you could be in love with her. It could be a yellow person, it could be a green person, but you might love the person . . .

[handwritten margin note: boys have problems too.]

The cultural dimension

Cultural preferences

Preferences in such matters as music, dress and food can act as powerful and pervasive ethnic boundary markers, insofar as the members of a minority group distinguish themselves from the majority along these lines. Some theorists have argued that, where the descendants of immigrants very visibly and self-consciously follow what they deem to be the cultural traditions of their forefathers, this signifies a nostalgic or romantic attachment to a way of life that has only intermittent bearing on their day-to-day behaviour. Such expressions of ethnicity among socially mobile 'ethnics' in the United States have been referred to by Gans (1979) as 'symbolic', and represent for Steinberg (1981) (also writing of the so-called 'ethnic revival' in the United States) a 'crisis of authenticity'. Taking these arguments into account, it becomes clear that it is important not to consider the 'cultural practices' element of my respondents' ethnic identities in isolation. It is only by looking at the various dimensions to their ethnicity that it is possible to understand that if their interest in 'cultural practices' can be described as symbolic, it is because these practices symbolise not only a perceived link with their family's place of origin and past, but also the many other meanings entailed by life as a 'Pakistani' or 'Asian'.

Among young people in Britain, taste in music is often seen as an extremely important marker of identity. Many researchers who have looked at South Asian communities in Britain have commented on the popularity of bhangra – a fusion of Punjabi folk with Western disco music – among young British Asians since the mid- or late 1980s.[9] A large majority of my respondents indicated that they enjoy listening to music which they described as Indian or Asian, differentiating sometimes between classical music, film music and bhangra.

Like taste in music, style of dress is often a strong expression of identity, and indeed can be, of course, an especially visible and literal marker of difference. During a discussion with two female respondents, one commented that she does not feel comfortable wearing the traditional *shalwar kameez* on the street. At this, the other looked surprised and asked her why not – was she ashamed of her culture? The significance of dress was emphasised also by Khalida (the respondent who had run away from home because of severe family problems). She remarked that Asian clothes are 'so glittery and over the top that I wouldn't be seen dead walking around the streets with them on'. As a child, she said, she had been forced to wear Asian clothes, but now that she is on her own she enjoys wearing what she wants. 'This is me', she said, gesturing at her clothes – a low-cut top, flared jeans and platform shoes. 'This reflects me.'

This kind of stated preference for Western clothes was, however, rare; a large majority of the young women specified a preference for Asian clothes, or said they enjoy wearing both Asian and Western dress.[10] It should be noted that the male respondents did not appear to be interested in traditional dress, although one – Adnan – was wearing *shalwar kameez* (with Doc Marten boots) when I spoke to him. He complained in the course of the interview that when he dresses in this style, his Pakistani friends ask him if he is on his way to the mosque.

The respondents can be said to express further the cultural dimension of their ethnicity in doing such things as watching Indian films and attending Asian cultural events like bhangra concerts or the *melas* (fairs) regularly held for Eid and other occasions in a local park. The vast majority of the young people indicated an attachment to Indian food; none said that they dislike it. A large majority told me that they attend cultural events, either with their families or their friends. With regard to Indian films, however, many appeared to have mixed feelings. Most said they watch the films at least occasionally, or that they used to in the past, but many complained that such films are boring or implied that they are always enjoyed more by the older than the younger generation.

In general, it is clear that the respondents maintain a strong interest in aspects of Pakistani or Indian culture; but also that this interest is itself the basis of a widening of ethnic boundaries in the sense that it promotes allegiance to a general Asian rather than narrower Pakistani community. The respondents generally did not discuss such matters as music, dress and food in terms that differentiate 'Pakistani' or 'Muslim' traditions from others. This apparent evolution of a cultural 'Asian' identity in Britain is particularly clearly manifest in the growing popularity of bhangra music which is, according to Gillespie, 'a focal point for the public emergence of a British Asian youth culture which transcends traditional divisions and aspires to a sense of ethnic unity'(1995: 45). The emerging Asian identity is evident also from the expansion of 'Asian' media and broadcasting.

Organisations such as the satellite television station TV Asia, the national radio station Sunrise Radio (a favourite jingle of which celebrates itself as 'The greatest Asian radio station in the world!') and newspapers such as *Eastern Eye* and *The Asian Times* (both of which are weeklies and are aimed specifically at the younger generation), along with the BBC television programme *Network East*, act to promote 'ethnic' films, music and fashion within the British Asian population. Some interest in various aspects of the British Asian media was expressed by a total of eighteen of my core respondents, of whom about half said that they sometimes or regularly read *Eastern Eye*.

The wider ethnic boundaries that are thus being constructed through the merging of various 'Asian' elements of culture are, in two ways, also becoming increasingly permeable. First, it is clear that the respondents' interest in Asian culture and traditions by no means precludes a liking for what are perceived as British or Western alternatives. The vast majority of respondents who spoke of enjoying Asian music, for example, stressed that they enjoy Western music also; and most of the female respondents told me that they like having the option of switching between Asian and Western dress. Second, various cultural practices which are described by the young people as 'Asian' are themselves influenced by Western or British styles. This intermingling of cultures is very evident in terms of fashion: Asian dress, as worn by many young people in Britain, is often 'adapted to more like a modern style now', as Sara put it. And, of course, observation alone would suggest that the kinds of Western clothes worn not only by young British Asians but by young people of all backgrounds are commonly influenced by Asian and other 'ethnic' modes of dress.

Again, it is interesting to consider here the significance of bhangra music, which provides a striking example of cultural fusion. Bhachu describes the evolution of bhangra as a 'process of appropriating facets of traditional ethnic cultural roots and recreating them to generate new forms that draw both from their Punjabi background and from whole sets of British subcultures' (1991: 409). The 'new forms' of musical expression have attracted young people to new forms of dance and socialising also: Asian discos and 'Asian nights' organised by mainstream night-clubs are growing in popularity (Dhingra 1994).

One might expect that this phenomenon is looked upon with alarm by many older members of the British Asian population. During my time in Waltham Forest I spoke with an especially devout older man who shook his head sadly as he

hat young Pakistanis in Britain have 'started adding Western spice' to the
f their parents. 'Not long ago you never heard of the name disco', he
nd now you hear of Asian discos.'

ld seem, then, that a new British Asian youth culture is emerging which
provides scope for resistance to older generation hopes and assumptions, while
drawing on many elements of culture that the older generation itself brought to
Britain. This process came clearly into focus for me during an evening I spent at a
Fashion Show held at the local Town Hall which was organised by a local Asian
women's association. The event attracted a large crowd of young Asian men and
women, who greeted with excited cheering the female models who, displaying
shalwar kameez in a dazzling array of colours, strolled across the stage. Every now
and then, the female models were joined by young men, who – as the audience
cheered more wildly – accompanied the women in choreographed flirtation, amid
clouds of dry ice and against the background thumping of Western pop. At one
point the powerful voice of Madonna filled the hall: 'Erotic! Erotic! Put your hands
all over my body!'

Language

Minority language use can be an especially explicit and concrete element of a
cultural boundary, in that it reinforces both the sense of belonging of group
members and the exclusion of outsiders. My respondents' comments about their
own use of language, however, seem to provide further evidence of what I have
described as the semi-permeability of ethnic boundaries. For while the mother
tongue continues to be used in conversations with parents and grandparents, and
may thereby promote some feelings of allegiance with the minority group, it is
rarely used by the young people outside the home.

The vast majority of respondents told me that they speak a mixture of English
and Punjabi or Urdu (or what was sometimes referred to as Urdu-Punjabi, by
which is meant, presumably, a blend of the two languages) within the home: they
talk mostly Punjabi or Urdu with their parents and English with their siblings.[11]
Only three of the core respondents mentioned that they sometimes speak Punjabi
or Urdu with their friends. My own observations of the local Pakistani community
support respondents' general accounts of patterns of mother-tongue usage: young
people talking among themselves seemed to speak English almost entirely; in
contrast, within mixed-age groups Punjabi or Urdu was the predominant
language, although English phrases were frequently inserted by the younger
people.

Intergenerational changes in language use and abilities have, according to some
researchers in this field, been a source of tension and even conflict within British
Asian families (for example, Saifullah Khan 1979; C. Ballard 1979). Although
none of the respondents talked directly about language problems causing a
communication barrier within the family – and very few told me that they can
speak little or no Punjabi or Urdu themselves – many did indicate that tension at

home is sometimes caused or fuelled by concerns with language. Some of the young people said, for example, that their parents often tell them to stop speaking English. Two of the respondents commented that their mothers claim not to know English, but will in fact understand anything that is said if they wish to. Mariam told me that when her parents are angry with her, they speak to her only in Urdu, and she replies only in English. And two young sisters told me that they speak Punjabi to their parents only 'when we want something; when we're sweet-talking them'.

Thus it seems that in general the linguistic element of ethnic boundaries is very obviously and rapidly undergoing profound change; and, as such, is perhaps open to an especially wide range of interpretations by the respondents and their peers. Some, apparently, see language as an element of ethnicity that is adaptable and fun: Tahmeena told me, for example, that she enjoys spending time with Asian friends because 'you can muck around with your own language'; and Faruq asserted that 'Punjabi is the best language in the world to swear in!' In contrast, a number of respondents expressed a serious concern with language matters: they talked, proudly, about their linguistic abilities, or discussed the interesting distinctions between Urdu and Punjabi.[12] For example, Zaheer told me, 'I speak about three languages, which a lot of people can't'; and Shahid remarked, 'I consider it to be rude to speak English to my parents. But some kids can't speak Urdu-Punjabi well at all – they just pick up broken words and stuff, and I don't like that at all.' On the subject of the relationship between Urdu and Punjabi, a young woman told me that Punjabi is a very 'frankful' and 'comfortable' language, in which it is possible to say exactly what you mean; whereas on the other hand Urdu is 'respectable' and 'disciplinary'. Ilyas said it is difficult to explain the differences between the two languages, and added, 'I put it as Urdu is neat, Punjabi is sweet'.

A few of the comments on the subject of language suggested that some of the young people fear that their own neglect of their mother tongue might reflect a kind of rootlessness. Majid was one of those who said they cannot talk Punjabi or Urdu; interestingly, his comment was 'I never picked up *my* language' [emphasis added]. Similarly, Nazia, while making a telephone call to a friend in my presence, said before the call was answered that she hoped her friend's mother would not answer because, 'Oh no, I can't speak in my own language right now – sometimes I forget my own language'. A few of the young people mentioned having language problems on visits to Pakistan. For example, Zareena, who had told me she was 'embarrassed' to admit that she speaks mostly English at home, said that when she was staying in Pakistan, 'They used to take the mick out of our accents and everything'.

During an afternoon I spent at an 'Asian sports day' in a local park, I spoke for a while with a young British Pakistani man whose comments seemed to associate linguistic problems with a wider sense of alienation from the culture of his parents. He said that although 'Punjabi is my language', he could not understand the running commentary on the sports that was being announced over a public address system, in Punjabi, as we spoke. He asked me if I knew what was going on at the event because he could not work it out. 'I'm trying to find it interesting, but I can't', he added.

'Postmodern' and ethnic identities

In the final part of this chapter, I wish to return to the question of the extent to which the findings presented above support the assertions of those theorists who argue that in the late twentieth century, or in the postmodern era, conceptions of identity are becomingly highly fluid, hybrid and malleable.

My findings with regard to the increasing flexibility in social patterns among British Pakistanis, the broader definitions of the minority that are gaining currency, and perhaps above all the diversifying expressions of ethnic culture, appear to endorse the claims of the postmodernists – discussed in Chapter 1 – that increasingly fragmented and hybrid identities are coming into being, as traditional boundaries between social categories are breaking down. I have argued above that an expanding British Asian youth culture, elements of which have been created through the fusion of diverse traditions, offers a challenge to the often conservative ideals of the older generation. The emergence, in this fashion, of 'new ethnicities' (a term apparently coined by S. Hall [1992b], and frequently used in literature on ethnic minority identities in Britain) also challenges to some extent the boundaries which define and demarcate Britishness, and thereby contributes further to the evolution of 'postmodern' patterns of social relations.

If we look beyond the immediate experiences and attitudes of my respondents, we can find further evidence of 'new ethnicities' in various public expressions of British Asian identity and youth culture; for example, in the fields of music, film and comedy. As far as music is concerned, it seems that cultural fusion has by no means reached its limits with bhangra: music which blends and adapts Afro-Caribbean with Asian and white styles has proved highly popular. This can be seen, for example, in the success of what has been described as the 'Asian Rock' of the highly successful singer Apache Indian, who 'performs and expresses himself through snatches of Jamaican patois, Punjabi and a unique form of English that is being generated by groups of young people who are growing up alongside each other in Birmingham' (Back 1996: 220). The 'Asian rap' music of groups such as Fun-da-mental, Kaliphz and the Asian Dub Foundation is a further manifestation of musical hybridisation.

British Asian comedy and drama, performed at *melas* (fairs), clubs and the theatre, has sometimes sought to address quite explicitly some of the potentials and problems of cultural fusion. For example, the London show entitled *D'yer Eat with your Fingers?!* attempted, according to the programme notes, to show that 'our culture, rather than being diluted by so many different influences, was in fact enriched by them'.[13] Some recent British films have taken on similar tasks in different ways: for example, *Bhaji on the Beach* (Channel Four Films 1994), which follows the exploits of a group of Asian women, of various ages and facing various difficulties, on a day-trip to Blackpool; and *Wild West* (Channel Four Films 1993), which is an account of a group of Asian teenagers in Southall who form a Country and Western band.[14] The work of Anglo-Pakistani writer Hanif Kureishi, for example his novels *The Buddha of Suburbia* (1990) and *The Black Album* (1995), also explores the diversity and dynamism of Asian identities in Britain.

As was suggested in Chapter 4, part of what we see in these new expressions of British Asian identity, and more narrowly in how my respondents spoke of what it is to be Pakistani or Asian, is increasing self-assertiveness and personal creativity. The ethnic boundaries are being actively reshaped by individuals who are ready to question and subvert many previously taken-for-granted notions of identity.

But it is clear also that these pre-existing social definitions continue to play a large part in the lives of the young people with whom I spoke. 'Who indeed', as Baumann asks, 'can claim freedom from reifications, even if such freedom were desirable or possible?' (1996: 30). Certainly my respondents feel more able than their parents have ever been to integrate within their conceptions of Asian ethnicity aspects of identity that they perceive to emanate from outside the group. But at the same time they do not believe they have the option of redefining themselves entirely. 'Yes, I'm British', Khalida told me – who of all my respondents was the only one who adamantly wished to dissociate herself from all facets of the minority culture and religion – 'But I don't think that white people would see me as British.' Back, in his study of 'new ethnicities' in London, draws our attention to the fact that while

> multiply inflected forms of social identity are being expressed within cities such as London . . . these are equally being met by multiply accented forms of popular racism that sometimes operate inside urban multiculture and at other times prey on these fragile forms of dialogue from outside.
>
> (1996: 7)

Among my respondents the new, 'multiply inflected' expressions of identity are constrained not only by racism, but also by the demands of traditionalist parents whose expectations, as we saw in Chapter 4, might be frequently resented but are rarely completely rejected. That it is by no means an easy matter to throw off communal constraints was made especially clear to me by the comments of Mumtaz, a worker in the Asian women's refuge at which the respondent Khalida was staying. Mumtaz told me that many of the young women who have run away from home, usually in order to escape physical and/or sexual abuse, must face the challenge of 'making up their own identities, selves, as they are going along', and find this process a painful and fraught one. Many of these young women, Mumtaz said, feel deeply perplexed and find it extremely difficult to come to terms with their experiences of being considered 'bad women' by the families and communities against which they have rebelled or been forced to rebel.

But I do not wish to argue simply that many who write of 'postmodern' identities are guilty of overlooking the significance of externally imposed restrictions on identity-formation. It is my contention that another flaw in much of what is said about processes of hybridisation is that it fails to consider the extent to which the individuals in question may themselves *not wish* to challenge some of the traditionalist conceptions of identity that they learn from their parents and indeed from wider society (although they do reject racist definitions of minorities). To differentiate between coercive, imposed social definitions and personal, creative expressions of group belonging is, I believe, to construct a false dichotomy.[15] It should be recognised that communities are created and recreated by the collective actions and attitudes of individuals who to varying degrees refer to and feel bound by (real or perceived) history and ancestry. As Berger and Luckmann have forcefully reminded us, in their exploration of the dialectical process by which 'reality' is socially constructed, the institutional world has for social actors a massive objectivity even while it is 'a humanly produced, constructed objectivity' (1967: 78).

To return to my respondents, it appears that they accept with ease some elements of ethnic or religious 'tradition' not simply because they are 'making the best of' social exclusion and parental restrictions, but also because they deem those elements to be inherently meaningful and, in Berger and Luckmann's terms, to have an objectivity. This has been demonstrated above, with respect to the young people's positive evaluations of much of what they see as the natural repercussions of being born and growing up within a Pakistani or Asian community. In Chapters 6 and 7, I shall write of the extent to which religious teachings that are perceived as fixed and universal are valued precisely because of their supposed fixity and universalism.

This chapter is best concluded with the observation that the ethnic boundaries which delineate the Pakistani community in Waltham Forest are undergoing a substantial degree of change but are showing no sign of dissolving. It might be expected that further, gradual evolution of the boundary elements over time will eventually ensure that the expressions of ethnic identity of future generations are quite far removed from those articulated by the young people with whom I have spoken. Here a comparison should be made with the religious boundaries maintained by my respondents and other young British Muslims. As we shall see, these latter boundaries are constructed in accordance with the demands of a distinct set of doctrines. As a result of this, they are relatively clear-cut, and have a logic, coherence and constancy that the ethnic boundaries never can. It seems to me, therefore, that the identities they encompass will survive in something like their present form for longer than the ethnic identities described above.

6

ISLAM AND GUIDANCE

This chapter and the next directly address the fundamental question which was the starting-point of this study: namely, how can one explain, in sociological terms, the persistence of religious commitment among young British Pakistanis? In order to understand the basis of this commitment, I have already considered, in Chapters 1 and 2 respectively, the notion of religion as a meaning system and the central tenets of Islam. Here, much more specifically, my task is to look at how and why it is that Islam acts as a significant source of meaning in the lives of my respondents and many of their peers.

I address this question by looking at two aspects to respondents' religious identities. First, I argue (in this chapter) that the religion should be conceived as a source of *guidance* in the young people's lives; guidance which allows them to undertake a 'quest for certainty', and thereby to resolve some of the ambivalence over identity engendered by their social circumstances. Second (in Chapter 7) I argue that the persistence of religious identities can be understood in terms of the *boundaries* which practising Muslims, by virtue of the demands of their religion, construct and maintain between themselves and others. In Chapter 5, I pointed out that as far as the respondents' expressions of ethnicity are concerned, there is some evidence of emerging fluid and hybrid identities; however, the discussions of religious guidance and religious boundaries will demonstrate that there is in general among the young people a certain disinclination to embrace the uncertainties of a postmodern world.

It could be argued that the commitment to religion of the respondents is simply the product of their upbringing and of the community within which they were born and bred. After all, Islam is for them an inescapable fact of life, as it is the religion in which they were raised and which, through its long-standing doctrines and rituals, binds them with their parents and grandparents and with the rest of the Muslim population of Britain and the world. In other words, we must understand that the young people find through their religion the guidance they seem to want, because, in the first place, it is available to them. However, this in itself is not a sufficient explanation for their attachment to Islam: after all, as we have seen from the findings presented thus far, the young people tend to be reflective and critical with regard to most aspects of their social environment. Indeed, as shall become

apparent from my discussion of their attitudes to religion, they frequently distance themselves from their parents' interpretations of Islam. It must thus be recognised that insofar as religion acts as a source of identity for the young people it comprises, like ethnicity, a host of pre-given elements which can be manipulated and invested with meaning in a wide variety of ways.

Overview of respondents' religiosity

The assumption that high levels of commitment to Islam persist among young British Pakistanis – an assumption which informed the research problem addressed by this study – is supported by much of what my respondents said about the part that Islam plays in their lives. Before going on to suggest some reasons for the continuing appeal of Islam, I shall provide an overview of the levels of religious commitment displayed by the fifteen male and eighteen female core respondents, by looking at their own accounts of their religious practices and involvement in learning activities. The more complex manifestations of the respondents' religiosity are described in the subsequent discussion.

Prayer
Male respondents: Six pray at least once a day; seven pray at least once a week (most of whom pray only on Fridays, when attending the mosque); two pray occasionally.

Female respondents: Eight pray at least once a day; two pray at least once a week; three pray occasionally; five do not pray.

(It should be noted, in addition, that many respondents commented that they pray much more regularly during Ramadan than at other times of the year.)

Reading the Qur'an (in English or Arabic)
Male respondents: Three read the Qur'an at least once a week; ten read from time to time; two do not read.

Female respondents: Six read the Qur'an at least once a week; eleven read from time to time; one does not read.

Mosque attendance (male respondents only: women rarely attend the local mosques)
Eleven attend a mosque at least once a week; two attend quite regularly but not every week; two attend occasionally. (One of those who said they only occasionally attend was Naveed, the only Shi'ite respondent, who told me that there are no local Shi'ite mosques.)

Fasting
Male respondents: All fifteen fast throughout the month of Ramadan every year, although four remarked that they do not usually manage to keep each day of the fast.

Female respondents: Twelve fast throughout Ramadan every year; four generally fast on-and-off over the course of the month; one does not fast because of health reasons, but did when she was younger; one never fasts.

Avoidance of alcohol
Male respondents: Fourteen never drink alcohol; one used to drink, but no longer does.
Female respondents: Sixteen never drink alcohol; two drink.

Eating *halal* meat
Male respondents: Twelve always eat *halal* meat; three sometimes eat non-*halal*.
Female respondents: Seventeen always eat *halal* meat, of whom four said that they have very occasionally eaten non-*halal* in the past; one does not eat *halal* meat.

Reading about Islam
Male respondents: Four often, and four from time to time, read books on the subject of Islam; seven do not.
Female respondents: Four often, and six from time to time, read about Islam; eight do not.

Attendance at religious talks and meetings organised by student Islamic societies and local and national Muslim associations
Male respondents: Four regularly, and six sometimes, attend religious talks or meetings; five do not attend talks or meetings.
Female respondents: Five regularly, and four sometimes, attend religious talks or meetings; nine do not attend talks or meetings.

It may be useful briefly to summarise the various findings by considering the general pattern of religious practice among the respondents. Eight of the young people – namely, Rafiq, Kabir, Shahid and Hanif among the men, and Zareena, Masooma, Ruksana and Ghazala among the women – could be described as devout, according to all or most of the above criteria. In contrast, Yusuf and Jamila could be labelled minimally religious, in the sense that they maintain low levels of practice; although both also asserted that religion is important to them. One respondent only – Khalida – is not at all religious: she professed no interest in practising Islam, and very little concern with the general subject of religion, which she dismissed as 'a man-made concept'. Among the respondents positioned between the devout and minimally religious poles, most commitment was shown with respect to fasting, eating *halal* meat, avoiding alcohol and, as far as the men are concerned, mosque attendance.

The general conclusion to be reached from the data described above is that the respondents, on the whole, exhibit a high degree of religious commitment. Although it is of course likely that in some cases there are discrepancies between respondents' claimed and actual levels of practice, it cannot be disputed that, at the very least, their accounts point to ready acceptance of the importance and value of religious observance. That there is widespread attachment to Islam among young Muslims in Waltham Forest generally was further supported by my own observations of mosque attendances and the many activities of (albeit small) numbers of especially devout young people engaged in religious organisations. Among the local community leaders and youth workers with whom I spoke during the field-work period, some reported a slow decline in religiosity within the younger generation, but more said that commitment remains high and several remarked that a growing minority of young Muslims are taking up their religion with renewed enthusiasm.

Guidance

In seeking to understand the religiosity of many of the respondents, one immediately confronts the apparent contradiction that this commitment to a clearly defined set of absolute and universal values coexists with varying degrees of ambivalence over identity which, I argued in Chapter Four, are engendered by the particular circumstances in which these young people grew up. It is my contention that this contradiction indicates that the religion flourishes because in situations where one is faced with deep-seated contradictions and dilemmas, a pre-existing set of doctrines that provide clear guidance in life can be all the more valued.

Respondents' accounts suggest that, as regards the role played by religion in their lives, it is appropriate actually to *define* Islam as guidance, within the broader conceptualisation of religion as a meaning-system. The respondents, quite evidently, have a tendency to perceive Islam – or what is set down in the Qur'an and *hadith* – as being, more than anything else, a complete and definitive source of information on how they should live their lives. That is, in delineating the parameters of moral behaviour, and outlining a detailed set of rituals which are the basis for personal expressions of religious belief and commitment, Islam is seen to provide clear rules for action. Though these rules may not be adhered to in many or even most instances, they are regarded by the young people as comprising a highly practical and solid frame of reference; a frame of reference not based on seemingly irrelevant parental anxieties or immoral Western values, but on ageless and ultimate truths.

Respondents' perceptions of Islam as, primarily, a source of guidance are clearly manifest in the terms in which they replied to general questions about the importance of religion in their lives and about the meaning that Islam has for them. As many as twenty of the core respondents answered such questions by referring principally to the impact of Islam on their behaviour: in terms of the practices they undertake, their observance of religious prescriptions with regard to daily, mundane activity and, perhaps most commonly, their adherence to a religiously oriented morality. The following three quotations are typical of the various responses given, in that they stress the notion of religion as a set of teachings which provide information as to how one should and should not act:

As a Muslim you've got to pray five times a day, you've got to fast during Ramzan [Ramadan] and all that. So I do all the things that I'm supposed to do as a Muslim now. It's how you think a lot – what you're supposed to be doing. It keeps you away from the troubles.

(Majid)

104

God has . . . given us, say, a manual, like a car manual, and if you follow the manual and you do everything as it's been told, your car will carry on and it will be OK.

(Amir)

I think everything the Qur'an says has something to do with what I'm doing in life. . . . It gears me to a different kind of lifestyle. I mean, I don't drink, I don't eat non-*halal* meat, I don't reveal my whole body . . .

(Sara)

Many of the young people emphasised their association of religiosity with behaviour by asserting that every aspect of their day-to-day lives is, or ideally should be, shaped by Islam. Frequently, and as in the examples given below, this conception of religion was in part conveyed by the statement that Islam is 'a way of life'.

I'd say religion plays the greatest part in my life. I certainly wouldn't do anything at all that would conflict with what my religion says. . . . It's a way of life for me. I eat, breathe and everything the way the religion tells me.

(Hanif)

It's not religion, is it – it's a way of life. It's interweaved with what you do every day. Like you can't define it in its own existence – that's how it is for us. Like if you eat pork, that's not religious; if you don't eat pork, that's religious.

(Adnan)

It's not religious – it's a way of life – the way you should be. Do certain things. Religion's not just praying and wearing a certain dress – it's the way you act, the way you act towards people. It's just – being human, basically.

(Nazia)

In explaining or developing their conceptions of religion as guidance, many talked in terms of the crucial role it plays in instilling a sense of morality, discipline and compassion in the lives of its followers. Islamic prescriptions for action, they feel, provide a basic ethical framework within which men and women must live if they are, at an individual or societal level, to enjoy a contented and harmonious existence. Islam means, said Waqar, 'Being honest. To be a good citizen. No bad habits.' Bushra told me, 'So much comes out of religion, you know. Discipline, manners, the way you treat people, respect for others, respect for yourself – which is so important. If you want to lead a happy life.' And Naveed remarked:

I try to use the Islamic values. Be good to your neighbour; be good to the next person as you would to yourself. I try to do that as much as possible, and I try not to lie – the basic values I believe help you to be a better Muslim rather than doing great deeds like feeding the thousands.

A few of the especially devout young people with whom I spoke expressed this kind of view in a somewhat different fashion: they asserted the need for Islamic law to enforce personal and public morality. For example, Tahir told me that 'Islam is really strict against crime. You've probably heard, some Third World Islamic countries are really strict with their punishment. It gives you a sense of moral virtues – keep away from crime.' Three young men whom I met at a mosque, on the occasion of the celebration of the Prophet's birthday, spoke of the necessity for religious laws which restrict sexual freedom: they talked about what they perceive to be the terrible social consequences of promiscuity, such as AIDS, abortion and high rates of illegitimacy. (There is a special Hell, one of them told me, for people who have sex before marriage.)

Many of the young people elaborated their understanding of religion as guidance by speaking of notions of divine judgement. Two-thirds of the core respondents made some reference to this dimension of religion, some of whom made it clear that, for them, the belief that one is rewarded or punished after death is central to their faith:

> They tell you when you're small if you do good things then you'll go to Heaven, and if you do bad things then you go to Hell, and that's what religion is – if you follow it properly, then you'll go to Heaven, and if you don't you'll go to Hell, innit.
>
> (Mustafa)

> I fear God. I really do. Sometimes I'm sitting there, and I'm thinking, oh God, I'm gonna die, and if I go to Hell, my nails are going to be pulled out, and I'm gonna have all these horrid things done to me.
>
> (Adnan)

> You'll go to Hell if you have done all the bad things in life – if you have drunk alcohol and that. If you do everything that is good in a Muslim life, you'll go to Heaven – if you've read your prayers five times a day. I'm always thinking – am I doing right? 'Cause believe me I don't reckon no one wants to go to Hell. 'Cause you hear it's like fire. They always say if you go to Heaven you're one lucky person.
>
> (Asya)

The respondents can be said to maintain a *behavioural perspective on Islam*, on the basis of their overwhelming tendency to regard it as a religion of conduct and social action. As should be clear from the above elaborations of their concepts of religious guidance, this perspective rests on faith in a transcendental God and a divinely ordained system of knowledge and morality: that is, there was little or no suggestion that the belief element of religious commitment is less important than conduct. However, the behavioural perspective seems, by and large, to preclude serious interest in theological debate.

The lack of concern with theology is evident from the fact that in the interviews and discussions very little of any substance was said about such matters as the nature of God and his revelations to the Prophet Muhammad, the relationship between God and man, or the process by which Islamic law, the *shari'a*, developed. Although, as I shall demonstrate below, many respondents appeared eager to take active steps to learn about their religion, this does not, apparently, entail a commitment to theological study. Those who told me about what they wish to learn tended to speak in quite general terms about wanting to know more of the history of Islam and its leaders, or to gain a more comprehensive understanding of the religion's fundamental teachings and the 'reasons' which underlie these.

Strategies of coping

I have argued above that a large part of the appeal of Islam to the respondents is that they feel their lives, in which much is contradictory, can benefit from the explicit guidance it offers. As I shall now go on to demonstrate, it is clear that not only does the religion, as the young people perceive it, provide universal rules for day-to-day behaviour, but also there are some circumstances where it acts as a resource which can be openly called upon in efforts to resolve conflicts which arise as a result of the differing demands of family and wider society. The clearest illustration of what might be termed the 'strategic use of religion' is provided by the comments of many of the female respondents about Islamic teachings on the status of women. According to Islam, they told me, women should be treated equally to men, should have the opportunity to be educated and to work outside the home, and should never be forced into marriage. These young women are thus able to feel justified in challenging the demands of their parents, brothers and others in the community that they lead sheltered lives.[1]

A majority of the female respondents mentioned that Islam guarantees many rights for women; and most stressed that this is a fundamental and especially appealing aspect of their religion. They also emphasised that throughout history Muslims have either wilfully or through ignorance misinterpreted Islam in such a way that they have denied women the freedoms and social standing that are rightfully theirs. Three examples of the forceful comments made on this broad subject follow:

> The teachings are OK. It's our people. These priests that are sitting in the mosque, and our parents, are so narrow-minded. They don't put the teachings right. It says that a girl is not allowed to be forced into marriage . . .
>
> (Zubaida)

culture nor Islam

If you read some of the books and everything – the Qur'an – it's men and women are equal. But it's the priests, you see. The ones who are not educated. They get their own ideas, and they put them all together, and then it's those ideas which have been going on for about – since Islam has been here.

(Abida)

A lot of people used to say, in Islam the girls aren't allowed to go out or anything – even for higher education. And I used to believe it at first. And now when I read the thing in the Qur'an it keeps on saying they *are* allowed to go out. I mean, for higher education, even if she has to go to another country.

(Masooma)

Several of the male respondents also spoke of how the religion is misused by many parents and grandparents, who invoke the name of Islam in denying people, and women in particular, the very rights and respect that it does in fact protect and promote. Again, the unIslamic nature of forced marriage was quite frequently pointed out; and some said also that, contrary to the views of many, Islam encourages education for women. Shahid, talking about the older generation, told me in exasperation,

They'll push religion at you when it suits their own needs, but when it serves the needs of somebody else they . . . try to twist and turn it. I think they're stupid, and they're the people that give us a bad name.

Zaheer, similarly, commented,

Parents bribe us through religion – oh, girls ain't supposed to go out after nine o'clock 'cause it's a sin. There's a lot of other things like that, I've picked them up and thought, that ain't a sin, that's just what our parents want us to do.

The findings of several other studies also indicate that many young British Pakistanis and other Muslims in Britain – and especially the women among them – are drawing on their religion in arguing against restrictions imposed upon them by families and communities. Shaw (1988), for example, in her account of the Pakistani community of Oxford, reports that there are numbers of young women who strive to justify to their parents the fact that they have careers by referring to Islamic teachings. She also writes of young people using 'Islamic' arguments in resisting their parents' marriage arrangements. Ali (1992) argues that substantial numbers of young Muslim women in the north of England are, likewise, resorting to what she refers to as 'Islamist subversion' in seeking to gain independence from their families.[2] Some other writers have discussed, in rather more general terms, the ways in which young British Muslims have found through Islam a kind of 'escape route' between the 'conflicting worlds' of their parents and modern British society (Clarke 1988).[3]

It is easy to understand that young people might find it helpful and even, particularly as far as women are concerned, liberating to use religious arguments in challenging attitudes maintained by the older generation. Such arguments allow individuals to reject certain of the more stringent demands made upon them, but do not entail an abandonment of the community and its values. Some might conclude from this that where young people appeal to Islam in such a way, this is a somewhat cynical ploy, rather than indicative of true faith; especially as calls for notions such as equal opportunities might be characterised as essentially 'Western' in content, if not in tone. One might also conclude that the religion is simply something which the youngsters fall back upon, when they find nothing else that can support them as they negotiate between conflicting demands. This may be what Mirza implies when she writes: 'Those who are born in England find it difficult to define themselves as Pakistanis. . . . The only option left for them to define themselves as distinct from the majority and the other Asian immigrants is to see themselves as Muslims' (1989: 23). Sahgal seems to propose something rather similar, in arguing that for many young Muslim women religious practice has provided 'a refuge rather than an empowering experience'; such that, for example, 'to be pious was to avoid the charge that in the eyes of the world you were dishonoured, because your intentions had remained pure' (1992: 193).

However, the overall picture of respondents' beliefs and practices appears to be more complex than is allowed for by a simple characterisation of the young people as manipulators of their religion, or as Muslims of last resort. The distancing of many of them from much that they perceive as 'Western', their high levels of religious practice and the eagerness with which they affirm their allegiance to Islam strongly suggest that many genuinely wish to retain values and a lifestyle they deem to be distinctly Muslim and, as such, intrinsically and immensely valuable. Hence it is apparent that if Islam provides a strategy for coping with culture clash, this should be regarded as a root cause of their sincere commitment to the religion, not as a reason for pretence. As Ali writes, whatever inherent contradictions there may appear to be in Muslim women's Islamist responses to their problems, it should be recognised also that this 'means to a form of personal liberation – albeit qualified – may arise naturally, organically, from one's experience of a community in which strong (and possibly increasing) emphasis is placed upon religion as a stabilizing force in an unstable world' (1992: 114).[4]

Quest for certainty

My primary concern in this chapter is to show that many of the respondents seem to find through Islam a sense of certainty, in that they feel the religion provides fixed and definite guidelines for action. But it cannot be assumed that religious faith necessarily implies confidence and conviction: it is clear that in modern conditions profound doubt can accompany belief, and any religious laws or teachings can be subject to extensive questioning and debate.[5] However, it would appear that for most of my respondents doubt is not an adjunct of faith; and it therefore seems appropriate to write of their attachment to and interest in Islam as manifestations of a quest for certainty.

Belief and certainty

When asked if there are aspects of Islam that they question or have significant doubts about, two-thirds of the core respondents replied in the negative. Of those who said that they do find it difficult to accept or understand certain religious teachings, most mentioned only quite minor issues; furthermore, they tended to talk about these in such a way as to suggest that they are convinced that it must ultimately be possible to find definitive solutions to any apparent contradictions within Islam.

To illustrate what I would describe as the general conservatism of the respondents, I shall cite various comments made on the theme of religious questioning and doubt. First, I quote Rafiq and Hanif, respectively: they are both very devout, and made it clear, in different ways, that they do not regard doubt to be a component of faith.

> I'm in no position to [question the religion] – we only have finite – how can I say it? – intellect. And if we only have finite intellect, if Allah makes a decision, you know it's best, so you just accept it. He knows better than you – you've no right to challenge what he says. . . . Otherwise you're just being a bit of an idiot, basically.

> You question [teachings] not because you think they're wrong, but to reaffirm your own belief. You work through the issues where the religion says so-and-so – you take the issue and you say, oh, let's break this issue down into what does it actually mean . . .

Zaheer and Yasmin are two respondents who practise their religion to a far lesser degree than Rafiq and Hanif, but also expressed certainty with regard to their religious beliefs:

> Everything I've been told about the religion has been true. There's not been something that I've thought about as being wrong, because when somebody tells you something right, you know it's right. You might not *want* it to be right, and you'd *hate* it if it was right, but still it's right.

> I believe in what the Qur'an says – what people say about it. I believe in it. I believe in it but I don't do it. I believe it. But I don't do it.

In the quotations that now follow, Adnan and Zareena explain that they do find some religious injunctions problematic, without giving any indication that such problems might provoke real doubt:

> They say, food additives such as E471, E472 are *haram*, we can't eat them. And other things such as gelatine, and whey – I dunno, they're really really small – should I or should I not eat them? Them things I'm really not sure about. 'Cause it's such a small thing. Like if there was pork there, OK, I definitely wouldn't eat that, 'cause I know that is religious.

> There's certain issues like . . . when you're praying, reading the Qur'an, hoping that the goodness you get from reading it will go to other people – a lot of people say it can be done, it's fine; a lot of people say it isn't – and I can't understand how it would work. So certain issues like that I just don't know, and I'm not sure how I'm ever going to find out.

Finally, I quote Ghazala, a very religious young woman, who was the only respondent to give the impression of being deeply engaged in an internal struggle over her beliefs. She refers here to health problems which have dogged her over recent years:

> When I've been ill, and I've had to go to hospital, thinking that every-thing's gonna be all right and sometimes it just does the opposite, and it makes me wonder why, because I think of all the people that do bad things get away with pure murder, and all the good people that don't do any harm to anyone keep suffering. And I don't like that. It makes me angry. My mum always says God's testing us, but I've always thought how much more does he want to test me, 'cause I've done everything he wants me to.

A further illustration of the young people's general unwillingness to look upon their religion with any kind of scepticism is provided by the finding that about two-thirds of the core respondents, including many who indicated relatively low levels of religious commitment, said that they feel they *should* follow their religion more than they do. Their failure to do so, they implied or said explicitly, is due not to problems inherent in the religion, but to their own personal weaknesses. In the following three extracts, such a point of view is clearly expressed:

> If I was really religious, I'd have to like – don't chat to girls and things like that. I'm not really religious, so I don't do that. But then afterwards you think – I shouldn't have done this, I should have done this.
>
> (Mustafa)

I am now going to ask you some questions about your religion —
Oh God – time for embarrassment now. . . . I don't read *namaz* [prayers] which is really bad – I'll be punished. I don't pray at all, no. It's terrible. I know.

(Bushra)

I feel so interested listening to [friends arguing about religion]. Then I feel guilty and I feel so sad that there are rules that are set, and I'm not going according to them. Then I feel depressed, and I feel so stupid that I do this stupid stuff. . . . I feel sad sometimes, 'cause I hear stories about what's gonna happen, like when it's judgement day . . .

(Yasmin)

Understanding the conservatism

One aspect of British Islam which might help explain the apparently conservative attitudes of the respondents is the essential traditionalism of most of the Muslim leadership and institutions in this country, which has been recorded previously in a number of studies.[6] It has been noted, for example, that a large majority of *imams* in Britain came to British mosques directly from the Indian subcontinent, with little knowledge of the English language or of British society in general. Also, methods of religious teaching in mosques and supplementary schools tend to be extremely traditional: the teachers are often authoritarian, frequently use corporal punishment, and generally encourage learning by rote and discourage questioning and debate. Furthermore, as Lewis (1994) stresses in particular, young British Muslims who have an interest in Islamic scholarship are likely to be put off by the fact that the amount of literature available in English is, to date, quite limited.

Such factors as these, however, cannot in themselves wholly account for why it is that among the young people I spoke to – who are, after all, in many ways happy to challenge the traditionalism of the older generation – there is such a reluctance to question the importance of any of the standard religious practices or the fundamental Islamic teachings on morality. (The views of the non-religious Khalida provide an exception to this general rule.) Perhaps it is useful here to consider the very nature of Islam itself: I would suggest that the conservatism of the young people to some extent reflects the key assumption of orthodox Islamic thought that the doctrines have been set out in the unchangeable and faultless form of the Qur'an; and that therefore any belief or practice can be challenged only insofar as it does not have a real basis in the original truths which were revealed to Muhammad.[7]

The emphasis upon continuity and permanence can be seen as a factor that has contributed to the relative impotence of reform movements throughout much of the history of Islam.[8] It can also be seen as a source of the religion's strength in the context of modern Britain. For in this society, where almost everything is open to question, it may seem all the more appealing or even essential to turn for meaning in life to a religion whose foundations have never pandered or succumbed to liberal attack. Little was explicitly said by the respondents on this undoubtedly complex subject, and it is hence difficult to determine to what extent the young people maintain the belief that the essence of Islam is an entirely fixed and perfect core of doctrines. However, it was emphasised by a few of the especially devout young people with whom I spoke that Islam is unchanging and that, therefore, any interpretation of the religion must look – or seek to return – to its *original* truths as these were revealed to Muhammad.

This view was expressed in various ways. For example, Rafiq spoke out against what he referred to as 'innovations': he commented, at one point in the interview, that a believer must only act as the Prophet acted, for 'if you're doing innovations you'll get nothing from it, because innovations will be rejected, and that's what the Prophet said'. Later on, Rafiq said of a religious group to which he belongs (one that is influenced by the teachings of the revivalist movement known as Wahhabism, which dates back to eighteenth-century Arabia):

> It's not a small sort of a sect – it has got major scholars from Saudi – you know, guiding it. So it's not sort of like guiding itself. And it is going according to the written text of what the Prophet did, what the Qur'an says. And it's not just interpreting it some ways.

This comment can be compared with what was said to me by a member of a rival group (namely, hizb-ut tahrir), with whom I had a brief discussion. He told me that Rafiq's group 'follows the Saudi way' and is 'unorthodox', whereas his own group is 'orthodox' and adheres to beliefs which 'go back to 1,300 years ago'.[9]

Some of the especially devout respondents stressed the difference between the Qur'an, which remains in its original form, and the scriptures of the Jews and the Christians, which do not. In the words of Amir: 'When you read [the Qur'an], you find that it don't knock the Bible, it don't knock the Torah, it just says that they've been tampered by man, and because they've been tampered they're not original.' Two young men selling Islamic literature told me that both Jews and Christians have 'messed up' their religions. The Christians, they said, have changed their religion so much that they are now able to 'follow any personal desires'. There are many different versions of the Bible, and even the Gospels do not give true accounts of Jesus' life. *Matthew* and *John*, they told me, are all right, but *Mark* and *Luke* are 'dodgy'.

Several of these devout respondents, in talking of how the message of Islam is perfect and unchanging, spoke about the relationship between religion and rational or scientific thought. It was stressed, in different ways, that Islam is not challenged or undermined by these supposedly 'modern' modes of reasoning; rather, an understanding of science or an attachment to rationalism can only reinforce one's appreciation of the religious truths. On the theme of science, I was told, variously, that scientists may one day find a reason for why one should not eat pork, just as they have found that drinking alcohol kills brain cells; that in the

Qur'an such things are described as the preservation of the bodies of the Pharaohs and the 'three stages of birth', which the Prophet could not have simply thought up for himself 1,400 years ago; that the Qur'an gives an account of the Big Bang and other 'scientific facts'; that 'if you ask someone who's studied the religion, he'd provide you with all the scientific explanations [for the religious teachings]'.

Ehsan, a highly articulate university student who was involved in a local Islamic group, spent a long time trying to convince me that if I would only think rationally I would come to see that Islam is the one true religion. Whereas Christianity, he said, is 'a matter of having faith . . . belief, dogma', Islam is 'not merely a dogmatic belief. It's a rational conviction. . . . You can arrive at conviction, rational conviction, through rational thought. A conviction, intellectual conviction.' A young teacher in a higher education college – who belongs to a Sufi group – complained to me that many of her Muslim students place too much emphasis on the importance of rational thinking, which she herself considers to be only one aspect of religion. To illustrate her point about the attitudes of young Muslims, she said that in her college she once came across Islamic Society posters claiming that there is 'proof that God exists'. When she asked a student what this was about, she was told she should come to the forthcoming Islamic Society meeting, where the 'proof' was to be shown on video.

Liberal responses?

Notwithstanding my account of the respondents' conservatism, I do not wish to give the impression that all the respondents opposed any kind of religious reform. I have already written of the eagerness of many of them to complain that Islam has been misinterpreted, most notably with respect to its teachings on women, by past generations of Muslims. Accusations of 'misinterpretation' might, indeed, be said to amount to a questioning of Islam itself. Certainly, the tendency among respondents to challenge traditional understandings of Islam has produced a range of views on the religion, including some that could be described as broadly liberal. This has been found also, as I have already noted, by other researchers who have looked at attitudes of young British Muslims. Among them, Lewis argues more strongly than most that 'aspects of belief and practice are now being contested *within* all the Islamic traditions' (1994: 187; original emphasis); and that the social control exercised by the traditional '*ulama*' is diminishing, as 'a British Muslim culture [is] developing with its own music, print and electronic media, and questioning ethos' [original emphasis] (1994: 202).

How might one explain the fact that numbers of my respondents appear to be evolving some quite liberal interpretations of Islamic teachings, despite what I would nevertheless regard as their general conservatism? Here, it is helpful to consider once again the possible repercussions of the common assumption that Islam originates in a set of fixed and explicitly defined core doctrines. This assumption of a 'fixed core', as I have already argued, seems on the one hand to encourage conservatism among British Muslims, and even extreme traditionalism among those who assert the superiority of Islam precisely on account of its unchanging nature.

On the other hand, this assumption can also promote some degree of flexibility, in that it provides scope for argument about the extent to which interpretations of Islam have, through the ages, distorted the true message that was revealed to Muhammad. Young Muslims who have some knowledge of Islamic scholarship can involve themselves in debates over the validity of certain of the *hadith*, the accuracy of translations of the Qur'an and *hadith* or the process by which the *shari'a* has been developed by the scholars of the past. And less scholarly young people (like the great majority of those to whom I spoke) can argue more generally about how the original truths contained in the Qur'an can best be understood and about the underlying meanings of Muhammad's actions and sayings.

Several of the female respondents used phrases like 'in the Qur'an' or 'it is written' when asserting that women's rights are protected by Islam, despite the contrary views or interpretations of many Muslims. Of all the young people I spoke to, Mumtaz, a youth worker, talked the most about the need for Muslim women to look directly at the Qur'an in order to develop an accurate understanding of their religion. But this is not easy to do, she said, because the Qur'an is in Arabic, and most translations may have been done in such a way that some of the true meanings are not properly conveyed.

According to Nielsen, the tendency for increasing numbers of young British Muslims to read the Qur'an and *hadith* for themselves, and to regard them as 'documents speaking directly to their own situation', does sometimes lead to a 'radical new formulation of Islamic ideals' (1987: 392). However, that there are no easy or self-evident openings for reform to be found through scrutiny of the texts is emphasised by Lewis in his discussion of some of the efforts being made by young Muslims in Britain to challenge the traditional thinking on women. Lewis argues:

> It is clear that apologetic is no substitute for research on the Qur'an, Sunna [Muhammad's example], the early history of Islam and the development of Islamic law. ... However uncongenial to the apologetic imagination, it might be less ahistorical to argue that 'patriarchal norms' are written into the Qur'an and Sunna, as traditionally understood, and that a huge task awaits those bold enough to challenge such venerable readings, enshrined in Islamic law.
>
> (1994: 195)

Radical Islam

While the young people with whom I spoke showed little or no interest in radical religious reform (despite the evidence of some tendencies or gestures towards a relative liberalism), many comments made in interviews and discussions suggested that there does exist a small but possibly growing minority of young Muslims in the local community who could be described as 'radicals' in the sense that they are

115

calling loudly for an increase in Islamic activities and single-minded religious commitment among their peers.[10] It is not possible to describe in specific terms the 'radical' perspective as it is manifest in the attitudes of young Muslims in Waltham Forest, for there is no particular movement or single set of characteristics that defines it. From what was said to me by the small number of respondents (including Rafiq and Majid among the core respondents) who could themselves be described as 'radicals', and by some others who spoke of having encountered extremism among people of their acquaintance, I received the impression that the radical fringe mostly comprises young men, who tend to operate within the frameworks of formal or informal religious groups.

The views of the 'radicals' on Islam seem to encompass a number of broad assumptions which, though not peculiar to these particular young people, are voiced by them with special fervour or emphasis. These assumptions, it should be noted, are related to issues that have been or are to be discussed elsewhere, and therefore I shall not consider them here in any depth. They include, most notably, the following beliefs and opinions: that Islam is not just a 'way of life' for individuals, but is a complete social system, and as such provides solutions to all the ills of human society; that 'the West' is not only unIslamic but has set itself up in opposition to Islam; that members of the older generation of Muslims in Britain are not committed to their faith and are unorthodox (this is a different kind of criticism from that which accuses the older generation of not taking into account the 'women's rights' and related dimensions of Islam); and that Muslims should engage in proselytising activities, in the confidence that the upsurge of interest in Islam that will follow will produce a better society. Also, as we have already seen, several extremely devout young people stressed to me their conviction that the teachings of Islam should and do remain unchanged through all time.

If it is indeed the case that the religious commitment of the young people to whom I talked is an expression of a 'quest for certainty', then perhaps it can only be expected that some of those young people will undertake this quest by means of recourse to an especially radical conception of Islam. The individuals who are the subjects of this study may, I have argued, be prone to feelings of uncertainty and general ambivalence over questions of identity, in the face of problems perceived to arise from racism, family conflict, life in the secular and immoral 'West', culture clash, or any combination of these and other factors. Where these individuals sense also that Islam enables them to resolve the dilemmas and contradictions they face, they may be inclined to seek to apply the solutions with extreme vigour. This is what F. Robinson would seem to suggest in arguing that

> Religious fundamentalism seems to flourish amongst those who are in a state of transition from one type of society to another, so, for instance, it is very much a phenomenon of urbanising societies in the Middle East and South Asia. We would expect it also to flourish amongst those who have and still make yet more transitions, from rural to urban areas, from South

Asia to Britain, and in their daily lives from Muslim home to Western school, factory and office.

(1988: 20)

Modood agrees with Robinson that the appeal of 'fundamentalism' is likely to grow among Britain's Muslims – even if as a political force it will continue to be no more than an 'ideological fringe' – and argues that this is due in part to their sense that since the publication of *The Satanic Verses* they have been abandoned by the Asian secular intelligentsia (1990: 156). Lewis is also concerned about the militancy of certain Islamic youth groups in Britain today, and comments that many of the pamphlets and books published by such organisations as hizb-ut tahrir – to which large numbers of Muslim students have easy access – are at worst 'either polemical diatribes against the West or simplistic appeals to return to the sources of the Qur'an and Sunna, which discount fifteen hundred years of history and disciplined reflection' (in press: 14). A.S. Ahmed draws attention to the oscillation between extremes which characterises attitudes of numbers of British-born Muslims and has 'produced, at one end of the spectrum, the young enthusiasts who supported the idea of an Islamic order in Britain and, at the other, the first Muslim strippers' (1992: 156).[11]

It is, however, important not to exaggerate the extent to which the younger members of the Pakistani community of Waltham Forest have taken up 'radical' religious beliefs. As I have already stated, only a small minority of the young people with whom I spoke (some of whom I actually met because of their involvement in religious activities) are, in any sense, 'radicals'. Furthermore, at least nine of the core respondents indicated that they feel uncomfortable with the strident and almost aggressive way in which some of their peers practise and speak about their faith. Tahir, for example, complained about the 'militant' members of a study circle which he had attended, who believe that 'we should start fighting this and we should start fighting that'. Faruq also spoke of the intolerance of some Muslims: 'Some people who are very religious,' he remarked, 'Muslims like that – some of them are awful, you know. Waving sticks everywhere and shouting "Kill Salman Rushdie!"'

Autonomy and Islam

At the end of Chapter 4, I suggested that many of the respondents appear to be quite independent-minded and self-assertive with respect to their ethnic and religious identities. This is, I argued, one consequence of the fact that they have been exposed, throughout their lives, to a wide variety of lifestyles and ways of thinking: circumstances which promote, as well as a certain amount of anxiety or uncertainty, the sense that one can make choices, consider options, determine one's own path of action. What I want to consider here is some of the ways in which this sense of personal autonomy is expressed with respect to religion.

In some ways the proposition that autonomy is expressed in their attachments to Islam may seem odd: after all, this is the religion into which they were born and brought up (as one respondent pointed out, even at the moment of a child's birth the *shahadah*, or profession of faith, is whispered in his or her ear). And as I state above, the teachings of Islam provide rules for behaviour and unambiguous 'truths' about reality, and thus might seem to militate against the development of a sense of autonomy. Indeed, the religion demands that the individual entirely submits to the will of God: we should remember that the Arabic word *islam* translates literally as 'surrender'. Respondents' apparent reluctance actively to question their religion indicates that they do, certainly, regard it as something which is given in a complete form rather than something to be worked out in accordance with their personal wishes and understandings.

Nevertheless it is my contention that the young people actually express a commitment to autonomy in making resolute efforts to become good Muslims, thereby consciously identifying and accepting the many limits on behaviour that that entails. The individual, in other words, is an *active self* in his or her attempts to undertake a 'quest for certainty'. The notion of this kind of active self is, clearly, very different from the notion of the postmodern self which thrives on change, ambiguity and confusion. My point here is, in fact, that many of the respondents are making the choice – the active choice – to emphasise continuity rather than change; certainty rather than ambiguity; order rather than confusion.

There are various ways in which, one can argue, the respondents' commitment to autonomy is manifest in their attitudes to Islam. Most generally, a majority of the core respondents – whether talking in an abstract way, or referring to their own or others' experiences – indicated that they believe a good Muslim must be prepared to make a self-conscious, well-thought-out and personal commitment to the religion. This approach to Islam demonstrates what Schiffauer, writing about (mostly first generation) Turkish Muslims in Germany, refers to as the 'individualization of religious practice' or, citing Nagel, the 'islamicization of the self'. In the immigrant or minority situation, Schiffauer argues, ritual practice 'no longer expresses . . . affiliation with the society as a whole'; and those who do practise are thus more likely than those living in an Islamic society to be following 'purely religious motivation' (1988: 151–2). As Metcalf notes, a special kind of religious self-consciousness is associated with Islamic practice in Western countries; a self-consciousness at the heart of which is a 'sense of contrast – contrast with a past or contrast with the rest of society' (1996: 7).

In the three interview extracts that follow, respondents quite distinctly place a special emphasis on the need for the individual, *as an individual*, to make active decisions with respect to religious belief and practice. These extracts also illustrate the tendency to focus on behavioural aspects of Islam.

> I was getting older, and there's so many bad things I could've done, which I didn't do, so I thought it's time to learn – get on the straight path, and then get into religion. . . . Before, I always wanted to do it, but my time wasn't there to do it.
>
> (Majid)

Since the day [my mother] came back from Mecca, since the day she came back, she's been practising. Non-stop. Every day. Which is excellent. It's amazing, because she never did. . . . Which goes to show, when you feel it, then you just do it straight away.

(Bushra)

They always say Islam says, you should do this and you shouldn't do this, but I think you shouldn't just put a pressure on somebody. OK, you should tell them what is right and wrong, but they should do it, if they want to, from their heart. . . . If you want to be a Muslim it's not that hard, but that's just if you wanna be it from your heart.

(Rasheeda)

The strongest views on the subject of personal responsibility were voiced by the very devout Ehsan who, as I have already reported, stressed that one should accept the teachings of Islam on the basis of 'rational conviction' rather than 'faith' or 'dogma'. He vehemently criticised the many Muslims, young and old, who 'claim to be Muslims merely because their parents were Muslims, merely because it's the environment they grew up in'. Moreover, Ehsan insisted that this study of mine is seriously flawed; for, as he understood it (and as is indeed inevitably the case, given its sociological framework), I was seeking to provide social explanations for belief. I should acknowledge, he said, that social factors do not – or should not – play a part in bringing people to Islam: 'You want to say that the environment, where I live, my family situation, and so on, is influencing my [Islamic] identity. But no. It's not.'

The importance of wearing a scarf, or *hijab*, was an issue talked about by several female respondents in a way that demonstrated their belief in the necessity for profound and personal commitment to religious practice. Rubina was wearing the full *hijab* when I met her, and told me this is something which is important to her and also very demanding. She complained that since she began to cover her head, she has noticed that people react 'coldly' on meeting her for the first time:

And then they're surprised when they hear my accent – I mean, 'cause I come out with a cockney accent! . . . That bit does weaken me, 'cause I haven't got a lot of will-power. If your will-power's strong, then it wouldn't bother you. But it does bother me quite a bit. You want to be liked – you know, you've got to live in this society.

Among the core respondents, one – Zareena – was already wearing the *hijab* at the time of the interview and six said that they genuinely intend to start doing so once they have acquired the necessary inner strength. For example:

You have to wear your scarf with pride. You mustn't feel intimidated. . . . It could take years – I mean, covering your beauty is difficult. I mean, you

have lovely hair yourself – imagine covering that up. Not letting men see
and admire. It's difficult.

(Bushra)

That's how you should dress – that's what Islam says, you should follow it.
It's for your own benefit anyway – not to restrict you. . . . Yeah, I think I
will [wear a scarf]. But if you'd asked me a few years ago, I'd say *no way* –
get outa my face! . . .

(Nazia)

A number of respondents expressed a keen interest in learning about their religion, thereby providing a further illustration of their tendency to assume that the responsibility for religious faith and understanding lies with the individual. Within the young British Muslim population as a whole there appears to be an increasing regard for religious learning, according to several other studies in the field; indeed, this might be said to be necessarily concomitant with the growing willingness of the young people to challenge certain traditional interpretations of Islam.[12]

The extent of the concern with learning among my respondents is indicated by the fact that, as I have stated above, more than half of them said that they at least occasionally attend religious talks or read books about Islam. Almost half of the core respondents spoke in strong terms about the importance of religious study; and many mentioned that they are particularly interested in reading the Qur'an in translation in order to acquire a better understanding of the bases of the Islamic teachings. A few of the young people also talked of their having a crucial role to play in teaching their own children or younger siblings about Islam. Three of the comments made on the subject of religious learning are quoted below:

I'd like to read a lot, if nothing else just to have a knowledge of Islam, so I
can argue in its favour, or against it if need be – which I doubt very much.
When you get together with friends and you talk about something – you
can't give an Islamic viewpoint if you haven't got enough knowledge.

(Naveed)

There's this computer program, by a couple of very highly-rated religious scholars, and I wanna get that on computer. . . . It gives you the
whole of the Qur'an, the translation, the meanings and that, and the
hadith, the actions, and what our Prophet said and done . . .

(Adnan)

I've got the English translation of the Qur'an. I try to read so I can understand. Sometimes you get told, oh you don't do this – but then, why? If
you know the reason why you shouldn't do these things – that helps.
'Cause if you understand *why* you don't wanna do it, it's better than you

120

just be *told* you don't wanna do it – it gives you that bit more scope of not wanting to do it . . .

(Sara)

Assertive identities

In this chapter as a whole, my aim has been to understand what I have deemed to be the significant role played by religion in the lives of my young British Pakistani respondents. It is, however, important to recognise that for some of the young people to whom I talked, and doubtless for a great many of their peers, the direct impact of Islamic teachings upon values and day-to-day behaviour is limited. As is clear from the earlier 'overview of respondents' religiosity', not all of them indicated very high levels of religious practice; and it was frequently acknowledged by my respondents and other contacts in Waltham Forest that there are significant numbers of local Muslims who neglect their religion.

On the basis of my own empirical findings and those of related studies, I have reached the conclusion that there are many young British Muslim males who have little interest in engaging in arduous religious practice, but who are nevertheless keen to proclaim, loudly and with pride, that they are Muslims. Because the self-definition of 'Muslim' has connotations of faith and even fervour, it seems that these young people perceive this to be an identity that is assertive and also, perhaps, more meaningful than one based on ethnicity alone. I do not wish to suggest that these individuals comprise a clear-cut category of Muslims or British Pakistanis. Rather, I am considering here a set of very general attitudes to religion – finding expression, in sum, in what I have termed the 'assertive Muslim identity'.

That the 'assertive Muslim identity' is a male phenomenon is probably due to the fact that men are able to take advantage of the relative laxity of parents to be largely irreligious in behaviour but Muslim in name. Young women, in contrast, rarely have the opportunity to rebel against the norms of the community and yet continue to be accepted as members of it. In fact, young women may, in a sense, become the targets of the assertive Muslim identity of their male peers, who find that a convenient way of emphasising their own 'Muslim' credentials is to insist upon the virtuous conduct of their wives, sisters and daughters.

I have already suggested that for a number of the young people with whom I spoke, and especially the women, Islamic teachings are thought to provide a means of resolving the contradictions which arise between the demands of family and the demands of wider society; and I have also suggested that some young people are inclined to seek a 'radical' religious response to the conflicts and ambivalence which may be part-and-parcel of lives spent within a Pakistani community in London. Those youngsters who have adopted the 'assertive Muslim identity' seem also to be drawing on their religion as a means of coping with culture clash and the problems of minority group membership. As far as they are concerned, however, the contents of the religious teachings are less important than the expressions and symbols of belonging to the minority community (even if the teachings, in

121

themselves, are by no means disbelieved or considered irrelevant). This form of identity is perhaps manifest to the ultimate extent in the music of the popular Asian rap group 'Fun-da-mental', a band whose name in itself conflates Islamic and aggressive idioms, and which has claimed 'to use music to articulate Islamic sentiments in general, and to defend the fatwa [against Salman Rushdie] in particular' (Lewis 1994: 181).[13]

Those young men who maintain the 'assertive Muslim identity' may be responding, above all else, to racism and to what they feel to be the widespread and often public denigration of their culture and religion within British society. By affirming their identity as Muslims they are thus engaging in what Leveau describes, in relation to French Muslims, as 'a form of "politics from below"'. Leveau argues that 'social actors who are deprived of other legitimate means of asserting their collective presence, have recourse to the means of expression that are closest to them at their cultural level' (1988: 107). Perhaps, most importantly, 'religious' protest permits an articulation of pride and honour as it entails not simply the rejection of the mainstream British way of life but also the affirmation of a viable and even potentially glorious alternative. This dual aspect of religious protest is discussed by Werbner, writing of the support for Saddam Hussein that a great many British Pakistanis voiced during the Gulf War:

> Theirs is a confrontational posture, as yet not fully worked out, more protest than actual action. The swings between temporary utopian hopes for Islamic dominance, and a sense of communal failure and total power-lessness, are more evident in British Muslims' attitudes than any determination to engage in sustained practical political action.
>
> (1994: 115)

The 'assertive Muslim identity' has been most evident in Britain in the wake of the Rushdie Affair: this was an issue of 'religious honour' which produced demonstrations and book-burnings that according to Modood were, above all, outbursts of 'spontaneous working-class anger and hurt pride' (1990: 145). One interesting aspect of the Rushdie Affair is that it provoked profound anger among large numbers of young men who, at least until that time, had not appeared to be especially interested in their religion. Samad points out that among Mirpuris in Bradford Rushdie's novel was seen as a 'gratuitous insult' and a cause of humiliation (1992: 516). He notes that although some moves towards radical Islam did occur among a minority of the Bradford Muslims, the majority did not exhibit an increased degree of religiosity, at least in the early days of the Rushdie Affair. Meanwhile, as race relations in the city deteriorated, increasing numbers of young people were drawing on Islam for 'metaphors [with which] to express their discontent against society which refused to accept them on an equal footing' (1992: 516).

Sahgal, like Samad, also writes of what I would describe as the 'assertive Muslim identity' in her discussion of the activities of young men who campaigned against *The Satanic Verses*. She argues that in the protests of the young Muslim men – and also in attitudes of militant Sikhs – one finds

> a crude anti-imperialism . . . combined with a specifically religious and ethnicized form of black identity. And when there is no white fascist enemy in sight – indeed, often when there is – young men, particularly in groups, appoint themselves the moral police of the women in their ambit.
>
> (1992: 180)

The phenomenon of the 'assertive Muslim identity' encompasses a wide spectrum of values and modes of behaviour. Certain aspects of it can be illuminated with reference to the comments made by four of my respondents – namely Yusuf, Waqar, Zaheer and Mustafa. These are four young men who indicated quite low levels of religious practice with regard to prayer, mosque attendance and reading the Qur'an. Furthermore, all four made it clear that they are not inclined to lead a lifestyle consistent with the stringent demands of Islamic teachings; for example, they told me that they regularly go to night-clubs and date girls. 'I've done a lot of bad things', Yusuf said to me. to emphasise the point. Three of these respondents (that is, all but Zaheer) told me without prevarication that they do not consider themselves to be religious. However, despite the fact that in their day-to-day behaviour there is much that suggests a lack of commitment to Islam, all four of the young men did talk of their religion in terms which imply that in many ways it is important to them; or, perhaps more crucially, that they value very highly the fact of being, in their own eyes, Muslims.

The comments made by these young men in relation to religious prescriptions on food, alcohol and fasting illustrate quite clearly their eagerness to express, through certain forms of behaviour, their identification with the Muslim community. All of them said that they fast for Ramadan, that they do not drink alcohol (although Waqar told me he used to drink when he was a little younger) and that they generally eat *halal* meat. Yusuf admitted that at times he does eat non-*halal* hamburgers, but added, 'I won't eat pork and that – bacon and that, I wouldn't eat that. That's well out of order. That's well wrong that is, to eat that.'

In talking in more general terms about the subject of religion, the four young men expressed in a wide variety of ways their underlying attachment to Islam and to their Muslim identity. Zaheer spoke the most about the part that religion plays in his life; he stressed, for example, that he finds that it disciplines him. Yusuf made it very clear that he takes it for granted that religion provides a fundamental sense of self: he said that he must teach his children about Islam because 'that is what our blood is'. He told me, also, that although he is not very interested in current affairs, he does follow stories in the news which involve Muslims; he mentioned, as an example, his concern about the war in Bosnia. Waqar commented, almost in passing, that 'you'll always believe in your religion'. He said that he had been to Mecca on *'umra* (the 'lesser pilgrimage'), which was 'a brilliant experience. . . . The atmosphere. You know, so many Muslims coming to this country. Just being there – it felt good.' He added that he wishes to learn the Qur'an by heart, since 'It's interesting, you know. If you learn the Qur'an by heart, and the meaning, you'll know more about life – what it has to offer.'

The four individuals in question can be said to display the 'assertive Muslim identity' not simply on the grounds that they expressed some attachment to Islam while acknowledging that their behaviour is largely irreligious. It is my contention that a vital aspect of the 'assertive identity' is its blending of religious awareness with rebelliousness, toughness or a degree of aggression. The four young men all gave the impression, throughout their interviews, of being somewhat hardened and street-wise. They also, most significantly, made a number of comments which suggest that they believe these personal characteristics easily go hand-in-hand with – or are even manifest in – sincere attachment to Islam. As might be expected, this perspective on religion is especially apparent in some of what was said about Salman Rushdie. 'I'm surprised he's still alive, really', Mustafa told me, when asked about the writer. He went on, 'I personally think he will die in a bad way – it's quite wrong what he done, you see . . . I think he should die, innit.' Just – someone kill him before he does something else stupid.' And Yusuf commented,

> Like he's Asian himself – saying them kind of things, man, and he hasn't got *no proof at all* that them things have ever happened like that – that's all wrong. That's stupidness. . . . If I had a chance – if I could get Salman Rushdie I would get Salman Rushdie.

Yusuf spoke again with a hint of bravado when he said, on the subject of abstinence from alcohol, 'That's stupid – drinking. It doesn't prove yourself a man if you drink, you understand?' Zaheer – who had also told me that he sometimes finds himself crying when he prays – left me with what was a particularly vivid impression of rebellious religiosity. He talked of having found himself, throughout his youth, in many dangerous and difficult situations, and said that he has been in prison more than once. He remarked that, during Ramadan, 'I used to fast in prison as well. And that's a hard thing to do, 'cause you don't get a lot of food in there anyway.'

In outlining the phenomenon of the 'assertive Muslim identity' I have drawn not only on the comments of those young people who themselves might be said to exhibit it, but also on remarks made by some others who spoke about young men of their acquaintance who proudly and publicly declare their allegiance to Islam, without leading, in any sense, the lives of devout Muslims. A youth leader, Karim, told me for example that many of the young Muslim men in his Asian youth group are rebellious, have been in various kinds of trouble and do not engage in much religious practice; and yet they consider their religion to be a significant aspect of their lives. When they feel that they are not accepted as British, Karim said, they will often turn to religion – and also, to a lesser extent, to 'culture' – for identity. Anjali, a student counsellor, told me that the female students she meets do not talk much about their religion, although neither do they say anything to suggest that they reject it. The male students, on the other hand, talk about Islam a great deal: 'I'm a Muslim and proud of it!' they say, and, 'We Muslims believe this!' and, 'This is part of our religion!'

Mariam spoke in the strongest terms about what I have called the 'assertive Muslim identity' of many of her male peers. She told me:

> A lot of people – this goes for guys more than girls – they'll go to the mosque on Friday and pray . . . and they'll come back and they'll just be fooling around. And I don't mean just little things – I'm talking bank jobs here and girlfriends and drugs and the works, really. And they're like gangsters and stuff. And it's weird . . . if you turn around and somebody says something to them, that is offensive to their religion or something, they'll go Allah this and Allah that, and come down like they're some pious, good man. . . . And this isn't a minority – it's about 60 per cent. Quite large. It's quite scary, actually.

double lives?

In the following extract, Faruq makes reference in a different way to what is effectively the same phenomenon. It is interesting to note, also, that in talking here about the reactions of young Muslims to the publication of *The Satanic Verses*, he acutely points to the circular relationship between reality and representation:

> The media put out these images – I mean the images of Muslims in most people's minds are fanatics, terrorists, Palestinians, bombers – things like that. That's the view that springs to mind. People are angry. But a lot of the kids, they like this image – it makes them feel powerful – come on, let's go round and kill [Rushdie]. There was rioting in London, wasn't there! Our lot started it – the Walthamstow lot – some of our boys!

reaction to stereo-type

7

RELIGIOUS BOUNDARIES

Religion and boundaries

My aim here is to show how mechanisms of boundary maintenance have acted to preserve Islam as a vital source of social identity among my respondents. In writing of boundaries, I am applying to my analysis of specifically religious phenomena a concept that is most commonly used in discussions of ethnicity. It should therefore be useful, at this stage, to consider some of the theoretical implications of this development of the notion of *religious* boundaries.

In Chapter 6, I have suggested that Islam survives as a source of meaning in the respondents' lives partly because the content of its messages is accessible and appealing to the young people. Most of the young men and women believe that they are able, or are potentially able, to shape their day-to-day behaviour in accordance with the teachings of their religion – and that the results of their doing so are, or would be, enormously beneficial. The persistence of religious identity among the respondents cannot, however, be explained solely by reference to this general perspective on Islam which the respondents maintain. Notwithstanding the apparent attractiveness of an Islamic way of life, a sociologist may be inclined to ask why it is that the respondents' attachment to their religion is not progressively weakened or diluted as a result of the fact that they are living in a non-Muslim society.

Writing of the changing place of religion within the West, Berger argues that there has been 'a severe rupture of the traditional task of religion, which was precisely the establishment of an integrated set of definitions of reality that could serve as a common universe of meaning for the members of a society'. The result is that we have, today, arrived at the situation where 'the potency of religion is . . . restricted to the construction of subworlds, of fragmented universes of meaning' (1969: 133). Of course, the 'rupture' to which Berger makes reference has occurred, dramatically, within the space of one generation in the case of the Pakistani community of Britain.

Berger goes on to develop the concept of the 'plausibility structure', by which term he refers to the social base which maintains the 'reality' of a religious worldview for its adherents. This social base comprises, in the words of Abercrombie,

126

'the set of significant others – supported by a chorus of less significant others – who, in their daily interactions, are chiefly responsible for repetitively confirming the individual's identity' (1986: 24). In secular society, religions may have to rely on extremely tenuous plausibility structures: in some cases, for example, families may act almost in isolation to protect and preserve their religious beliefs. By contrast, Luckmann writes, for most people in most past eras 'the entire social structure supported the sacred cosmos and the sacred cosmos legitimated the entire social structure' (1983: 129).

It is my contention that we can understand how the religious identities of my respondents survive and even thrive within what is at best an indifferent social environment if we look at the ways in which the plausibility structure upon which these identities rest is reinforced by boundary mechanisms. The boundaries which define the distinctiveness of Muslims guarantee that there exists a certain social distance between the minority religious group and the majority; and also that some sense of solidarity exists within the Muslim community (whether this 'community' is perceived to be a local or nation-wide grouping, or even the entire Muslim *umma* which transcends both history and nations). Thus individual Muslims are likely to be somewhat insulated from external pressures which might otherwise bring about the gradual erosion or even, ultimately, the abandonment of their traditional beliefs and practices.

In order to understand why the religious boundaries should act so successfully to protect and enhance the respondents' attachment to Islam, it is necessary to consider the actual processes of boundary construction and maintenance. Like the ethnic boundaries which, according to my earlier discussion, are upheld by the young people, religious boundaries comprise those aspects of the respondents' lives which ensure that the individuals are identified both by themselves and others as members of the minority (in this case, the minority religious) group. Religious boundaries *differ* from ethnic boundaries in that whereas the latter appear to be becoming increasingly permeable and subject to redefinition, religious boundaries are, by comparison, clear-cut and pervasive.

The religious boundaries owe their clarity and pervasiveness to the very nature of Islam; more particularly, to the emphasis that, according to most interpretations of the religion and certainly those of my respondents, its teachings place upon rightful action. This emphasis upon action means that to be a devout Muslim, one must behave in certain explicitly defined ways. Therefore a Muslim is obliged to express his belonging to the Muslim community, and detachment from non-Muslim society, in an especially concrete and unequivocal manner. Furthermore, Islamic prescriptions for action do not relate to one, specifically 'religious' sphere of life. Rather, they involve all aspects of social existence: even the mundane activities that fill a day can and should be permeated with religious meanings. Thus the social differences that distinguish observant Muslims from non-Muslims tend to be demonstrated in normal interaction and on an ongoing basis, rather than merely from time to time.[1]

It is useful to consider three levels of religiously oriented action that influence day-to-day interaction between Muslims and non-Muslims, although these are not hard-and-fast, mutually exclusive categories. First, at the level of formal practice, the stringent demands made upon Muslims – most particularly regarding the five daily prayers and fasting – ensure that non-Muslims are made aware of the activities of devout Muslims with whom they have social contact. Second, at the level of routine behaviour, such matters as Islam's dietary laws and prohibition of alcohol are likely to have an effect upon patterns of interaction between Muslims and non-Muslims. Third, at the level of general social conduct, the religious-based morality to which devout Muslims must adhere proscribes many forms of social behaviour that are regarded as fully acceptable within most segments of a predominantly secular, Western society.

At no point in this book have I asserted that my respondents, along with their peers, lead lives that in all ways accord with the demands of their religion. Nor am I claiming that a majority, or even a substantial minority, of the respondents are constantly engaged in the process of defining themselves, unambiguously and publicly, as Muslims. What I do wish to argue is that many actions of these young people contribute to the collective construction and maintenance of the religious boundaries which encompass the Muslim population of Britain.

I would also suggest that part of the strength of Islam in Britain lies in the fact that those individuals who do not practise their religion to a great extent have available to them, as a paradigm or ideal towards which they can strive, a conception of life within embracing and clear-cut religious boundaries. Thus, even the less religious young Muslims who do not preserve a real social distance from their non-Muslim peers are likely to maintain, at the very least, some kind of 'psychological distance', as long as they are aware of the numerous demands that are made of them but not of outsiders. This 'psychological distance' can assume an almost tangible form where the young Muslims undertake certain, rather minimal, gestures – such as occasional mosque attendance or abstinence from alcohol – which indicate their underlying commitment to the minority community.[2]

This contemporary construction of boundaries is consonant with the entire history of Islam. Although the teachings of Islam present universal truths for the whole of humanity, the religion has evolved in and through its opposition to alternative versions of reality. Muslims have thus always defined themselves in terms of what they are not as well as what they are. Armstrong argues that there are for this reason clear parallels between ethnic boundary processes and the modes of Muslim identification which emerged in the early centuries of Islamic history. He writes: 'Christendom was bound to be the main contrasting environment by which Moslems defined the limits of their own civilization, just as ethnic groups define themselves by contrast to neighbors' (1982: 57). F. Robinson (1979: 85–6) also discusses how the notion of community, which is so central to Islamic thought, rests in large part upon the eagerness shown by Muslims, from the earliest days of their religion, to assert their distinctiveness from and indeed superiority to non-Muslim groups. Robinson writes that the Muslims first established themselves as a separate community when they fled to Medina in 622; here, Muhammad told them, 'You are the best nation raised up for men'.

In this discussion of boundaries, reference should be made to the comments in Chapter 6 about the tendency for a commitment to autonomy among the respondents to be manifest in their expressions of religious identity. To say that many of my respondents and their peers are taking upon themselves the responsibility of working out what it means to be a Muslim, is to say also that they believe that they must actively and with clear intentions draw the boundaries within which they are required to live as Muslims. Although they are not in this way *creating* their own self-definitions as Muslims – or, as the postmodernists might suggest, constructing new, diverse and fluid conceptualisations of what it is to be Muslim – the boundaries require energy, not passivity, if they are to be sustained in a meaningful form in Britain. In a sense ethnic boundaries can, in contrast, be maintained in a passive manner, to the extent that the exclusion of ethnic minorities from notions of Britishness acts to sustain minority identity.

The construction of boundaries

To elaborate the arguments outlined above, I shall now consider the extent to which my empirical findings indicate that the respondents indeed engage in patterns of behaviour and social interaction which enhance their social distinctiveness as Muslims.

Formal practice

From the data presented in Chapter 6, we can see that a large majority of the respondents engage in some form of regular religious practice; almost all of them, for example, tend to fast during Ramadan, and most of the men attend a local mosque for Friday prayers. Although they said little about whether or not they feel that their involvement in these activities has an impact upon their wider social relations, it seems clear that such forms of religious practice inevitably entail some kind of public statement of difference from non-Muslim peers. Furthermore, among the less observant respondents *feelings* of difference from the majority are likely to be enhanced if they accept – as most seem to – that regular and formal practice should be, and ideally will become, a significant element of their own daily lives.

The extent to which ritual practice can, where an individual is especially devout, directly impinge upon relationships with non-Muslims was demonstrated by Amir, who talked at some length about his decision to leave a job as a shop manager for the position of bus driver, because the latter occupation would allow him more time for saying his five daily prayers. He told me,

> When I was a manager, say if I stopped to do one of my *salats* [prayers], and if for any reason the area supervisor come in, they could be very

upset that I would be basically praying. . . . It's a case where I could choose out of earning the money or worshipping Allah – God. And I had an opportunity to join the buses . . . and things started to work out. In my breaks, I pray – like for instance in my lunch break, or if I drive from Tottenham, which is where the garage is based, to Victoria, I'd pray on the bus at Victoria – only takes five, ten minutes . . .

In writing of formal religious practice as an aspect of boundary construction I am not simply referring to a process which is an aggregate of individual acts, but rather, given the emphasis within Islam upon communal worship, to something that is intrinsically collective in nature. A striking illustration of this occurs in certain areas of Waltham Forest on Friday afternoons: at this time every week, large numbers of the local shops close down, and crowds of Asian men and boys of all ages, many dressed in *shalwar kameez* but more in casual dress, make their way by foot and by car to the local mosques for Friday prayers. Any non-Muslim passing by one of the mosques is thereby made acutely conscious of the existence of an apparently thriving, tightly-bound minority religious community. In the Western world the mosques themselves, of course, 'now announce a Muslim presence' (Metcalf 1996: 16).

Eid is also a time when Muslims in Waltham Forest quite publicly celebrate their belonging to a community. Within what is generally a relaxed, holiday atmosphere, families dress up for the day and spend time calling on each others' houses. Some attempts are made by borough institutions to make Eid celebrations inclusive rather than exclusive or potentially divisive social affairs: all schoolchildren, for example, have holidays on the two Eid days each year; and the posters which advertise Eid *melas* held in the local showground typically assert, 'The Eid Festival Committee welcomes all communities to the Eid Festival'. Such efforts at inclusion can hardly mask the ethnic and religious differences that occasions like Eid, or indeed the month of Ramadan, bring to light; but it should not be assumed that hostility or unease on the part of the majority or other minority populations is inevitably promoted by collective processes of boundary-drawing.

'Are you fasting? And are you feeling all right? You must be careful, you know', I heard a neighbour of mine – a middle-aged, working-class, white woman – say solicitously to the young daughter of a Pakistani neighbour during Ramadan. And a few days before Eid I overheard a white shopkeeper remark to a customer who was buying a suitcase from her, 'Oh, you're going to Pakistan? Oh yeah, it's coming up to your Christmas, isn't it?'

Routine behaviour and boundaries

As a religion which provides prescriptions for action encompassing all aspects of daily life, Islam ensures that the boundaries defining Muslim identity emerge in routine, mundane behaviour as well as through explicitly 'religious' activities. Here there are parallels with Judaism, in that 'the thrust of Jewish sacramentalism is to diminish the sacred–secular dichotomy by investing all routines of life with sacred significance' (Sklare and Greenblum 1967: 46). A devout Muslim who seeks to follow to a full extent the *sunna* will shape almost every aspect of his day-to-day life in accordance with the example set by Muhammad: he will, for example, eat with his hands and primarily his right hand, sit on the floor while eating, leave and enter a house with his right foot first, say a prayer or *du'a* on leaving and entering a house, and sleep on his right side and on the floor.

Such small details of behaviour were rarely if ever referred to in my research interviews. However, the respondents did make it clear that they regard as highly important the fundamental religious prescriptions on food and drink; that is, the prohibition of alcohol and of pork, and the insistence upon ritual slaughter of animals. These teachings (which have some common ground with Jewish dietary laws with respect to ritual slaughter and the prohibition of pork) provide a clear example of how routine behaviour can be permeated with religious meanings. As Sklare and Greenblum write in relation to Jewish laws: 'They invest the act of eating with sacred significance, and they provide every believer with recurring opportunities to show his obedience to God's will' (1967: 46).

Douglas, among others, has discussed the extent to which religious laws relating to food, such as the Jewish prohibition of pork and, formerly, Friday abstinence among Catholics, can promote the social distinctiveness of religious communities. While some religious practices such as Sabbath observance and circumcision are essentially private affairs, dietary laws inevitably entail a 'refusal of commensality' and thus a meaningful 'rejection of social intercourse'; these teachings therefore tend to 'gain significance as symbols of allegiance simply by their lack of meaning for other cultures' (1970: 40).

As I made clear in Chapter 6, it seems that the large majority of the core respondents follow the injunctions of their religion relating to meat and alcohol. Thus, with respect to what they eat and drink, both the more and the less obser-vant respondents are engaged in a collective process of boundary construction and maintenance. As far as the especially devout respondents are concerned, this is only one of many ways in which they maintain a real sense of difference and distance from non-Muslims and strong feelings of solidarity with the minority. For the less devout young people, adherence to Islamic dietary laws may be a symbolic gesture of belonging to the group that does not (at least at this stage in their lives) translate into a willingness to create a significant social distance between them-selves and their non-Muslim peers.

Many of the male respondents spoke at some length or in strong terms about their abstinence from alcohol, thereby indicating that this is an especially mean-ingful (if, in many cases, essentially symbolic) statement of identification with the Muslim community. Some talked of how drinking is a central aspect of the social lives of most young Britons, and of their own consequent isolation as Muslims. For example, Shahid commented,

When I'm with my English friends at university, the primary conversation used to always revolve around how drunk they were the night before! And you just sat there – oh, right, OK, yeah. And then they'd talk about something else – but it'll always come back to drink . . .

Several of the male respondents, in speaking about the differences in socialising patterns between themselves and their non-Muslim friends, made it clear that as a group the Muslims (or, sometimes, 'Asians' or 'Pakistanis') with whom they mix tend not to drink. For example, Zaheer told me that his Pakistani friends 'might drink when they're on their own, or they're with other friends, but when they're with Muslim friends they wouldn't drink, because they know that we'd look down on them'. Adnan told me that he used to visit a pub owned by a Sikh friend of his, but that when he went there 'the Pakistanis didn't drink – only the Sikhs and the Hindus out of us lot drank. There was a pool table there – we just messed around with the pool.' And Naveed told me,

What Asian people regard as going out – maybe we'd go bowling – English people'd regard as boring, because they'd rather go for a drink, which slightly clashes with culture, because we can't – well, there's no Asians who'd go for a drink with anyone, so maybe we'd tag along to the pub and play pool, but it's not a very comfortable situation in which they're all drinking, and we're just playing pool.

That the Islamic laws relating to *halal* meat are, like the prohibition of alcohol, a constant and concrete reminder of one's membership of the religious minority was evident from the ways in which many respondents of differing levels of religiosity spoke about food. Four women, for example, who talked of having eaten non-*halal* meat in the past indicated that they regard this as a serious error; several respondents of both sexes mentioned that they try to avoid eating anything that contains animal fat; and some of the young people indicated that they are somewhat constrained when they eat out with friends. These kinds of issues are raised in the following extracts:

If a food's got animal fat in it, I think – I can't throw it away. When I'm in a good mood I'll throw it away. If I'm hungry I'll eat it. Sometimes you just make a mistake and you've bought it – you have to eat it then.

(Ilyas)

When people go out eating, I can't go with them and get a burger. But I have done. My mum knows about it. My brother still does it. Now I would stop myself, 'cause I know I can't eat it.

(Amina)

A couple of weeks ago, I didn't know Opal Fruits have gelatine, and I was eating it and my friend goes that's got gelatine in it, and I ate the whole packet, and I was thinking shit – I've carried on eating it!

(Asya)

I used to love McDonald's Fillet, and somebody said no no, they fry the fish in animal fat. . . . Now I've stopped – I don't even think about it, because I know that pizzas are OK! Pizza Hut's OK!

(Zareena)

General social conduct

A broader issue than that of the potential repercussions for social relations of Islamic teachings on formal practice and routine behaviour is the question of whether, in the general conduct of their social lives, many of the respondents adhere sufficiently closely to an Islamically defined morality to give rise to a sense of distance between themselves and their non-Muslim peers. In seeking answers to this question, one could consider a wide range of behaviours in which my respondents do or do not engage. Two activities which seem especially relevant to this discussion – given the demands of Islam, the social pressures exerted on all young people in Britain today and the ages of my respondents – are dating members of the opposite sex and going to night-clubs.

Not surprisingly, fewer respondents are evidently prepared to shape their entire social lives in accordance with Islamic principles than are willing to adhere to the basic religious prescriptions concerning food and drink. Nevertheless, a majority of the respondents did say that they avoid such blatantly unIslamic forms of behaviour as dancing and forming relationships with members of the opposite sex: among the core respondents nine of the fifteen young men told me that they generally do not go out on dates or that they did not date prior to marriage; and seven that they do not go to night-clubs. Among the women, a higher proportion apparently tend not to engage in these activities: fourteen of the eighteen said they do not go to clubs, and thirteen that they do not date, or did not prior to marriage.

These findings suggest that one element of religious boundary maintenance, at least among the more devout respondents, is an avoidance of social activities that they consider to be 'typical' among the majority of young Britons. However, the fact that many of the respondents do not date and do not go to clubs cannot be explained purely in terms of religious constraints. It is obvious, from much of what was said to me by the young people about their socialising patterns, that the motivations underlying their behaviour in this regard are extremely varied and often mixed. Some of the respondents who talked of having quite narrowly circumscribed social lives explained this explicitly by reference to moral or religious concerns; others said, more simply, that they do what their friends do, or referred to personal preferences and notions about what they see as typical behaviour for

'Asians'; many of the young women in particular also mentioned parental and community restrictions. It is interesting to note also that some of the respondents who admitted that they engage in unIslamic social activities indicated a certain ambivalence or hesitation with regard to these habits.

The only conclusion it seems possible to reach from such diverse data is that a substantial number of respondents socialise in such a way as to contribute, but with widely varying levels of commitment and explicitness, to the establishment of religious boundaries. Below I quote a range of comments made by respondents on the subjects of dating and night-clubs which provide evidence of this very general process:

> No I don't go to clubs – I'm not really that sort of dancing type. . . . When they all go to the raves and that – that's not really for me, 'cause I sort of – yuk – shameful though, isn't it. I feel embarrassed.
>
> (Rafiq)

> Sometimes I go to clubs. But it's not that much accepted – in our religion. Music – people dancing and things. Music should really be kept to a minimum, but – [*laughs*]
>
> (Ilyas)

> My mother says, until we've all become successful we shouldn't interact emotionally with a girl. Which is understandable, I suppose. I can see her point of view – it distracts a person from his studies. . . . And I've personally upheld this, and I haven't ever got involved with a girl – I make sure that I don't.
>
> (Naveed)

> I don't believe in dating and that sort of thing. So whenever I meet [boys], it's not rude – I mean it's pleasant enough, but there is this barrier that you're not going to get too familiar. And I think that works out best. Because that's the way I've been brought up, and that's what I understand and know, and agree with.
>
> (Zareena)

> The thing is, with me, in my religion – they don't believe in [dating], so it's something I couldn't do really. . . . No [I don't date], because if I do it will just be a big thing – like if an Asian girl does, they'll probably get her married off or something, or they'll just send her back home.
>
> (Amina)

The way in which an individual dresses is another aspect of general social conduct which can potentially foster religious boundaries, in the sense that certain styles of dress – in particular, modest female dress – may be associated with religious commitment by the individual herself and by others around her. A large majority of both the male and the female respondents asserted that it is important for women to dress modestly; although definitions of what is 'modest' varied from person to person: a few of the men and also, as we have seen, some of the women favour (in principle, at least) the *hijab*; some talked more generally about the importance of not wearing revealing clothes; and some drew the line at 'short skirts'.

However, attitudes to modest dress, like other aspects of the respondents' general social conduct, are not a straightforward or simple manifestation of religious boundaries. For example, those male respondents who insisted that women should dress modestly are, in a sense, making a statement of allegiance with the minority community that does not require, on their own part, any active construction of social difference. It is noticeable that some of the young men who are quite irreligious as far as their own behaviour is concerned – such as Yusuf and Zaheer who are quoted, respectively, below – did not appear to perceive any double standard when they talked of how women should behave:

Yeah, women have got to cover themselves. They have to, really. But then, when they grow up they learn themselves what to do, what not to do. Our job is to tell them – teach them that way.

They can dress as they want. But not too revealing and that, and not too like tomboyish, like short haircuts. . . . Yeah, like short skirts, and things like that, you should just tell them no.

For women, the subject of dress raises various issues. Some, when talking of how they dress, and in a similar manner to how they spoke about socialising, indicated that their behaviour is constrained more by family and community pressures than by their own moral or religious judgements. A few of the women, when telling me that modest dress is important, talked in essentially rationalistic terms about how women are perceived by men. Also, as I have discussed previously, many of the female respondents clearly feel that they express their 'Asian' ethnicity, rather than or as well as their religious commitment, in how they dress. The following quotations illustrate the ways in which religious and other factors can merge in views about modest dress:

Yeah, I suppose it is [important for women to dress modestly]. I mean, I don't go out wearing low-cut things. But I just wear T-shirts and trousers. *Do you wear skirts?* No. I wouldn't be allowed from my father's respect. But I wouldn't wear them anyway.

(Tahmeena)

The way I see it, no one should be told how to dress. If there's a rape, for instance, and they're like – oh she's asking for it, the way she's dressed – that's a load of rubbish. But personally, I try to be as modest as possible.

(Bushra)

Women should dress how they feel comfortable. But then, on the other hand you have to think – you get real crazy people round nowadays, crazy guys, and you could get yourself into a mess . . .

(Ghazala)

Attitudes and boundaries

I have up to this point focused on the manifestations of religious boundaries in the behaviour of the respondents. However, as members of a religious minority, these young people are set apart from the majority population of Britain not only in terms of their religiously oriented actions, but also on account of the beliefs and values on which these actions are based. Few of them, however, spoke explicitly of the 'belief' aspect of difference; indeed, several pointed to the commonalities of Muslim and Christian belief systems, indicating that they feel that at the level of ultimate values, at least, little differentiates them from members of the (nominally) Christian majority. It is interesting that the one respondent – Asya – who asked me in some detail about my own beliefs was most surprised to hear that I do not consider myself at all religious, as can be seen from the following exchange:

Are you a Christian?
No – I wasn't brought up in any religion.
Really? You haven't got no religion whatsoever?
No.
Do you believe in God, though?
Not really.
What about your parents, are they Christian or what?
No, they're also not religious.
What about your brothers?
Also not.
Do you believe in God – do you actually believe in the God up there?
Not really . . .
So what about when someone dies or something – do you pray and that?

But we should remember that one issue has recently brought into sharp relief differences in attitudes, if not basic religious beliefs, between Muslims and non-Muslims in Britain: this was the Rushdie Affair. Those young people who feel strongly that Rushdie was wrong to have written *The Satanic Verses* are resisting the mainstream British media's backing of the author, and maybe be flying in the face of the views of non-Muslim friends and acquaintances who are unsympathetic to Muslim anger. We have already seen, in Chapter 4, that several respondents complained about the failure of white Britons to understand the viewpoints of aggrieved Muslims.

Over two-thirds of the core respondents expressed a firm conviction that the book was a real and hurtful affront to Islam and to Muslims. Like some other aspects of boundary maintenance which have already been discussed, the views of some of the less religious respondents on this issue could be interpreted as a gesture of general but largely inactive allegiance to the minority community. One of the most vivid denunciations of Rushdie that I heard was uttered by a young woman – casually dressed in leggings and a T-shirt – who indicated in various ways that she is not strongly committed to Islam. She told me that someone had once read her some extracts from *The Satanic Verses* which had made her extremely angry: 'It's like someone stabs a Muslim in the stomach, and he is supposed to just sit there and watch the blood flow out.'

The comments about Rushdie tended to focus on the vulgarity and offensiveness of his language: it appears that the objections to his novel were primarily on the grounds that it was insulting, especially of the Prophet, rather than simply critical of Islam. This view is made clear in the following quotations:

> There was a part where he actually said the Prophet Muhammad's daughter must have been a whore, and that is asking for trouble with Islam 'cause according to us he's the last prophet sent by God, and his daughter's given a very very high opinion in Islam basically.
>
> (Tahir)

> He said things about our Prophet that was so wrong. I mean, I'm not allowed to say them. But he really degraded him, and put him down – with the whores, etcetera. Which was really wrong. God forgive me.
>
> (Zubaida)

Of the core respondents who mentioned Khomeini's *fatwa* against Salman Rushdie, ten expressed (sometimes qualified) support of it and ten argued against it. Other points frequently made were that the book should be banned and that Rushdie will be punished by God for what he has done.

> I wouldn't want to do a life sentence for killing him, because I've got my own life to live. And our God is the same – he'll get judged on his day, and I just think, let him live his life in hiding. He's suffering, isn't he.
>
> (Zaheer)

> Islam is never a violent religion, it means peace. The *fatwa* is to bring him to Islamic court, to bring him to trial, 'cause he's attacked the Prophet himself. They shouldn't outright cold-blooded kill him; they should bring him to trial, and then let him have his punishment.
>
> (Kabir)

137

If there was a way of eradicating the book completely, that would be fine with me – so that there was not a copy left, for anybody to read and get the wrong idea, then I wouldn't mind so much.

(Zareena)

Disengagement or engagement?

The boundaries defining the religious identities of devout British Muslims are, I have argued, manifest in their day-to-day social activities, with the result that the plausibility structure on which allegiance to Islam relies is strengthened. The all-encompassing nature of Islamic faith can, however, simultaneously be problematic for boundary maintenance. In particular, it might be expected that devout Muslims will experience psychological stress on account of their continuous exposure to alternative and possibly tempting modes of behaviour. The social or psychological distance these young people preserve from non-Muslims is likely to diminish but not eliminate social pressures to undertake unIslamic activities and to neglect religious practice.

A large majority of the respondents talked of facing some kind of internal conflict or temptation arising from the contradictory pressures of religion and wider society. Comments made on this subject tended to focus on the importance of being resolute in the face of distraction; the specific issue that was most commonly raised in this context was the difficulty, at times, of adhering to Islamic prescriptions on food and alcohol. As we can see from the following examples, the young people's remarks about the necessity of resisting temptation are further examples of their tendency (discussed in Chapter 6) to express a commitment to autonomy in their attitudes to Islam.

What sort of things do you like doing in your spare time?
What things I *like* doing in my spare time, and what sort of things I *do* in my spare time are different. . . . 'Cause, like in Islam you can't do certain things, like you can't listen to music, you can't go out – so usually I just go round the mosque, or go with my friends.

(Rafiq)

Are there times when you're tempted to go against your religion, but you don't?
That's all the time, I suppose. Like if your mate offers you a drink, then I don't go against it. Or if your mates are all half pissed and having a good time – no, I won't have a drink. Are you sure? Then half an hour later when they're all drunk and they feel like shit, then you think, good! Serves them right! There's temptations there all the time, though. Like I went to party recently, and a woman came on to me.

(Naveed)

Several of the young people made the point that the influence of wider society,

or of what Zaheer called the 'fast life' of Britain, is so great that they inevitably do not behave all the time as good Muslims should: temptation, in other words, cannot be entirely overcome. 'Because I live in a Western society', Kabir told me, 'it pulls you down. Because you see other people not doing it, you think, ah, he's not doing it, I'll not do it.' And Jamila said,

> I'm a bit confused. I can't live the proper way. I can't do it. My lifestyle just doesn't suit it. At the same time I respect it. . . . You see a different life here and you get influenced, and then you can't totally go the orthodox way that you're supposed to, according to the Qur'an.

Some of the young people talked in what can be described as a general or reflective manner about the problems of negotiating between religious and other demands. For example, one young man told me that it is a positive thing to be a Muslim in Britain, 'Because here, there's more temptation to stray from religion. . . . But because it's harder here, there's more virtue in it.' The very devout Ehsan – with whom I spoke in the coffee shop of the local shopping centre – told me forcefully,

> We've agreed that it's an attribute of human nature – people are influenced by their environment. Why oh why should someone come amongst all of this [*he gestures with a flourish at the shops surrounding us and the mass of shoppers hurrying past*] – this – the technology, the wealth, the confidence this society has in its secularist ideas – why should someone fervently believe, have this conviction [in Islam], when it's always portrayed as being bad, awful, backwards. Why should someone – out of all of this! [*again he holds out both arms as if to embrace our surroundings*] – why should someone believe? And then even claim the belief is rational!

As would be expected, given the broad conservatism of those I spoke to, none suggested that the problems of accommodating religious with secular needs can be resolved by fundamentally reformulating the teachings of Islam. Mariam was one respondent who did, however, seem to suggest that some degree of rethinking by Muslims is required, in order to make Islam more relevant to those who live as members of minorities within Western society:

> I don't think this is possible, but I'd like to see an update of the Qur'an – one that was set within society which isn't really Islamic. I'd like to see some kind of structure there in religion. Because at the moment it's just people deciding amongst themselves what they think is right, and what they think is – religion. I mean, you've got people who – the only thing they religiously believe in is that there is only one God and Muhammad is his messenger, and they call themselves Muslims. And then there's other people, who are just so extremely strict that they wouldn't even eat a take-

away, in case it might have some chemical in it that somewhere originated from an animal.

Given that, for devout British Muslims, 'ordinary life' is necessarily tightly interwoven with religious practice, it seems that the only way they could entirely avoid conflict between their religious and other social needs would be by widening the social distance between themselves and non-Muslims to such an extent that they would be thoroughly segregated from the mainstream. Some minority religious groups in the West have quite successfully maintained their distinctiveness by taking up an extremely isolationist stance. For example, the Amish people of Pennsylvania are what Banton refers to as an 'incapsulating minority': that is, they comprise a group which has resisted assimilation by organising 'the central features of its life so as to strengthen both its inclusive and exclusive boundaries, making it difficult for those born into the community to leave it, and even more difficult for outsiders to join' (1983: 157). Sharot (1982) describes communities of Hasidic Jews of the United States as examples of 'introversionist groups' which, like the Amish and also the Hutterite communities, seek to disengage themselves completely from their wider social environment.

However, none of the Muslims with whom I was in contact indicated any desire to retreat behind boundaries so exclusive and restricting that, for example, their work and study, as well as their socialising, would be carried out only within Muslim circles and institutions. It could indeed be argued that the very nature of Islam makes it unlikely that a highly isolationist stance would be favoured by any significant segment of the British Muslim population. In particular, the awareness of British Muslims of their belonging to a global community of believers, the *umma*, makes the option of retreat undesirable. Christie points out that for Muslims in the non-Muslim world, retreat might be seen as the invocation of the Muslim principle of *hijra* or 'emigration' (which Muhammad introduced with his flight from Mecca to Medina), but carries with it the danger that 'the universal imperative that lies at the heart of Islam will atrophy, and that the internal *hijra* will over time become merely the defence of the specific culture of a specific ethnic group' (1991: 460).

The likelihood of retreat by British Muslims is further diminished by the fact that Islam is a politicised religion. Although my respondents did not themselves indicate a strong interest in the political campaigns in which British Muslims are currently engaged (briefly discussed in Chapter 2), it might be supposed that the theocratic nature of Islam means that devout and politically active Muslims will wish to influence rather than disengage from the British state, in the hope of introducing state structures that can allow some measure of Islamic governance for its Muslim citizens.

Another aspect of Islam which, like its universalistic ideology and political nature, militates against any tendency among British Muslims to be inward-looking is its emphasis upon proselytisation. As I have mentioned in the discussion of the field-work process in Chapter 3, the fact that some of the more radical young men with whom I came into contact sincerely wished to persuade me of the

140

benefits of becoming a Muslim occasionally posed a problem for me. On quite a number of occasions during my time in Waltham Forest – and not only when I was talking to these radical individuals – I was told about the many white and black British people who have made the decision to turn to Islam. The example of Cat Stevens – the former pop singer who converted and is now called Yusuf Islam – was mentioned to me several times.

Peer pressure

As the concept of plausibility structures suggests, the key function of the boundary process *vis-à-vis* a minority religious identity is to create a social space within which religious beliefs are shared. In this part of the discussion of religious boundaries, I wish to consider the ways in which peer pressure can operate among young British Muslims to reinforce, from within, the boundaries encircling the religion's social arena.

A majority of the respondents indicated that they are encouraged or pressurised by Muslim friends and peers to take their religion more seriously than they otherwise might. They indicated that peer pressure can take various forms and have differing levels of impact. Peer pressure can be manifest, for example, in a sense of shame that is induced when others behave in a way that is perceived as more appropriate than one's own behaviour; or in everyday – and even jokey – conversation and debate with Muslim friends about religion and the rights and wrongs of certain actions; or in a motivation to study the religion, pray, fast or attend the local mosque because that is what one's friends are doing:

> If we [friends] was all together, and something was to be said or done, religion would come into it, like you'd advise your friend – oh, d'you know that's a sin if you do that. But then again, you just say that a lot, when you're with your friends, just to make him feel guilty of what he's doing. Like say he's going out with a girl, and he has sex with her or something, we'd turn around and laugh and say, d'you know you've just done a sin?
>
> (Zaheer)

> A lot of the youngsters nowadays are really going into the religion and I've come across them, and I tend to keep away, 'cause – I can't disagree with them, 'cause what they're saying is right, according to religion. 'Cause I can't practise it, they end up looking at me like – you're really sinful, you haven't got a scarf on your head.
>
> (Jamila)

> Yeah, I fasted this year. Miracle, innit! I had to this year, because of the guys in my class. They would've killed me. That's the only reason, I swear!
>
> (Yasmin)

Conflict between groups.

141

Peer pressure can also be generated by the work undertaken by the religious groups run by young people which are located or have branches in Waltham Forest, and which explicitly strive to promote interest in and knowledge of Islam among young people. A substantial number of both formal and informal religious associations evidently exist in the local area, the members of which are primarily engaged in distributing leaflets, selling religious texts and literature, and organising study circles run from private homes and talks and meetings held in mosques and community centres. Some study circles are organised by and for women, but most of the active work of the groups is, it appears, carried out by young men. Although the numbers of men and women participating in group activities clearly amount only to a small minority of the local young Pakistanis and other Muslims, the groups maintain a conspicuous presence in the area, and thus it might be expected that they exercise a considerable influence over the less active majority. It is important, however, to remember that a number of my respondents find the strident approach of some of these groups quite distasteful and off-putting, as I have pointed out in my discussion of 'radicalism' in Chapter 6.

Six of the core respondents, including two women, spoke of being or having been in the past involved in some form of locally based group activity (this number does not take into account several who mentioned their membership of college or university Islamic societies). The six included the very devout Rafiq, who told me that he had been wary of joining the group of which he eventually became a part ''cause you've heard stories about sects and everything', but who was satisfied when he found that the group members follow 'proper scholars'. The other respondents who mentioned involvement in groups indicated that this has been limited to participation in informal study circles: Majid explained, for example, that 'we just sit down and we talk and we read, that's all. . . . It's some people from the mosque. These are young boys, not old men.'

A few respondents indicated that they are very aware of the existence of local religious groups, but that they do not themselves participate in these. Ruksana, for example, told me that her mother does not want her to get too involved in any Islamic group 'because she feels that I'm gonna get, er, brainwashed by their views, like some people they go to the extreme of something – she thinks I might turn into one of those people. But I know I won't!' Kabir complained at some length about the proliferation of various religious factions in the local area, which are based in mosques:

> There's three types of people come to my college, because of our different views. . . . Specially the Francis Road mosque, they say you must have the trousers above your ankles, you must have a beard. . . . They're sects. You've got the Lea Bridge Road mob, you've got the Francis Road mob, you've got the Queen's Road mob.

The kind of rivalry between groups to which Kabir referred was evident in a conversation I had with three young men selling Islamic literature. One of the three indicated his disapproval of the organisation hizb-ut tahrir: 'We could introduce you to the HTs – but maybe not. They'd just talk a load of rubbish to you. They'd tell you to start setting up an Islamic state right now.' Another said that he could give me some telephone numbers of the 'Lea Bridge Road lot' (that is, young people who attend the Lea Bridge Road mosque), but that I would have to be careful of what they told me. For them, he said scornfully, 'Religion is totally entwined with culture'. *crucial*

During the period that I spent living in Waltham Forest I found that the local Islamic groups made themselves most visible by running stalls at local 'Asian' events and in the open-air Walthamstow market. I discovered that a spot in the main market square was occupied on Saturday afternoons first by one group (seemingly hizb-ut tahrir) manning a small stall and then by another, rival group; both stalls, like others one was liable to come across, sold religious books and texts, together with video- and audio-tapes of lectures and recitations by Islamic scholars. Such stalls also distributed leaflets which publicised local talks and meetings to be held, or which gave educational messages varying from the sober ('Alhamdulillah, we see the wearing of hijab by more sisters as an indication of the growing awareness of Islam. However, we find that still a large proportion of sisters are ignorant of this Islamic duty . . . ') to the semi-jaunty ('Life's short and then you die. That's when the real fun starts. Judgement Day and Hellfire await. And all that time you acted as if you were made of asbestos'). *extremism !!*

The hizb-ut tahrir stall in Walthamstow Market regularly sold, for some time, T-shirts bearing the slogan 'NOT EAST NOT WEST ISLAM IS THE BEST!' and mugs proclaiming 'KHILAFAH' (the establishment of *khilafah*, or Islamic rule, is hizb-ut tahrir's stated aim). The young men running the rival stall sometimes made use of a loudhailer to ensure that none who strolled by could entirely ignore their message. '*And* the Prophet Moses, peace be upon him!' an urgent voice rang out one day, as I walked past; '*And* the Prophet Jesus, peace be upon him! *And* the Prophet Muhammad, peace be upon him!'

Local Muslims and non-Muslims alike were made further aware of the commitment of Muslim activists when a large green and white sign was erected on a gable end of a house on the main street in Walthamstow (above a billboard advertising Heineken Export) which pronounced: 'READ AL-QURAN, THE LAST TESTAMENT'. Some time later, again on the main street, a religious book shop opened for business: this was a brightly lit, well-stocked store staffed by young men. Its clean and tidy shelves made a stark contrast with the shabby, cluttered interior of a shop around the corner which was run by an old man and sold tattered volumes on Islam alongside Urdu-language textbooks for children.

Distinguishing between religion and ethnicity

In the final section of this chapter I will look at what was said by many of the respondents about the importance of distinguishing between religion and ethnicity as sources of social identity. It appears that the nature of this distinction is itself a vital manifestation of the particular force of religious identity, and of the boundaries which encompass that identity, in the lives of the young British Muslims with whom I spoke.

The distinction rests on the notion that whereas Asian or Pakistani ethnicity is an aspect of life which relates to a particular people and place, Islam has universal relevance and applicability. The respondents make two kinds of distinction between the particularism of ethnic and the universalism of religious identity; these are based on two different, but interrelated and overlapping, understandings of ethnicity.

First, there is a perception of ethnic identity as an attachment to a set of traditions or customs that are non-Islamic in origin and are associated with the minority group. According to this view, one should distinguish between the universal applicability of religious teachings and the limited relevance or usefulness of 'culture'. The assumption here is that while religious commitment expresses one's acceptance of a set of absolute truths, recorded for all time in the Qur'an and *hadith*, ethnic identity is not much more than loyalty to disparate customs from distant places, such as the traditions which the older generation of British Pakistanis brought with them to Britain from the Indian subcontinent. This way of differentiating between religion and ethnicity can be termed the *religion–ethnic culture distinction*.

The second means of distinguishing religion from ethnicity is based on a perception of ethnic identity in terms of national origins or descent; here, then, we can talk of the *religion–ethnic origins distinction*. Thus, while one's ethnic identity (or self-definition as, for example, 'Asian' or 'Pakistani') denotes one's attachment to a country or region of origin, one's religious identity as a Muslim signifies belonging to a global community and, indeed, commitment to a set of doctrines which asserts the intrinsic equality of men across all boundaries of race and nation.

The religion–ethnic culture distinction

At least half of the core respondents made some kind of reference – often at length – to the need to distinguish, as a framework within which to live one's life, Islamic teachings from 'culture', 'traditions' or 'customs'. Most frequently, the matter was discussed in terms of what the young people regard as the tendency among Pakistanis in Britain and/or in Pakistan to engage in certain forms of behaviour which are the product of long-standing traditions of the Indian subcontinent or, more specifically, Hindu or Sikh teachings, but which have no basis in Islam. A number of the young people made the point that some 'cultural' attributes of the minority community are beneficial and can be enjoyed, though they should be recognised as non-Islamic. Others argued that many such forms of behaviour are at best unimportant or somewhat inappropriate in the context of lives spent in Britain, and at worst morally reprehensible.

The respondents mentioned a wide range of behaviours which they deem to be 'traditional' or 'cultural' rather than 'religious', including practices relating to

caste, dowries, dress, arranged marriage, marriage ceremonies and unequal treat-
ment of men and women:

> Culture is a way of living in a society. Religion is living on your own. Our
> culture it's like – at a religious wedding there'd be a little bit of music, just
> that, but in our culture, it's getting away from religion – they have a henna
> night, they have an oil night . . . that's culture, that's custom. Our
> customs are getting away from religion.
>
> (Ilyas)

> Most things we tend to do are culture, rather than the religion. Religion is
> – five times a day prayer, being good, whereas culture is getting married
> in red, and arranged marriages. So I got married in shocking pink!
>
> (Sara)

Many of the respondents who criticised their parents' overly confining interpretations of Islam based their arguments on the notion of there being a
distinction between the ethnic culture to which their parents adhere and the true
teachings of Islam:

> The Muslim religion, it doesn't say that girls should stay at home. Like my
> dad goes a lot – this is our culture, and I go, no dad, you shouldn't be
> talking culture – you should be talking religious terms here. And reli-
> giously I *can* do this, I *can't* do that.
>
> (Amina)

We have already seen that several other researchers who have looked at the
subject of British Muslim identity have found that increasing numbers of young
people and especially young women are appealing to Islamic teachings as they seek
to resist parental and community restrictions on behaviour. These researchers
have also drawn attention to the fact that the resistance often takes the form of a
rejection of parents' narrow conceptions of culture and tradition in favour of the
'global appeal of intellectual Islam [which] offers the possibility of a wider world
in which to live' (Ali 1992 113). Nielsen points out that in Britain there are
frequent encounters between Muslims of different ethnic backgrounds, which lead
inevitably to a certain reappraisal within the Muslim population of what can be
understood as truly 'Islamic' and what can be discounted as 'tradition': 'The experience of meeting other modes of Islamic cultural expression with equally strong
claims to validity as one's own raises questions as to the exclusive legitimacy of any
one particular mode' (1984: 16).[3]

Rather than referring to specific forms of behaviour, some of my respondents
talked more generally of how 'Pakistani culture' – as it exists in Pakistan itself and
as it has been articulated in Britain – is a fusion of various elements of Hindu and
Sikh religion and indigenous customs, even though the state of Pakistan was

founded in the name of Islam. It should be remembered that, as I pointed out in Chapter 1, Islam in the Indian subcontinent has a long history of incorporating diverse elements of pre-existing customs and traditions, and indeed that the involvement of Muslims in South Asia in localised 'unorthodox practices' is still today the object of criticism by some religious leaders. Furthermore, the Barelvi movement, within which much emphasis is placed on such practices as worship at shrines, has been highly influential in Pakistan and among Pakistanis in Britain. Thus, when young British Pakistani Muslims complain about the hybrid nature of Pakistani culture and Pakistani 'versions' of Islam, their arguments have some basis in historical reality.[4]

The following are examples of comments made by three of the respondents about the general nature of Pakistani culture and society:

> How would I describe Pakistani culture? Um – touch of Islam. Hindu and Sikh culture and tradition, with a bit of the British Empire some-where in there. Something like this. It's to do with them three.
>
> (Adnan)

> [Pakistani culture is] very backward. I mean, basically because they don't follow Islam. That's what our culture's about, yeah. And they manipulate tradition. If they were to follow Islam it would be pretty good, but they don't. Just tradition.
>
> (Nazia)

> Islam is much more easily accessible in this country than it is back home, because of a lot of cultural influences which are actually totally wrong. And so practising Islam is a lot easier here. Like if I went back in *hijab*, I'd have all sorts of stick from my family.
>
> (Zareena)

The assertion by young British Muslims that it is possible to divorce religion from ethnic culture might remind one of the assumption within orthodox Islam (briefly discussed in Chapter 6) that the religion comprises a fixed and perfect core of doctrines; and that, following from this, 'reform' within Islam should take the form of attempts to return to *original* truths. Underlying the religion–ethnic culture distinction made by many would seem to be a view that it is possible and necessary for Muslims in Britain to establish greater orthodoxy in their beliefs and practices by purifying Islam of all cultural accretions. Religion is constant, it was sometimes said by the respondents, whereas culture is always open to change.

This view was rarely explicitly articulated. Of all the individuals I spoke to, the very devout Rafiq expressed in the most outspoken terms the view that Muslims must seek to return to a pure, culturally free Islam. He told me that Pakistan has

ended up being a country full of Muslims who are deviated. Following their own whims and desires. . . . You know, taking up saints, and then going to graves to worship them. And that's what the Hindus are doing. . . . And that should be cleaned up somehow.
How do you think that should be done?
Well – the same way it was done in Saudi Arabia. . . . Basically they just – destroyed all the graves, and they – um – killed all the people, who were sort of like innovating into the religion. Things that shouldn't be there.

Whatever the ambitious goals of numbers of young Muslims in Britain, it can certainly be suggested that there are few or no prospects for the emergence of an Islam in Britain that is free of forms of 'culture' alien to its original order. Here as elsewhere values embedded in the majority society inevitably have their impact upon expressions of religious belief and practice. Furthermore, it is inevitable that Asian Muslims will continue, for another generation or two at the very least, to be influenced by cultures and customs emanating from the Indian subcontinent. As far as my respondents are concerned, the whole context within which they practise their religion is, after all, a Pakistani one: not only because they learn about Islam first and foremost from their Pakistani parents, but also because Pakistanis are the dominant group within the local Muslim community. For all those who are used to hearing Urdu spoken in the mosque, to eating Pakistani food and wearing Pakistani clothes at religious festivals, to following Pakistani customs at weddings and other 'religious' ceremonies, to abiding by or railing against definitions of 'moral' behaviour which have more to do with the norms of Pakistani village life than anything else – for all of them, the interconnections between ethnic culture and religion are dense and intricate.

The religion–ethnic origins distinction

A global identity?

Given that Pakistan was founded with the explicit purpose of being a homeland for India's Muslims, one might expect that the objections to 'cultural' interpretations of Islam would not prevent the majority of the young people I spoke to strongly associating being Pakistani with being Muslim. However, only eight of the core respondents talked in a positive manner – and they generally briefly – about the link between Islam and Pakistan.

It may be fair to assume that many of the respondents make an implicit association between Pakistaniness and Islam that simply was not articulated in the course of the interviews. Indeed, some of the young people seemed to relate not merely being Pakistani but also being 'Asian' with a Muslim identity, judging from the fact that a small number of them appeared to use the terms 'Muslim' and 'Asian' interchangeably, and some others occasionally slipped between them. For example, Yusuf told me, with regard to Salman Rushdie: 'The things he said was totally wrong – and that's being Asian himself saying that'. And Tahmeena, when asked what her religion means to her, told me, 'I wouldn't want to be anything else. I think I'd prefer to be an Asian.' She also commented, in another context, 'I suppose every Asian should know how to read the Qur'an.'

In contrast, some of the respondents appear to make a conscious effort to distinguish between 'Pakistani' or 'Asian' as ethnic labels which signify one's place of origin and 'Muslim' as a global identity. This is in some ways a natural corollary of the religion–ethnic culture distinction, although in general it seemed to be accorded less importance than the latter. Ten of the core respondents gave the impression that they regard Islam as a source of global identity, in stressing that they like to define themselves by reference to religion rather than ethnic origin. In some of these cases, furthermore, self-definitions in terms of British nationality were also described as somewhat insignificant.

> [I would identify myself] hopefully as a Muslim! That's how I'd like to be recognised – not as a Pakistani or as a English man or – a British person or anything. As a Muslim.
>
> (Majid)

> *How would you describe your identity?*
> Muslim. And a Pakistani. But somebody in England. No, I wouldn't say that! . . . I'd just say I'm a Muslim, and it doesn't really matter what country. At the end of the day it's really religion – don't you reckon?
>
> (Asya)

> I'm a Muslim first. That should be promoted first. That's what's impor-tant – not the fact where you're from. Because that also creates divisions, you see. Because when you start promoting your own countries, that's when people will start thinking, oh we're better, because we're from Pakistan.
>
> (Bushra)

Where young British Muslims maintain a view of religious identity as cross-cutting ethnic or national affiliations, this can be described as an effort to *widen* the religious boundaries beyond the narrow definitions of Islam held by their more parochial parents. For young British Muslims, as Gardner and Shukur write in relation to British Bengalis, the fact that the 'collective ideal' contained within Islamic rhetoric is not confined to Britain but encompasses the world is a powerful motivating force. It allows these young people to feel that they are part of 'a worldwide trend which links them politically and financially to the global *umma* . . . ' (1994: 163). In this way, the boundaries defining Muslim identity – and the plausibility structure they delineate – are strengthened: the young

Muslims are likely to feel that although within British society they are members of a relatively small and weak minority, their religious beliefs and practices traverse the globe and history and are, thus, components of what is a vast and (potentially at least) powerful force.

The existence of the *umma* can be said to provide for young Muslims a sense of belonging and continuity that is analogous to that entailed by membership of an ethnic group, despite the fact that a global Muslim identity is not based on notions of shared ancestry (only a tiny minority of Muslims claim descent from the Prophet or his tribe). And even the lack of shared ancestry is, in a sense, compensated for by the habit among the more religious young people of referring to their co-religionists as 'brothers' and 'sisters'. It seems, therefore, that the sacred history through which the *umma* has evolved provides a sense of kinship which tightly binds individuals together; even if there are none of the assumptions of a literal kinship which tend to cement social relations within ethnic groups (and which are also often articulated through the use of family words like 'brother' or 'cousin', as Horowitz [1985] points out).

Furthermore, the emphasis within Islam on sacred places – most particularly Mecca – and communal worship can heighten one's awareness of being a small but integral part of something far greater than oneself.[5] The respondent Majid described his experience of going on *'umra* (lesser pilgrimage) to Mecca in the following terms:

> There's only Muslims allowed, so just to see them – at prayer time, to just see the people coming from all angles. It's masses of people, just gather in one place, to pray. It's such a good thing. You can't explain it. Not even to a Muslim, you can't explain it – you've got to go there to learn what it's like.

Solidarity with Muslims overseas

Some of the young people with whom I spoke indicated an attachment to the notion of a global Muslim community by expressing some feelings of solidarity with Muslims overseas. In general, the comments which were made about the international community tended to focus on current conflicts which involve Muslims. For several of the more devout young people in particular, an awareness of the struggles in which Muslims in various parts of the world are engaged seems to be a central aspect of faith.

The only specific international issue that was regularly mentioned in interviews and discussions was the war in Bosnia. Other issues which were raised from time to time were the Palestinian question, the Gulf War, the destruction of the Ayodhya mosque in India and the situation of Muslims in Kashmir.[6] The fact that a global perspective on the religion often entails a recognition of the suffering and oppression of Muslims overseas appears to promote the notion of a single international community and to increase the emotional intensity of feelings about that community. Commitment to the *umma* may, furthermore, be born of the explicit or implicit hope that it will one day relive its glorious past.

That it is not possible to maintain a neutral or complacent stance with respect to international issues is evident from the three major themes which emerged in my respondents' discussions of the *umma* and its current condition. One theme was the importance of being compassionate towards Muslims overseas who are in trouble, and of recognising their need for financial and political support. Bushra, for example, told me that her religion

> is very dear to me – like if anybody will say anything it will hurt. I mean, I remember I was on the train and somebody was complaining about how we were helping the Muslims in Bosnia, and I just thought – they're people that are dear to me, and they're being totally decimated, and how can you even think that? And I was very angry. All the Muslims are very dear to me in the world.

Local fund-raising activities in aid of Muslims overseas provide further evidence of the awareness of the problems facing the global community: Muslim and Asian organisations in Waltham Forest have organised events in aid of Bosnian Muslims, for example; and an Islamic Relief stall at most local *melas* draws attention to the suffering of Muslims in many distant and not-so-distant places. One of my respondents, Amir, was extensively involved in raising money for Bosnians: at the time I met him he was, as his wife explained to me, extremely busy collecting money on behalf of some friends who had travelled to Bosnia a few months previously and had just contacted him to say they had run out of supplies.

The second theme that was raised in discussions of international issues concerned the apparent hostility that Muslims face throughout the world, and their consequent vulnerability – even in Britain. This viewpoint was expressed in various ways. A young man at a religious stall, for example, told me that Marxists 'haven't learnt the lessons of history' and that Marxism may grow in strength again, once 'everyone has forgotten the fall of Russia'. When that happens, he said, 'the Marxists will line up with fascists against us. That's what's happening in Algeria now.' Faruq talked at some length about the Gulf War:

> That really is like the turning point for many Asians in this country. That's what's really jolted them – made them realise what the world is about. . . . Also, it was right near Mecca, and the excuse was – oh we think Saddam Hussein's going to invade Saudi Arabia. It was a turning point – little things in this country we noticed, like the papers came out with this racism, mosques were firebombed, Asians were beaten up. . . . And 'Muslim' became a dirty word.

Adnan spoke of the repercussions of the Bosnian conflict for some Muslims' perceptions of their status in Britain: 'In Yugoslavia, Muslims are being slaughtered by the Serbs. . . . And [my mum] is going – I told you it can happen – look it's happening there.' This sense of vulnerability in the face of the Bosnian war was made apparent to me in another context. A teacher at a local sixth-form college arranged for me to conduct interviews with some of his students, but told me that a few of them had not wanted to take part in my research. One had said to him, 'What about Bosnia?', and then explained that research could be used against Muslims in this country – in the same way that in Germany statistics had been used in the efforts to round up and kill the Jews.

The third theme relating to international affairs was the impotence and guilt of the so-called 'Islamic' countries themselves. A few young people told me that Western governments alone are not to blame for the suffering of Muslims: 'Islamic' governments have failed their own people and the Muslims of other nations. No particular state or group of states was, however, consistently identified in the interviews as being at fault. Naveed commented, for example,

> If there was one proper Islamic state in the whole world with an ounce of authority things like that [Ayodhya] would not have happened. They would have had some sort of political pressure applied to India to stop that sort of thing. Political pressure applied to Bosnia, and political pressure applied to Israel.

The same young man who had told me that in the future the Marxists and the fascists will line up against the Muslims complained at some length about the weakness of 'Islamic' governments. He also talked of how the radical organisation in which he is involved has to operate underground in many 'Islamic' countries. It is sad and strange, he said, that in Britain he can sell literature which he could never circulate in such places as Saudi Arabia and Jordan. Those who have tried to do so have been shot and killed; or they have had their hands and feet cut off and been left to die in the desert. Another of my respondents complained with some vehemence about specific regimes:

> What [Salman Rushdie] did – he incited people – he was just one among many evils in the world, you know. No more evil than all the other ones, like Saddam Hussein and that lot. Or the other ones, like the one in Syria – Asad – they're all pretty horrific, horrible people. Or – the Ayatollah. They're all horrible. You'd better not show this tape to no one – no Shi'ites, otherwise – [laughs]. Don't show that tape to no Shi'ites!

CONCLUSION

My aim in these last few pages is to highlight briefly some of the findings of my study which seem to be of most significance and to have a relevance to broad questions about how individuals living in contemporary Western societies define the social collectivities to which they belong.

Much of what was said to me over the course of my field-work, and which has been recounted and commented upon in the book, has demonstrated that the very concept of 'identity' is difficult to elucidate. As I have reported, many social theorists are today disputing the validity of 'essentialising' notions of identity which assume that individuals have consistent, core self-definitions based, for example, on ethnicity or nationality. And, indeed, many of my young respondents spoke in such a way as to suggest that they themselves feel that the process of identity-formation is necessarily open-ended: that there can be no concrete answers to questions such as 'Who am I?' and 'Where do I belong?' Certainly, because of their particular circumstances the children of immigrants – like my respondents – may be more likely than most to feel that identity is an ambiguous and slippery concept; but perhaps for every one of us who lives in a nation-state which contains an ethnically diverse and cosmopolitan population and is well integrated within the global and ever-expanding network of communications, questions of identity are increasingly difficult to resolve.

It seems that for my respondents the question of how to define the British 'nation' or British identity is particularly problematic. Again, this partly arises because these individuals are in an especially ambivalent position with regard to their own British identity, given that there are plenty of popular notions of Britishness which equate being British with being white or having a British heritage (whatever way that heritage is defined). However, the concept of the British nation appears to be one that is highly contested within a great many spheres of society. For example, concerns regarding the ongoing process of European integration, the impact of nationalist movements in Scotland, Wales and Northern Ireland, and perhaps even the repercussions of notions of a 'north–south divide' within England, fuel both popular and political debates about the nature of 'Britishness'.

Notwithstanding the evidence that, for my respondents and for others, many aspects of social identity are no longer as sharply delineated as they may have been in the past, a recurring theme throughout this book has been the argument that theorists should be careful not to overestimate the extent to which aspects of identity are malleable and subject to reinterpretation. It seems to me vitally important to recognise that there are certain limits to the extent to which individuals can redefine themselves and the groups to which they belong; or that, at least, even if theoretically it is possible to challenge in countless ways such limits, they are very often accepted and hence, in practice, they exist.

For my respondents, Pakistani ethnicity as a basis of identity is not something that they can shape at will. It comprises a host of different elements – ways of thinking, feeling, understanding, acting and being – some of which the young people question and even jettison, but others of which, in contrast, they see as fixed and constant. Thus while they challenge much of what their parents say about what it means to be Pakistani, they also tend to feel that they are bound in a meaningful way to the culture and the place from which their parents came to Britain, and to the other people who share that culture and (original) home. The fact that this sentiment can take a variety of forms and emerge in a variety of ways does not diminish its force or significance both for individuals and for the minority group as a whole.

Furthermore, the sense of the inescapability of ethnicity is likely to be greatly enhanced if there is an awareness, as there seems to be among the young people with whom I spoke, that many white Britons regard the minority group as immutably foreign or alien. This perspective on the part of members of the majority population is, of course, itself a clear manifestation of the fact that fixed or essentialist conceptualisations of identity, however adverse their consequences can be, are still maintained by ordinary social actors.

From what was said by my respondents, it is evident also that while concepts of ethnicity tend to set certain limits on one's potential to redefine oneself, commitment to a religious faith can establish parameters of identity of a different kind. For my respondents, ethnic identity is largely a 'natural' or 'given' fact of life: one acquires an ethnic identity, first and foremost, by being born into it. Religion, on the other hand, is regarded by the young people as more of a matter of personal choice – despite the fact that Islam was the religion of their forefathers and is something which, therefore, connects them with their families' and indeed their ethnic group's past. It is increasingly common, it appears, for young British Muslims like my respondents to assert that true commitment to Islam does not arise out of the circumstances of one's birth: it must be based on reflection and on self-conscious determination.

The emphasis within British Islam upon the need for the individual to develop a personal approach to faith has parallels with modern developments within a great many other religious traditions in the West. Within many branches of mainstream Christianity, for example, there is plenty of scope for individuals to engage in far-reaching reinterpretations of key doctrines. The emergence, since the 1960s, of what are collectively known as 'New Age' beliefs and practices provides another, very different, example of individual-oriented religiosity. This latter phenomenon has involved the exploration and revival of elements from diverse and often ancient Eastern and Western traditions of belief, learning and healing.

The trend towards personal expressions of religiosity has often been seen as one dimension of a gradual and general process of secularisation. It can also be argued that in many cases it gives rise to religious identities which – and here we return to arguments about the nature of all social identities – are highly malleable, since there apparently remain few clear-cut limits to belief or practice. But the attitudes to Islam of the young people I interviewed do not in any way provide evidence of the proliferation of fluid identities. Rather, these young Muslims tend to combine an emphasis on the role of the individual with unquestioning belief in the absolute 'truths' contained in the teachings of Islam; truths which, indeed, inform Muslims of the predetermined, unambiguous and constant constraints within which they all should live.

X   I have argued in this book that there is so much that is fixed and certain in my respondents' beliefs partly because the very nature of orthodox Islamic thought provides limited scope for radical reformulation: most crucially, the view that the teachings of Islam are unchanging and unchangeable logically follows from the belief that the Qur'an comprises the unmediated words of God. Furthermore, the teachings themselves are a source of precise guidelines on all aspects of behaviour and thereby ensure that a relatively clear-cut and pervasive social boundary separates Muslims from non-Muslims. I have concluded that it is because so much in the young people's lives is open to question, including many aspects of other potential sources of identity, that the certainties contained within Islam hold so much appeal. And thus Islam in Britain seems, for the time being at least, to be resisting the secularising trends that are manifest in wider society.

On a more general note, I hope that this book illustrates some of the benefits of undertaking social research by means of a detailed and thorough examination of what the subjects of the study themselves think and say about the issues at stake. In any public debate – whether conducted by academics, politicians, policy-makers or journalists – about complex and sensitive subjects such as racism and multiculturalism, it appears all too easy for the participants to allow their personal or political viewpoints to prevent them from listening carefully to what is being said by the individuals most affected by the matters under discussion. Those who claim to speak on behalf of members of ethnic minorities may, for example, be too eager to voice some anti-racist dogma or to express their liberal or postmodern discomfort with certain aspects of minority identity, to pay attention to the details of what individuals believe and care about.

This book has not set out to offer answers to political or policy-related questions; but in giving a great deal of space to what its subjects have to say it has, I trust, provided material that can inform debates about identity and ethnic and religious minorities in contemporary Britain. Most of all, in writing of my respondents I hope to have demonstrated that the young people who are central to such debates – but who are often portrayed simply as, for example, 'victims' of racism or the defenders of a potentially threatening religious ideology – are likely to be, in diverse ways, reflective, attentive and as interested as anybody else in discussing and grappling with issues that matter to them. I hope that I have conveyed also my respondents' expectations of tolerance from, and their desire to be tolerant towards, those who are different from themselves, even while they know and indeed hope that some of the differences will remain.

As a final comment on how in Britain today greatly different social groupings meet, merge, compete for our hearts and minds, and produce powerful and discrete collective identities, I shall close this discussion with an account of a scene I came across one spring afternoon in the market in Walthamstow's High Street.

I was making my way through the crowd that every Saturday converges on the market when I heard music from its central square, and went to investigate. I soon made out the words of the song's chorus: 'Jesus! Jesus! Jesus is our friend!' A line of black and white men and women on a make-shift stage belted out the song, banged tambourines, blew trumpets and swayed their hips. A fair-sized crowd had gathered in front of them, some members of which jigged about half-heartedly. A long-haired, long-skirted young white woman pressed a leaflet into my hand which implored me to 'march for Jesus'. The singing died down for a while, and a man came forward with a microphone, to tell us that Jesus had died for our sins and that we ought to get to know Him.

To one side of the square, unnoticed by the crowd, eight or nine young, bearded Asian men stood behind a table upon which Islamic literature and video-tapes were displayed. The young men were chatting quite cheerfully among themselves, seemingly unconcerned at being (literally) overshadowed by the dancing, singing evangelicals. They showed no interest in me when I peered at their books.

As I left the market square, another flyer was handed to me: this one invited me to 'march against racism'. The demonstration was to take place the next day; it was to start in Leyton and would finish in a local park at the 'Festival for Racial Harmony'. The message was repeated in Urdu on the other side of the leaflet.

NOTES

1 Social identities

1 For development of Tajfel's social identity theory see, for example, Brown (1988), Tajfel (ed.) (1978), J.C. Turner *et al.* (1987).
2 Talai's complaint relates to that made by Mahmood and Armstrong (1992) about general anthropological tendencies in studies of ethnicity. They point out that theorists, having generally agreed that it is not possible to produce any list of traits or features which define ethnic groups, have tended to argue that it is inappropriate to describe specific groups in terms of their 'cultural realities', despite the fact that the members of any given group themselves clearly assume that their identification has a concrete basis in culture. Writing in relation to two specific ethnic communities, Mahmood and Armstrong argue that 'since in social life what people accept as real is real in its consequences, this means that on some important level Québecois and Frisian cultures exist. The problem is to find a methodology capable of revealing this reality' (1992: 8).
3 For the Durkheimian and Weberian perspectives on religion see, for example, Durkheim (1954) and Weber (1948).
4 Spiro, for example, defines religion as 'an institution consisting of culturally patterned interaction with culturally postulated superhuman beings' (1966: 96).

2 The background

1 There are various collections of *hadith*, six of which were compiled in the ninth century and are regarded as especially authoritative by Sunni Muslims. Questions of the validity of particular *hadith* and collections of *hadith* have been a constant source of debate and disagreement in the Muslim world.
2 The most fundamental division within Islam is that between 'orthodox' or Sunni Islam and Shi'ism, which dates back to the assassination of the fourth caliph or 'successor' to Muhammad, his son-in-law, 'Ali. The 'party' (*shi'a*) of 'Ali demanded, after his death, the reinstatement of his family as rulers; subsequently, Shi'ism developed a distinct theological content. Shi'ites, who today make up about 10 per cent of the world's Muslim population, place special emphasis upon the role of 'Ali and his descendants, the twelve *imams* or spiritual leaders, who alone are believed to have access to the hidden meanings of the Qur'an.
3 See F. Robinson (1988) for a clear outline of the major movements which grew up in South Asia in the face of the challenges of British colonialism.

4 To calculate the number of converts to Islam in Britain is almost impossible, as Nielsen (1992) points out; he has offered a quite conservative estimate of 5,000 converts, among whom most are students and a large number are of Afro-Caribbean origin.

5 My respondents tended not to make reference to theological distinctions between different Islamic traditions, although, very occasionally, the Shi'ah–Sunni divide was stressed as significant (one respondent was himself a Shi'ite). On the occasions where I encouraged respondents and informants to tell me something about divisions within Sunni Islam, I was either told that no such divisions existed or that conflicts within the (local) Sunni Muslim community are endemic but arise out of the trivial, political interests of the individuals and groups concerned, rather than out of concerns over interpretations of Islam.

   The terms 'Barelvi' and 'Deobandi' were never spontaneously mentioned in any discussion at any point in the field-work. The one time that I specifically questioned a senior community leader as to whether the local mosques are Barelvi or Deobandi he replied, firmly, that 'I would rather not mention such things, because the differences [between mosques or religious groupings] are very slight, and if you talk about them some people might not like it.' The overall impression that I received was that there is among the older generation a reluctance to admit publicly to the existence of theological divisions in the local Muslim community; and that within the younger generation there is generally a lack of interest in such matters, other than among those who belong to organised religious youth groups which themselves tend not to be aligned with the traditional movements of the subcontinent.

   It should nevertheless be noted that according to Nielsen support for the Deobandi and Barelvi movements in Britain 'has been so deep-rooted that conflicts over control of mosques and associated resources are almost stereotypically presented as Deobandi–Barelvi conflicts' (1992: 45). Modood (1990), similarly, writes that sectarian clashes between the Barelvis and Deobandis have been widespread throughout Muslim communities in Britain.

6 Andrews (1994), Ellis (1991), Hiro (1991), Joly (1995), Lewis (1994), Mirza (1989), Nielsen (1987), Sahgal (1992) and Shaw (1988) all make some reference to the fact that many young Muslims are displaying an interest in improving their understanding of Islam and challenging certain traditional views held by older Muslims.

7 Researchers who have drawn attention to the extent to which, in some situations at least, religious identities are being prioritised by young British Muslims are Ali (1992), Eade (1990), Gardner and Shukur (1994), Knott and Khoker (1993), Mirza (1989) and Nielsen (1984) and (1987).

8 There is little literature on British Muslims which explicitly deals with what I have termed the 'assertive Muslim identity'. However, various studies looking at related issues create an overall impression of the burgeoning of this form of religiosity. See, for example, Samad (1992) on youth anger in Bradford over *The Satanic Verses*, Modood (1990) also on the anti-Rushdie campaigns among working-class British Pakistanis, Werbner (1994) on general Muslim opposition to the Gulf War, Lewis (1994) on the Muslim Asian rap group 'Fun-da-mental', and Sahgal (1992) on protest among Muslim and also Sikh young men.

9 For mostly brief mentions of radical or militant Islamic activities among British Muslims see A.S. Ahmed (1992), Hiro (1991), Lewis (in press), Modood (1990), Rex and Josephides (1987).

10 This information was supplied by a personal communication from the Office of Population Censuses and Surveys (OPCS), London.

11 For further details on YM and its activities see Andrews (1992) and, particularly, Lewis (1994).

12 Indeed, the militancy of hizb-ut tahrir has provoked much debate in the media. For example *First Sight* (BBC 2, 20.4.95) reported on tensions and occasional incidents of violent conflict, seemingly in part encouraged by militant Islamic groups and especially hizb-ut tahrir, between Muslim and non-Muslim students on some college campuses. *Public Eye* (BBC 2, 25.7.95) also reported on hizb-ut tahrir, and emphasised that there exists within British Islam considerable opposition to the group, with the result that it has, for example, been banned from several mosques in various parts of the country. An edition of *Witness* (Channel 4, 8.4.97), entitled 'The Tottenham Ayatollah', profiled Omar Bakri Mohammed who was formerly a leader of hizb-ut tahrir and since January 1996 has headed a breakaway faction by the name of Al-Muhajiroun (see Ronson 1997).

13 See Christie (1991) for a brief discussion of possible political responses of Muslims in the West to their minority status; a status which has come about by virtue of the fact that 'they have emigrated – normally for economic reasons – into the heart of the Western world'. Christie points out that these Muslims have, by moving '*into* rather than *away from* the non-Muslim world . . . challenged the basic Muslim concept of Muslim solidarity exemplified by Muhammad's own *hijra* [flight] from Mecca to Medina' [original emphases] (1991: 459).

14 One illustration of the wide impact of the controversy is the enormous amount of literature it has produced. In addition to numerous articles, the literature includes several collections of papers and commentaries, such as Ahsan and Kidwai (eds) (1991) (which maintains a pronounced anti-Rushdie perspective), Bowen (ed.) (1992) and the CSIC *Research Paper* (1989). The legal and social policy implications of the Rushdie Affair in relation to multiculturalism in general and, more specifically, the blasphemy laws and questions of free speech are considered in publications such as Lee (1990), Webster (1990) and the reports of three CRE seminars on these issues (1989, 1990a, 1990b). Other books published on the Rushdie Affair include Akhtar (1989) which seeks, in the author's own words, to explain the 'anguish' of Muslims like the illiterate woman who is told by her daughter's schoolteacher that Rushdie's novel is 'great literature'; Sardar and Wyn Davies (1990) which, also from a Muslim perspective, looks at the history of anti-Muslim sentiment in the West and details the reactions of non-Muslims to the Rushdie Affair; and Ruthven (1990) which explores, from the angle of a non-Muslim and informed journalist, the background to the anger of British Muslims.

15 It is not possible to determine accurately the levels of support for the Ayatollah's *fatwa*; but certainly the majority of British Muslims and their leaders did not actively distance themselves from it. Hiro (1991) cites a poll commissioned in September 1989 by BBC Television which shows that 79 per cent of the 674 Muslims questioned favoured action against Rushdie, of whom 35 per cent (45 per cent among those aged 16–20) supported the death sentence.

16 See Samad (1992) for an account of the militancy of young Pakistanis in Bradford in the wake of the Rushdie Affair; militancy which, Samad argues, must be understood in the context of deteriorating race relations in the city.

17 See Parker-Jenkins (1991) and Joly (1995) for accounts of Muslim educational needs. The *British Muslims Monthly Survey* also provides reports of Muslim campaigns over educational (and many other) issues across Britain.

18 See, for example, 1996 and 1997 issues of the *British Muslims Monthly Survey*.

3 The field and field-work

1 General information about the London Borough of Waltham Forest that is presented here is taken from the Waltham Forest *Borough Profile 1994*; and figures relating to the

ethnic minority population from the Waltham Forest *1991 Census Newsletter*, No. 13 (1993b).

2 The figures cited in this part of the Appendix all derive from the 1991 census, and are taken from the Waltham Forest *1991 Census Newsletter*, Nos 6 and 13 (1993a and 1993b), and the *Waltham Forest Economic Overview* (1994b). The *Economic Overview*, which is the source of the information about employment-related matters, provides figures based on an analysis of a 10 per cent sample of the full borough population.

   I do not provide here a general overview of the Pakistani population of Britain, since this kind of broad information is readily accessible in many other texts. For an account of the current social and economic circumstances of Pakistanis and other South Asians in Britain, see Owen (1994); for the history of emigration to Britain from the Indian subcontinent see, among others, R. and C. Ballard (1977), R. Ballard (1990), Shaw (1988); for patterns of settlement of South Asians in Britain see V. Robinson (1986); for discussion of the social networks established by Pakistani immigrants in Britain see Dahya (1974), Anwar (1979).

3 It might be expected that the low rate of economic activity among Pakistani women relates in part at least to certain cultural norms of the minority which discourage employment among women. For an account of many of the factors which determine the positioning of South Asian Muslim women in the British labour market, see Brah and Shaw (1992).

4 This brief discussion of community leaders and local politics is based on observations made throughout my period of field-work in Waltham Forest. Many of the community leaders with whom I spoke both complained bitterly about the existence of internal political conflict and at the same time made evident their own involvement in conflict, by openly criticising certain individuals whom they regard as their rivals. Two of my respondents – Mariam, whose parents have both been involved in local politics, and Jamila, who was herself attempting to set up a young women's group – also spoke to me at some length about the pervasiveness, intensity and pointlessness of the competition between local factions. For a detailed examination of the roles played by community leaders within ethnic minority communities in Britain, see Werbner and Anwar (eds) (1991). Baumann (1996) also discusses the notion of the community leader, and points to the in-fighting and creative alliances in Southall local politics which are inevitable consequences of the fact that community leaders are in competition with one another for scarce resources.

5 I had made the decision, at the outset of the project, that the time that would be needed to acquire a working knowledge of Punjabi or Urdu would not be well spent, since the study was to focus on attitudes among young people who have grown up speaking English.

4 The circumstances

1 Both for practical reasons and because of the nature of my basic research questions, my field-work in Waltham Forest did not incorporate an investigation of attitudes held by members of the older generation (apart from my discussions with community leaders, whose views may not have been highly typical); thus, my intention in this section of the chapter is to discuss my respondents' *assessments* of their parents' views, rather than those views in themselves.

2 Having experienced many years of conflict with her parents, Jamila now feels that she has established her own independence within her family, with the result that, for example, her efforts to start a small jewellery-making business have been supported, and her parents have accepted her intended marriage to her boyfriend.

3 See, for example, Anwar (1981), C. Ballard (1979), R. and C. Ballard (1977), James (1974), Saifullah Khan (1977, 1979), Thompson (1974), Wilson (1984). It is interesting to note that Ballard (1994) argues that the earlier researchers never did suggest that it was useful to describe young British Asians as finding themselves 'between two cultures'; and that this term has been given such credence partly on account of its inappropriate and 'unfortunate' use as the title of Watson's influential volume (1977) on minorities in Britain (to which Ballard himself was a contributor).

4 See also R. and C. Ballard (1977), Bhachu (1985), Drury (1991), Rex and Josephides (1987), Shaw (1988), Thompson (1974) for discussion of persisting family loyalties within the younger generation of British Asians.

5 Tebbit's stated concern, which led him to raise the question of the 'cricket test', was with what he saw as the threat to the British identity emanating from 'the waves of newcomers intent on importing their nationality to our nation' (cited in Solomos 1993: 229).

6 My usage of the term 'race' here is informed by van den Berghe's definition of a 'racial group' as

> a human group that defines itself and/or is defined by other groups as different from other groups by virtue of innate and immutable physical characteristics. These physical characteristics are in turn believed to be intrinsically related to moral, intellectual, and other non-physical attributes or abilities.

Thus for van den Berghe a 'race' is 'a group that is *socially* defined but on the basis of *physical* criteria' [original emphases] (1967: 9).

7 Narrow, ethnic definitions of Britishness, even within their own limited frames of reference, clearly lack coherence. The history of the British Isles is of course such that the very concept of British national identity is necessarily contested and multifaceted: given that this is a history which has seen successive waves of invaders make their homes in these islands prior to the twelfth century, the incorporation of the separate 'nations' of Scotland, Wales and Ireland (today, Northern Ireland) together with the dominant England within a single political entity, and the establishment and subsequent loss of an empire that straddled much of the globe. See, for example, Robin Cohen (1994), Dodd (1995), Haseler (1996), Samuel (ed.) (1989), for discussion of many of the complex dimensions to official and popular conceptions of British and English national identity today.

8 It is interesting to note that when referring to white Britons, the respondents variously used the words 'white' and 'English' (eighteen of the thirty-three core respondents employed the two words interchangeably) and, less commonly, 'British'. 'British' was employed more frequently as a term which potentially encompasses ethnic minorities (a usage partially prompted by my phrasing of questions); and the ambivalence of many respondents regarding their Britishness was reflected in inconsistent use of the word. Indeed it was sometimes simultaneously employed as an exclusive and inclusive term. For example, Mustafa, shortly after stating quite unequivocally that he himself is British and not Pakistani, answered a question about his views on 'British society' with the comment, 'It's all right, actually. I've got quite a few friends that are British, and they're all right. Like quite good, enjoyable people.'

9 The interviews provided very little evidence of participation by the respondents in political activities devoted to combating racism. Only one respondent mentioned involvement in an anti-racist organisation: Mariam said that she attends meetings and demonstrations organised by the group 'Youth Against Racism'. Another indicator of

the low level of political mobilisation around issues of racism was that only Khalida among all the respondents described herself as 'black'. The use of the word 'black' as an inclusive term to describe members of all non-white ethnic groups in Britain, which could thus provide the basis of unified political action against racism, has been advocated by anti-racists since the late 1970s. More recently, the concept of 'political blackness' has found less favour among campaigners partly because there has seemingly been a reluctance on the part of British Asians to identify themselves as 'black'. See Modood (1994) for an extensive discussion of 'political blackness' and what he regards as its negative implications for British Asians; see also Baumann (1996) for an account of public debate in Southall over the question, 'Are Asians Black?'

10 In 1996 the Runnymede Trust launched the 'Runnymede Commission on British Muslims and Islamophobia'; its initial consultation paper was published in February 1997.

11 Drury (1991), Gardner and Shukur (1994), K. Hall (1995) and Hewitt (1990) also give accounts of what can broadly be termed 'code-switching' or 'cultural translation' among young British Asians.

5 Ethnic boundaries

1 Writing in 1979, C. Ballard asserted that for first-generation Asians in Britain, 'the extended family, with its common identification with the village or area of origin, is still the most important focus of social interaction' (1979: 112). Werbner (1990) has written extensively of the persistence of caste (or *zat*) divisions among first-generation Pakistanis in Manchester, although she notes that, very often, caste becomes significant to individuals only once they are concerned with their children's marriage prospects. See also Shaw (1988) on caste and, particularly, kinship groupings among Pakistanis in Oxford.

2 In a study of ethnic minority identities in Britain, Modood *et al.* (1994) found that among their sample of forty-nine South Asian respondents, most favoured a religious or narrower ethnic self-categorisation over the broad label 'Asian'. However, more of the second-generation than the first-generation respondents identified themselves as Asian; among the younger people, some regarded this as a negative ethnic label, but more saw it as a positive or simply as a descriptive term.

3 Ahmed and Donnan write in relation to the Muslim diaspora that the fact of large-scale emigration from certain regions of the world challenges and disrupts traditional perceptions of 'home' even for those who themselves have never migrated. For they are inevitably 'faced with the fantasy if not the reality of moving', and encounter the different perspectives of returned migrants (1994: 6).

4 See, for example, Breton and Pinard (1960) for a discussion of some of the general theoretical concerns of researchers who have carried out work in this area. See also Davey (1987), who conducted a review of British studies on interethnic friendship patterns; he argues that these studies reveal, on the whole, that children show a preference for in-group friendships from an early age, and that this preference often becomes stronger as children grow older.

5 *The Fourth National Survey of Ethnic Minorities* (cited in Modood 1997a) found that 54 per cent of married Pakistani and Indian Muslim respondents, and as many as 64 per cent of the younger Pakistanis, were married to a cousin (including non-first cousins). It is noted also that the practice of family marriage is class-related: twice as many manual workers as non-manual workers had married cousins. For an account of the impact on immigration patterns of first cousin marriage among Mirpuris see R. Ballard (1990).

See also Werbner (1990), who writes of marriage customs among Pakistanis in Manchester.

6 In challenging parents' criteria for marriage partners, the respondents are also, of course, questioning the traditional system of arranged marriage. The subject of arranged marriage is a large one, and there is insufficient space here to explore it. It should be noted, however, that although a few of my respondents spoke at some length about conflict they had had with parents who had sought to deny them the opportunity to choose their own partners, the majority did not express a great deal of anxiety about the matter. It was frequently said that there is nothing or little wrong with the idea that parents should help one find a partner; but that 'forced marriage' is unacceptable. Thus it appears that a modified arranged marriage system is gradually emerging within the local Pakistani community; as seems to be the case within other South Asian communities in Britain according to the literature on the subject. See, for example, Bhachu (1985) Gardner and Shukur (1994), Gillespie (1995), Modood (1997a), Rex and Josephides (1987).

7 R. Ballard (1990) discusses this dimension to Mirpuri marriage patterns which, he writes, is meeting with increasing resistance among the younger generation in Britain. Despite the resistance, however, most parents continue to feel obliged to fulfil their family duties, which include marrying their children to the children of their siblings who remain in Mirpur.

8 A recent study carried out in Birmingham (cited by Kingman 1993) has found that the prevalence of cousin marriage within the Pakistani community is one factor contributing to a higher incidence of illness and disability among Pakistani children in comparison to white children. The research findings have encouraged local health workers to offer genetic counselling to Pakistani families, to which there has been some opposition from the older generation, but a favourable response from many young women.

9 See, for example, Bhachu (1991), Drury (1991), Gillespie (1995) and Hiro (1991).

10 *The Fourth National Survey of Ethnic Minorities* (cited in Modood 1997a) found that as many as 72 per cent of Pakistani female respondents always wear Pakistani clothes, while 2 per cent never do.

11 Urdu is the national language of Pakistan, and is looked upon by respondents and informants as the language spoken by the more educated and high-status Pakistanis. Thus, for example, Yusuf indicated a certain ambition in telling me that he speaks Punjabi with his parents and Urdu with his children.

12 While a relatively small number of my respondents professed a particular interest in language, Modood *et al.* found among many first- and second-generation South Asians a belief that 'the ability to speak their ethnic group language was of crucial importance in how they saw and described themselves' (1994: 39). The authors point out, however, that widespread belief in the importance of a given minority language is not necessarily reflected in actual knowledge and use of that language; one might conclude, therefore, 'that just at the time when these languages become of less instrumental importance, their importance as bearers of ethnic heritage grows' (1994: 43).

13 The theatre company Moti Roti, in its production *Maa*, likewise sought to challenge the 'out-dated and out-moded images' of an Asian community concerned with shop-keeping and arranged marriages, and to demonstrate instead the 'vivacity, vibrancy and difference that is emerging from our communities'. The original production of *D'yer Eat with your Fingers?!* ran at the Theatre Royal Stratford East, London, in 1994; *Maa* was performed at the Royal Court Theatre, London, in 1995.

14 Gillespie (1995: 5) points out that

The names 'Wild West' and 'Apache Indian' represent playful puns on 'Indian' and 'West' and 'East'. At once affirming their 'Indian' (sub-continental) identity and redefining it in terms of the (doubly) 'Western' popular cultural stereotype of 'cowboys and indians', the protagonists of these British Asian cultural expressions are inventing names for their identity which announce them as 'familiar others'.

15 For one such example of false dichotomisation, consider K. Hall's account of the 'ideologies' of 'family honor' and 'British cultural purity' encountered by young British Sikhs, which reflect 'a commonly shared desire for social wholeness, a desire to impose order and boundaries . . . in a world of cultural flow and flux'. These ideologies, K. Hall claims, do no less than 'halt the forward march of social and cultural change' (1995: 248).

6 Islam and guidance

1 There are certainly no definitive answers to the question of to what extent women's 'rights' are affirmed by Sunni Islam in the ways the respondents argued. For extensive discussion of the status of women in Islam see, among much else, L. Ahmed (1992), Fawzi El-Solh and Mabro (eds) (1984), Hussain (ed.) (1984), Kandiyoti (ed.) (1991), Mernissi (1985) and (1991).

2 See also Andrews (1994), Lewis (1994), Nielsen (1987) and Sahgal (1992) for more on the ways in which some Muslim women in Britain have found, through their religion, a means of rejecting or rethinking traditional gender roles.

3 See also Mirza (1989) and Ellis (1991), who conducted research within the Muslim communities of Bradford and Coventry, respectively. Both spoke to young people who are inclined to reject aspects of their parents' interpretations of Islam, and in so doing are finding the religion to be a highly positive and valuable basis of identity. Geaves writes of young Muslims in Leeds for whom 'Islam has been used . . . to resolve identity questions which have arisen from sitting astride two cultures' (1995: 14).

4 Shaw (1988) argues in a similar vein when she describes the views of a young British Pakistani man who justifies the freedoms enjoyed by his wife by making reference to Islamic teachings. She writes that his justification does not appeal to 'Western' concepts of equality because this would not convince his parents; and nor, in all likelihood, would he thus convince himself.

5 Many sociologists of religion, seeking to understand patterns of religious change in the West, have pointed to the increasing tendency of ordinary Christian believers to perceive that it is possible or even necessary for them to question and criticise much of what has passed in previous ages as self-evident and objective religious truths. Bellah argues, for example, that today 'for many churchgoers the obligation of doctrinal orthodoxy sits lightly indeed, and the idea that all creedal statements must receive a personal reinterpretation is widely accepted' (1976: 41). This process of 'privatization of religion' (Roof 1978) means that the individual Christian has allowed himself – and often with almost explicit permission from mainstream churches and churchmen – increasing scope in establishing his own views on religion. For Luckmann, religion has thus become a private reality, such that, eventually, 'the *prevalent* individual systems of "ultimate" significance will consist of a loose and rather unstable hierarchy of "opinions" legitimating the affectively determined priorities of "private" life' [original emphasis] (1967: 105). (See also Berger [1969], B. Martin [1981] and D. Martin [1978], among others, for more on these general themes.)

6 See, in particular, Joly (1988), Ruthven (1990), Raza (1991) and Lewis (1994) for discussion of this and related issues.

7 This key assumption is succinctly expressed by D. Martin:

> In Islam the incarnate word is the Quran. It follows from this that the Quran represents the essence of revelation and thus is irrefragable. Of course, there are all kinds of sources of secondary hermeneutic, even including reason, but the emphasis of Islam pushes in the direction of fundamentalism.
>
> (1990: 13)

8 The subject of reformist or modernist movements within Islam is a vast one which can hardly be broached here. It is, however, interesting to consider that there have always been severe tensions within Islamic modernism. Smith has noted that, with respect to religious reform in general, the inherent conflict between reason and revelation within reformist movements inevitably brings about some acceptance of 'the individual's right to reinterpret the tradition for himself' and, very often, produces the situation where 'rationalism may easily triumph and bring with it the dissolution of all tradition and religion' (1979: 37). This profound problem has been of concern to Nasr, writing from a Muslim perspective. He draws a distinction between what he terms 'the movement of reform' within Islam which has sought 'to recreate and reshape human attitudes and social institutions so as to make them harmonious with the *Shari'ah*' and 'modern movements' which, in contrast, 'seek to reform the Divine Law rather than human society' and are thus, in Islamic terms, anomalous. To be a modernist and, at the same time, a true Muslim is impossible in the eyes of Nasr, for 'the modern mentality, which originated in the West with its Christian background, cannot conceive of an immutable Law which is the guide of human society' (1966: 96).

Rahman, who himself has sought to promote a modernist view of Islam, has argued that

> the movement inspired by the initial modernist impulse split into two developments moving in two different directions: one in the direction of almost pure Westernism and the other gravitating towards fundamentalism or what has been called 'Revivalism'. From approximately the second decade of the present century onwards the history of the spiritual and intellectual development of Islamic society is a story of the tension between these two trends.
>
> (1966: 222)

9 For discussion of Islamic youth organisations in Britain in general and in Waltham Forest in particular, see Chapters 2 and 7, respectively.

10 These young people could be referred to as 'fundamentalists', but it is important to note that this is a contested term. The phrase 'fundamentalist Islam' is used, in Britain today, in popular discourse and especially in the media, in an ill-defined sense but with great frequency to imply fanaticism and militancy.

11 What can be described as Islamic radicalism is also mentioned by Rex and Josephides (writing before the Rushdie Affair), who comment on the 'emergence of groups of young men in their early twenties who have an almost missionary zeal about the propagation of Islam among their peers' (1987: 30). The rise of radical Islam in Britain since the Rushdie Affair is also referred to by Hiro, who writes of the 'inner belief in the superiority of Islam over all other religions' maintained by many young British Muslims (1991: 188).

12 Interest in religious study and learning is mentioned specifically by, among others, Ellis (1991), Hiro (1991), Lewis (1994), Nielsen (1987) and Rex and Josephides (1987).

13 According to *Melody Maker*, Fun-da-mental's

> live performances are more like political rallies than gigs. Samples of Louis Farrakhan, Malcolm X and Enoch Powell's 'Rivers of Blood' speech and the fact that the group dress like PLO terrorists further fuel the excitement . . . their tracks have, however, not been welcomed by their community elders and the group were recently banned from two Asian music TV shows. As well as being unhappy with their Islamic chanting and the extracts from the Koran . . . the programme producers were livid at the fact that 'Righteous Preacher' openly supports the fatwa against Salman Rushdie.
>
> (cited by Lewis 1994: 180)

7 Religious boundaries

1 McCloud expresses a similar idea in noting that 'Muslims' submission of their will to God ideally reappropriates space and reorganizes temporality.' She elaborates this idea by explaining that '*Salat* (formal prayer) requires space both physically and mentally. Fasting makes demands of mental and spiritual space, while altering temporality. The Hajj demands its space and time' (1996: 65). McCloud's article is one of a collection entitled *Making Muslim Space* (edited by Metcalf) which, as its name suggests, explores various aspects of the private and public use of space by Muslims.

2 De Vos and Romanucci-Ross use the term 'psychological distance' in writing of how, in modern pluralistic society, minor symbols of difference may be vital if ethnic groups which are in constant and intense contact with one another are to remain distinctive (1975: 369).

3 Developing the same point as Nielsen, Metcalf points out that some Muslim leaders in the West have entertained the hope 'that in a new setting, particularly when Muslims from different areas were joined together, individuals would examine their practices in the light of scriptural norms and focus on what was sanctioned and could be common to all' (1996: 10). See also Ellis (1991), Knott and Khoker (1993), Mirza (1989) and Nielsen (1987) for more on the process whereby, in the words of Ellis, 'perceptions of ethnic difference are giving way to an identification as British Muslim' (1991: 370).

4 It can be argued, however, that it is inappropriate to regard as inherently problematic the fact that Islam in India incorporated elements of local customs. First, it would not have been possible for Islam, particularly since it was a minority religion, to retain any kind of cultural 'purity' in India – a 'purity' which in any case would have been a false notion, since the religion was, after all, originally established within and partially shaped by a particular cultural milieu. Secondly, as A.S. Ahmed suggests, the fusion of Islamic with Hindu traditions can be seen as 'one of the most remarkable developments of South Asia . . . [which] added to the richness of both cultures' (1993: 92).

5 For Muslims across the globe, as Metcalf writes, 'It is themselves, and their fellow Muslims as embodiments of Muslim ritual and practice, that define any place as Muslim space' (1996: 11). One might find certain parallels here with the situation of the Jews, in the way in which some sense of unity out of the diverse and scattered expressions of Islamic belief is established through, in part at least, adherence to collective ritual and allegiance to sacred places. Paine writes of the paradox that once the State of Israel was created, cultural differences between Jews became highly salient; whereas

> while widely dispersed throughout the Diaspora, Jews went to elaborate ritual lengths to overcome, symbolically, differences of time and place between them as Jews. . . . All turned towards Jerusalem to pray, and in synagogues

across the globe and across the centuries the salutation would ring out: 'Next year in Jerusalem'.

(1989: 121)

6 Despite the fact that many of the Pakistanis in Waltham Forest originate from the Mirpur district in Kashmir and from nearby Jhellum, the Kashmiri conflict was mentioned to me only occasionally. Among the core respondents only Faruq appeared to be especially concerned with this matter. In general, notwithstanding the appearance of a stall raising money for the 'Kashmir Fund' at a few local events, there was little evidence that Kashmir is regarded as an issue of importance, at least as far as the young people are concerned. This finding accords with that of Joly (1995), who discovered that young British Pakistanis in Birmingham were largely non-committal in relation to the Kashmiri situation, even though this has been an issue which has mobilised many members of the older generation.

BIBLIOGRAPHY

Abercrombie, N. (1986) 'Knowledge, order and human autonomy' in J.D. Hunter and S.G. Ainlay (eds) *Making Sense of Modern Times: Peter L. Berger and the Vision of Interpretive Sociology*, London: Routledge & Kegan Paul.

Abrams, D. and Hogg, M. (1990) *Social Identity Theory: Constructive and Critical Advances*, Hemel Hempstead: Harvester Wheatsheaf.

Ahmed, A.S. (1992) *Postmodernism and Islam: Predicament and Promise*, London: Routledge.

—— (1993) *Living Islam: From Samarkand to Stornoway*, London: Penguin.

Ahmed, A.S. and Donnan, H. (1994) 'Islam in the age of postmodernity' in A.S. Ahmed and H. Donnan (eds) *Islam, Globalization and Postmodernity*, London: Routledge.

Ahmed, L. (1992) *Women and Gender in Islam: Historical Roots of a Modern Debate*, New Haven: Yale University Press.

Ahsan, M.M. and Kidwai, A.R. (eds) (1991) *Sacrilege and Civility: Muslim Perspectives on 'The Satanic Verses' Affair*, Leicester: The Islamic Foundation.

Akhtar, S. (1989) *Be Careful with Muhammad! The Salman Rushdie Affair*, London: Bellew.

Ali, Y. (1992) 'Muslim women and the politics of ethnicity and culture in northern England' in G. Sahgal and N. Yuval-Davis (eds) *Refusing Holy Orders: Women and Fundamentalism in Britain*, London: Virago.

Andrews, A.Y. (1992) 'Sociological analysis of Jamaat-i-Islami in the United Kingdom' in R. Barot (ed.) *Religion and Ethnicity: Minorities and Social Change in the Metropolis*, Kampen: Kok Pharos.

—— (1994) 'Muslim women in a western European society: Gujarati Muslim women in Leicester' in J. Fulton and P. Gee (eds) *Religion in Contemporary Europe*, Lampeter: Edwin Mellen Press.

Anwar, M. (1979) *The Myth of Return: Pakistanis in Britain*, London: Heinemann.

—— (1981) *Between Two Cultures: A Study of Relationships between Generations in the Asian Community in Britain*, London: Commission for Racial Equality.

—— (1991) *Muslims in Britain: Some Recent Developments*, Berlin: Berliner Institut für Vergleichende Sozialforschung.

Armstrong, J.A. (1982) *Nations Before Nationalism*, Chapel Hill: University of North Carolina Press.

Back, L. (1996) *New Ethnicities and Urban Culture: Racisms and Multiculture in Young Lives*, London: UCL Press.

Ballard, C. (1979) 'Conflict, continuity and change: second-generation South Asians' in V. Saifullah Khan (ed.) *Minority Families in Britain: Support and Stress*, London: Macmillan.

167

Ballard, R. (1990) 'Migration and kinship' in C. Clarke, C. Peach and S. Vertovec (eds) *South Asians Overseas: Migration and Ethnicity*, Cambridge: Cambridge University Press.

—— (1994) 'Introduction: the emergence of desh pardesh' in R. Ballard (ed.) *Desh Pardesh: The South Asian Presence in Britain*, London: Hurst.

Ballard, R. and Ballard, C. (1977) 'The Sikhs: the development of South Asian settlements in Britain' in J.L. Watson (ed.) *Between Two Cultures: Migrants and Minorities in Britain*, Oxford: Blackwell.

Banton, M. (1983) *Racial and Ethnic Competition*, Cambridge: Cambridge University Press.

Barth, F. (1969) 'Introduction' in F. Barth (ed.) *Ethnic Groups and Boundaries: The Social Organization of Culture Difference*, London: Allen & Unwin.

Bauman, Z. (1991) *Modernity and Ambivalence*, Cambridge: Polity Press.

Baumann, G. (1996) *Contesting Culture: Discourses of Identity in Multi-Ethnic London*, Cambridge: Cambridge University Press.

Bellah, R.N. (1969) 'Religious evolution' in R. Robertson (ed.) *Sociology of Religion*, Harmondsworth: Penguin.

—— (1976) *Beyond Belief: Essays on Religion in a Post-Traditional World*, New York: Harper & Row.

Berger, P.L. (1969) *The Social Reality of Religion*, London: Faber & Faber.

Berger, P.L. and Luckmann, T. (1967) *The Social Construction of Reality*, London: Penguin.

Bhachu, P. (1985) *Twice Migrants: East African Sikh Settlers in Britain*, London: Tavistock.

—— (1991) 'Culture, ethnicity and class among Punjabi Sikh women in 1990s Britain', *New Community* 17, 3: 401–12.

Billig, M. (1995) *Banal Nationalism*, London: Sage.

Bowen, D.G. (ed.) (1992) *The Satanic Verses: Bradford Responds*, Bradford: Bradford and Ilkley Community College.

Brah, A. and Shaw, S. (1992) *Working Choices: South Asian Young Muslim Women and the Labour Market*, Research Paper no. 91, London: Department of Employment.

Breton, R. and Pinard, M. (1960) 'Group formation among immigrants: criteria and processes', *Canadian Journal of Economics and Political Science* 26: 465–77.

British Muslims Monthly Survey, Birmingham: CSIC, Selly Oak Colleges.

Brown, R. (1988) *Group Processes: Dynamics Within and Between Groups*, Oxford: Blackwell.

Cairns, E. (1982) 'Intergroup conflict in Northern Ireland' in H. Tajfel (ed.) *Social Identity and Intergroup Relations*, Cambridge: Cambridge University Press.

Christie, C.J. (1991) 'The rope of God: Muslim minorities in the West and Britain', *New Community* 17, 3: 457–66.

Clarke, P. (1988) 'Islam in contemporary Europe' in P. Clarke (ed.) *The World's Religions: Islam*, London: Routledge & Kegan Paul.

Cohen, A. (1974) 'Introduction: the lesson of ethnicity' in A. Cohen (ed.) *Urban Ethnicity*, London: Tavistock.

Cohen, Robin (1994) *Frontiers of Identity: The British and the Others*, London: Longman.

Cohen, Ronald (1978) 'Ethnicity: problem and focus in anthropology', *Annual Review of Anthropology* 7: 379–403.

Connolly, J. (1989) 'Identity and difference in global politics' in J. der Derian and M.J. Shapiro (eds) *International / Intertextual Relations: Postmodern Readings of World Politics*, Lexington: Lexington Books.

CRE (1989) *Law, Blasphemy and the Multi-Faith Society: Report of a Seminar*, London: Commission for Racial Equality.

—— (1990a) *Free Speech: Report of a Seminar*, London: Commission for Racial Equality.

—— (1990b) *Britain: A Plural Society*, London: Commission for Racial Equality.

CSIC (1989) *The 'Rushdie Affair'. A Documentation*, Research Papers: Muslims in Europe no. 42, Birmingham: CSIC, Selly Oak Colleges.

Dahya, B. (1974) 'The nature of Pakistani ethnicity in industrial cities in Britain' in A. Cohen (ed.) *Urban Ethnicity*, London: Tavistock.

Davey, A.G. (1987) 'Inter-ethnic friendship patterns in British schools over three decades', *New Community* 14, 1/2: 202–9.

de Vos, G. and Romanucci-Ross, L. (1975) 'Ethnicity: vessel of meaning and emblem of contrast' in G. de Vos and L. Romanucci-Ross (eds) *Ethnic Identity: Cultural Continuities and Change*, Palo Alto: Mayfield.

Dhingra, D. (1994) 'Bombay Nights', *Independent*, London, 4.5.94.

Dodd, P. (1995) *The Battle over Britain*, London: Demos.

Douglas, M. (1970) *Natural Symbols: Explorations in Cosmology*, New York: Pantheon Books.

Drury, B. (1991) 'Sikh girls and the maintenance of an ethnic culture', *New Community* 17, 3: 387–99.

Durkheim, E. (1954) *The Elementary Forms of the Religious Life*, London: Allen & Unwin.

Dwyer, C. (1993) 'Constructions of Muslim identity and the contesting of power' in P. Jackson and J. Penrose (eds) *Constructions of Race, Place and Nation*, London: UCL Press.

Dwyer, C. and Meyer, A. (1996) 'The establishment of Islamic schools: a controversial phenomenon in three European countries' in W.A.R. Shadid and P.S. van Koningsveld (eds) *Muslims in the Margin: Political Responses to the Presence of Islam in Western Europe*, Kampen: Kok Pharos.

Eade, J. (1990) 'Nationalism and the quest for authenticity: the Bangladeshis in Tower Hamlets', *New Community* 16, 4: 493–503.

Ellis, J. (1991) 'Local government and community needs: a case study of Muslims in Coventry', *New Community* 17, 3: 359–76.

Eriksen, T.H. (1991) 'The cultural contexts of ethnic differences', *Man* 26, 1: 127–44.

Esposito, J.L. (1991) *Islam: The Straight Path*, New York: Oxford University Press.

Fawzi El-Solh, C. and Mabro, J. (eds) (1984) *Muslim Women's Choices: Religious Beliefs and Social Reality*, Oxford: Berg.

Friedman, J. (1997) 'Global crises, the struggle for cultural identity and intellectual porkbar-relling: cosmopolitans versus locals, ethnics and nationals in an era of de-hegemonisation' in P. Werbner and T. Modood (eds) *Debating Cultural Hybridity: Multi-Cultural Identities and the Politics of Anti-Racism*, London: Zed Books.

Gans, H. (1979) 'Symbolic ethnicity: the future of ethnic groups and cultures in America', *Ethnic and Racial Studies* 2, 1: 1–20.

Gardner, K. and Shukur, A. (1994) '"I'm Bengali, I'm Asian, and I'm living here": the changing identity of British Bengalis' in R. Ballard (ed.) *Desh Pardesh: The South Asian Presence in Britain*, London: Hurst.

Geaves, R. (1995) *Muslims in Leeds*, Community Religions Project Research Papers no. 10, Leeds: University of Leeds.

Geertz, C. (1993) *The Interpretation of Cultures: Selected Essays*, London: Fontana.

Gillespie, M. (1995) *Television, Ethnicity and Cultural Change*, London: Routledge.

Gilroy, P. (1987) *There Ain't No Black in the Union Jack: The Cultural Politics of Race and Nation*, London: Hutchinson.

169

Glazer, N. and Moynihan, D.P. (1970) *Beyond the Melting Pot: The Negroes, Puerto Ricans, Jews, Italians, and Irish of New York City*, Cambridge: MIT Press.

Greeley, A. (1973) *The Persistence of Religion*, London: SCM Press.

—— (1992) 'Religion in Britain, Ireland and the USA' in R. Jowell *et al.* (eds) *British Social Attitudes: The Ninth Report*, London: SCPR.

Hall, K. (1995) '"There's a time to act English and a time to act Indian": the politics of identity among British-Sikh teenagers' in S. Stephens (ed.) *Children and the Politics of Culture*, Princeton: Princeton University Press.

Hall, S. (1992a) 'The question of cultural identity' in S. Hall, D. Held and T. McGrew (eds) *Modernity and its Futures*, Cambridge: Polity Press.

—— (1992b) 'New ethnicities' in J. Donald and A. Rattansi (eds) *'Race', Culture and Difference*, London: Sage.

Hardy, P. (1987) 'Islam in South Asia' in M. Eliade (ed.) *The Encyclopaedia of Religion*, New York: Macmillan.

Haseler, S. (1996) *The English Tribe: Identity, Nation and Europe*, London: Macmillan.

Hewitt, R. (1990) 'A sociolinguistic view of urban adolescent relations' in F. Rogilds (ed.) *Every Cloud has a Silver Lining: Lectures on Everyday Life, Cultural Production and Race*, Copenhagen: Akademisk Forlag.

Hiro, D. (1991) *Black British, White British: A History of Race Relations in Britain*, 3rd edn, London: Grafton.

Horowitz, D.L. (1985) *Ethnic Groups in Conflict*, London: University of California Press.

Hussain, F. (ed.) (1984) *Muslim Women*, London: Croom Helm.

Hutnik, N. (1985) 'Aspects of identity in multi-ethnic society', *New Community* 12, 2: 298–309.

—— (1986) 'Ethnic minority identification and social adaptation', *Ethnic and Racial Studies* 9, 2: 150–67.

—— (1991) *Ethnic Minority Identity: A Social Psychological Perspective*, Oxford: Clarendon Press.

James, A.G. (1974) *Sikh Children in Britain*, London: Oxford University Press.

Jenkins, R. (1986) 'Social anthropological models of inter-ethnic relations' in J. Rex and D. Mason (eds) *Theories of Race and Ethnic Relations*, Cambridge: Cambridge University Press.

Joly, D. (1988) 'Making a place for Islam in British society' in T. Gerholm and Y.G. Lithman (eds) *The New Islamic Presence in Western Europe*, London: Mansell.

—— (1995) *Britannia's Crescent: Making a Place for Muslims in British Society*, Aldershot: Avebury.

Kandiyoti, D. (ed.) (1991) *Women, Islam and the State*, Basingstoke: Macmillan.

Kaye, R. (1993) 'The politics of religious slaughter of animals: strategies for ethno-religious political action', *New Community* 19, 2: 235–50.

Kingman, S. (1993) 'Why cousins can be just too close', *Independent*, 6.7.93.

Knott, K. and Khoker, S. (1993) 'Religious and ethnic identity among young Muslim women in Bradford', *New Community*, 19, 4: 593–610.

Kureishi, H. (1990) *The Buddha of Suburbia*, London: Faber & Faber.

—— (1995) *The Black Album*, London: Faber & Faber.

Lee, S. (1990) *The Cost of Free Speech*, London: Faber & Faber.

Leveau, R. (1988) 'The Islamic presence in France' in T. Gerholm and Y.G. Lithman (eds) *The New Islamic Presence in Western Europe*, London: Mansell.

Lewis, P. (1994) *Islamic Britain: Religion, Politics and Identity among British Muslims*, London: I.B. Tauris.

170

—— (in press) 'British Muslims and the search for religious guidance' in J. Hinnells and F.W. Menski (eds) *From Generation to Generation: Religious Reconstruction in the South Asian Diaspora*, London: Macmillan.

London Borough of Waltham Forest (1993a) 'Initial findings on black and ethnic minorities in LBWF', *1991 Census Newsletter* no. 6, London: Waltham Forest Policy Analysis Unit.

—— (1993b) 'Ethnic minorities in Waltham Forest', *1991 Census Newsletter* no. 13, London: Waltham Forest Policy Analysis Unit.

—— (1994a) *Borough Profile 1994*, London: Waltham Forest Policy Analysis Unit.

—— (1994b) *Waltham Forest Economic Overview*, London: London Research Centre with Waltham Forest Policy Analysis Unit.

Luckmann, T. (1967) *The Invisible Religion: The Problem of Religion in Modern Society*, London: Collier-Macmillan.

—— (1983) *Life-World and Social Realities*, London: Heinemann.

McCloud, A.B. (1996) ' "This is a Muslim home": signs of difference in the African-American Row House' in B.D. Metcalf (ed.) *Making Muslim Space in North America and Europe*, Berkeley: University of California Press.

McGuire, M.B. (1992) *Religion: The Social Context*, Belmont: Wadsworth.

Mahmood, C.K. and Armstrong, S.L. (1992) 'Do ethnic groups exist?' *Ethnology* 31, 1: 1–14.

Martin, B. (1981) *A Sociology of Contemporary Cultural Change*, Oxford: Blackwell.

Martin, D. (1978) *A General Theory of Secularisation*, Oxford: Blackwell.

—— (1990) 'Fundamentalism: an observational and definitional *Tour D'Horizon*', *Political Quarterly* 61, 2: 129–31.

Mead, G.H. (1964) *On Social Psychology: Selected Papers*, ed. A. Strauss, Chicago: University of Chicago Press.

Mernissi, F. (1985) *Beyond the Veil: Male–Female Dynamics in Modern Muslim Society*, rev. edn, London: Al Saqi Books.

—— (1991) *Women and Islam: An Historical and Theological Enquiry*, Oxford: Blackwell.

Metcalf, B.D. (1996) 'Introduction: sacred words, sanctioned practice, new communities' in B.D. Metcalf (ed.) *Making Muslim Space in North America and Europe*, Berkeley: University of California Press.

Mirza, K. (1989) *The Silent Cry: Second Generation Bradford Muslim Women Speak*, Research Papers: Muslims in Europe, no. 43, Birmingham: CSIC, Selly Oak Colleges.

Modood, T. (1990) 'British Asian Muslims and the Rushdie Affair', *Political Quarterly* 61, 2: 143–60.

—— (1994) 'Political blackness and British Asians', *Sociology* 28, 4: 859–76.

—— (1997a) 'Culture and identity' in T. Modood *et al.* (eds) *Ethnic Minorities in Britain: Diversity and Disadvantage*, London: Policy Studies Institute.

—— (1997b) ' "Difference", cultural racism and anti-racism' in T. Modood and P. Werbner (eds) *Debating Cultural Hybridity*, London: Zed Books.

Modood, T., Beishon, S. and Virdee, S. (1994) *Changing Ethnic Identities*, London: Policy Studies Institute.

Murphy, D. (1987) *Tales from Two Cities: Travel of Another Sort*, London: Penguin.

Nash, M. (1989) *The Cauldron of Ethnicity in the Modern World*, Chicago: University of Chicago Press.

Nasr, S.H. (1966) *Ideals and Realities of Islam*, London: Allen & Unwin.

Nielsen, J.S. (1984) 'Muslim immigration and settlement in Britain', *Research Papers: Muslims in Europe* No. 21, Birmingham: CSIC, Selly Oak Colleges.

—— (1987) 'Muslims in Britain: searching for an identity?' *New Community* 13, 3: 384–94.

—— (1992) *Muslims in Western Europe*, Edinburgh: Edinburgh University Press.

Osmond, J. (1988) *The Divided Kingdom*, London: Constable.

Owen, D. (1994) 'South Asian people in Great Britain: social and economic circumstances', *1991 Census Statistical Paper*, no. 1, Warwick: Centre for Research in Ethnic Relations, University of Warwick.

Paine, R. (1989) 'Israel: Jewish identity and competition over "tradition"' in E. Tonkin, M. McDonald and M. Chapman (eds) *History and Ethnicity*, London: Routledge.

Parekh, B. (1990) 'Britain and the social logic of pluralism' in *Britain: A Plural Society*, London: Commission for Racial Equality.

—— (1995) 'Introduction', *New Community* 21, 2: 147–51.

Parker-Jenkins, M. (1991) 'Muslim matters: the educational needs of the Muslim child', *New Community* 17, 4: 569–82.

Peach, C. and Glebe, G. (1995) 'Muslim minorities in western Europe', *Ethnic and Racial Studies* 18, 1: 26–45.

Rahman, F. (1966) *Islam*, London: Weidenfeld & Nicolson.

Rath, J., Groenendijk, K. and Penninx, R. (1991) 'The recognition and institutionalization of Islam in Belgium, Great Britain and the Netherlands', *New Community* 18, 1: 101–14.

Raza, M.S. (1991) *Islam in Britain: Past, Present and the Future*, Leicester: Volcano Press.

Rex, J. and Josephides, S. (1987) 'Asian and Greek Cypriot associations and identity' in J. Rex, D. Joly and C. Wilpert (eds) *Immigrant Associations in Europe*, Aldershot: Gower.

Robertson, R. (1990) 'After nostalgia? Wilful nostalgia and the phases of globalization' in B.S. Turner (ed.) *Theories of Modernity and Postmodernity*, London: Sage.

Robins, K. (1991) 'Tradition and translation: national culture in its global context' in J. Corner and S. Harvey (eds) *Enterprise and Heritage: Crosscurrents of National Culture*, London: Routledge.

Robinson, F. (1979) 'Islam and Muslim separatism' in D. Taylor and M. Yapp (eds) *Political Identity in South Asia*, London: Curzon.

—— (1988) *Varieties of South Asian Islam*, Research Paper no. 8, Warwick: Centre for Research in Ethnic Relations, University of Warwick.

Robinson, V. (1986) *Transients, Settlers and Refugees: Asians in Britain*, Oxford: Clarendon Press.

Roff, W.R. (1987) 'Islamic movements: one or many?' in W.R. Roff (ed.) *Islam and the Political Economy*, London: Croom Helm.

Ronson, J. (1997) 'Oh, what a lovely jihad', *Guardian*, 29.3.97.

Roof, W.C. (1978) *Community and Commitment: Religious Plausibility in a Liberal Protestant Church*, New York: Elsevier.

Runnymede Trust (1997) *Islamophobia – Its Features and Dangers: A Consultation Paper*, London: Runnymede Trust.

Rushdie, S. (1991) *Imaginary Homelands: Essays and Criticism 1981–1991*, London: Granta.

Rutherford, J. (1990) 'A place called home: identity and cultural politics' in J. Rutherford (ed.) *Identity: Community, Culture, Difference*, London: Lawrence & Wishart.

Ruthven, M. (1990) *A Satanic Affair: Salman Rushdie and the Wrath of Islam*, London: Chatto & Windus.

Sahgal, G. (1992) 'Secular spaces: the experience of Asian women organising' in G. Sahgal and N. Yuval-Davis (eds) *Refusing Holy Orders: Women and Fundamentalism in Britain*, London: Virago.

Saifullah Khan, V. (1977) 'The Pakistanis' in J.L. Watson (ed.) *Between Two Cultures: Migrants and Minorities in Britain*, Oxford: Blackwell.

—— (1979) 'Migration and social stress: Mirpuris in Bradford' in V. Saifullah Khan (ed.) *Minority Families in Britain: Support and Stress*, London: Macmillan.

Samad, Y. (1992) 'Book-burning and race relations: political mobilisation of Bradford Muslims', *New Community* 18, 4 507–19.

Samuel, R. (ed.) (1989) *Patriotism: The Making and Unmaking of British National Identity, Volume I: History and Politics*, London: Routledge.

Sardar, Z. and Wyn Davies, M. (1990) *Distorted Imagination: Lessons from the Rushdie Affair*, London: Grey Seal.

Schiffauer, W. (1988) 'Migration and religiousness' in T. Gerholm and Y.G. Lithman (eds) *The New Islamic Presence in Western Europe*, London: Mansell.

Sharot, S. (1982) *Messianism, Mysticism and Magic: A Sociological Analysis of Jewish Religious Movements*, Chapel Hill: University of California Press.

Shaw, A. (1988) *A Pakistani Community in Britain*, Oxford: Blackwell.

Sklare, M. and Greenblum, J. (1967) *Jewish Identity on the Suburban Frontier: A Study of Group Survival in the Open Society*, Chicago: University of Chicago Press.

Smith, A.D. (1979) *Nationalism in the Twentieth Century*, Oxford: Martin Robertson.

—— (1995) *Nations and Nationalism in a Global Era*, Cambridge: Polity Press.

Solomos, J. (1993) *Race and Racism in Britain*, 2nd edn, Basingstoke: Macmillan.

Spiro, M.E. (1966) 'Religion: problems of definition and explanation' in M. Banton (ed.) *Anthropological Approaches to the Study of Religion*, London: Tavistock.

Stack, J.F. (1986) 'Ethnic mobilization in world politics: the primordial perspective' in J.F. Stack (ed.) *The Primordial Challenge: Ethnicity in the Contemporary World*, New York: Greenwood.

Steinberg, S. (1981) *The Ethnic Myth: Race, Ethnicity, and Class in America*, New York: Atheneum.

Tajfel, H. (1978) 'Interindividual behaviour and intergroup behaviour' in H. Tajfel (ed.) *Differentiation Between Social Groups: Studies in the Social Psychology of Intergroup Relations*, London: Academic Press.

Talai, V.A. (1989) *Armenians in London: The Management of Social Boundaries*, Manchester: Manchester University Press.

Thompson, M. (1974) 'The second generation – Punjabi or English?' *New Community* 3, 3: 242–8.

Turner, B.S. (1991) *Religion and Social Theory*, 2nd edn, London: Sage.

Turner, J.C. with M. Hogg *et al.* (1987) *Rediscovering the Social Group: A Self-Categorization Theory*, Oxford: Blackwell.

van den Berghe, P.L. (1967) *Race and Racism: A Comparative Perspective*, New York: John Wiley & Sons.

Wallman, S. (1978) 'The boundaries of "race": processes of ethnicity in England', *Man* 13, 2: 200–17.

Watson, J.L. (ed.) (1977) *Between Two Cultures: Migrants and Minorities in Britain*, Oxford: Blackwell.

Weber, M. (1948) 'The social psychology of the world's religions' in H.H. Gerth and C. Wright Mills (eds) *From Max Weber: Essays in Sociology*, London: Routledge.

Webster, R. (1990) *A Brief History of Blasphemy: Liberalism, Censorship and 'The Satanic Verses'*, Southwold: Orwell Press.

Werbner, P. (1990) *The Migration Process: Capital, Gifts and Offerings among British Pakistanis*, Oxford: Berg.

—— (1994) 'Islamic radicalism and the Gulf War: lay preachers and political dissent among British Pakistanis' in B. Lewis and D. Schnapper (eds) *Muslims in Europe*, London: Pinter.

—— (1997) 'Introduction: the dialectics of cultural hybridity' in P. Werbner and T. Modood (eds) *Debating Cultural Hybridity: Multi-Cultural Identities and the Politics of Anti-Racism*, London: Zed Books.

Werbner, P. and Anwar, M. (eds) (1991) *Black and Ethnic Leaderships in Britain: The Cultural Dimensions of Political Action*, London: Routledge.

West, C. (1990) 'The new cultural politics of difference' in R. Ferguson *et al.* (eds) *Out There: Marginalization and Contemporary Cultures*, Cambridge: MIT Press.

Wilson, A. (1984) *Finding a Voice: Asian Women in Britain*, London: Virago.

INDEX